BRIAN **WOOD** . JORGE **COELHO** . DOUG **GARBARK**

RoboCop™
CITIZENS ARREST

ROSS RICHIE CEO & Founder
JOY HUFFMAN CFO
MATT GAGNON Editor-in-Chief
FILIP SABLIK President, Publishing & Marketing
STEPHEN CHRISTY President, Development
LANCE KREITER Vice President, Licensing & Merchandising
PHIL BARBARO Vice President, Finance & Human Resources
ARUNE SINGH Vice President, Marketing
BRYCE CARLSON Vice President, Editorial & Creative Strategy
SCOTT NEWMAN Manager, Production Design
KATE HENNING Manager, Operations
SPENCER SIMPSON Manager, Sales
SIERRA HAHN Executive Editor
JEANINE SCHAEFER Executive Editor
DAFNA PLEBAN Senior Editor
SHANNON WATTERS Senior Editor
ERIC HARBURN Senior Editor
WHITNEY LEOPARD Editor
CAMERON CHITTOCK Editor
CHRIS ROSA Editor
MATTHEW LEVINE Editor

SOPHIE PHILIPS-ROBERTS Assistant Editor
GAVIN GRONENTHAL Assistant Editor
MICHAEL MOCCIO Assistant Editor
AMANDA LaFRANCO Executive Assistant
JILLIAN CRAB Design Coordinator
MICHELLE ANKLEY Design Coordinator
KARA LEOPARD Production Designer
MARIE KRUPINA Production Designer
GRACE PARK Production Design Assistant
CHELSEA ROBERTS Production Design Assistant
SAMANTHA KNAPP Production Design Assistant
ELIZABETH LOUGHRIDGE Accounting Coordinator
STEPHANIE HOCUTT Social Media Coordinator
JOSÉ MEZA Event Coordinator
HOLLY AITCHISON Operations Coordinator
MEGAN CHRISTOPHER Operations Assistant
RODRIGO HERNANDEZ Mailroom Assistant
MORGAN PERRY Direct Market Representative
CAT O'GRADY Marketing Assistant
BREANNA SARPY Executive Assistant

ROBOCOP: CITIZENS ARREST, November 2018. Published by BOOM!
Studios, a division of Boom Entertainment, Inc. ROBOCOP ™ & © 1987
Orion Pictures Corporation. © 2018 Metro-Goldwyn-Mayer Studios Inc.
Originally published in single magazine form as ROBOCOP: CITIZENS
ARREST No. 1-5. ™ & © 1987 Orion Pictures Corporation. © 2018
Metro-Goldwyn-Mayer Studios Inc. METRO-GOLDWYN-MAYER is a trademark of Metro-Goldwyn-Mayer Lion Corp. © 2018
Metro-Goldwyn-Mayer Studios Inc. All rights reserved. BOOM!™ Studios™ and the BOOM! Studios logo are trademarks of Boom
Entertainment, Inc., registered in various countries and categories. All characters, events, and institutions depicted herein are
fictional. Any similarity between any of the names, characters, persons, events, and/or institutions in this publication to actual
names, characters, and persons, whether living or dead, events, and/or institutions is unintended and purely coincidental. BOOM!
Studios does not read or accept unsolicited submissions of ideas, stories, or artwork.

For more information regarding the CPSIA on this printed material, call (203) 595-3636 and provide reference #RICH – 812282.

BOOM! Studios, 5670 Wilshire Boulevard, Suite 400, Los Angeles, CA 90036-5679. Printed in USA. First Printing.

ISBN: 978-1-68415-270-4, eISBN: 978-1-64144-132-2

PRIME DIRECTIVES

SERVE THE PUBLIC TRUST.
PROTECT THE INNOCENT.
UPHOLD THE LAW.

WRITTEN BY
BRIAN WOOD

ILLUSTRATED BY
JORGE COELHO

COLORED BY
DOUG GARBARK

LETTERED BY
ED DUKESHIRE

COVER BY
NIMIT MALAVIA

BACK COVER ART BY
PIUS BAK

SERIES DESIGNER
MARIE KRUPINA

COLLECTION DESIGNER
JILLIAN CRAB

ASSISTANT EDITOR
GAVIN GRONENTHAL

EDITORS
ERIC HARBURN & SIERRA HAHN

SPECIAL THANKS
KAROL MORA

ONE

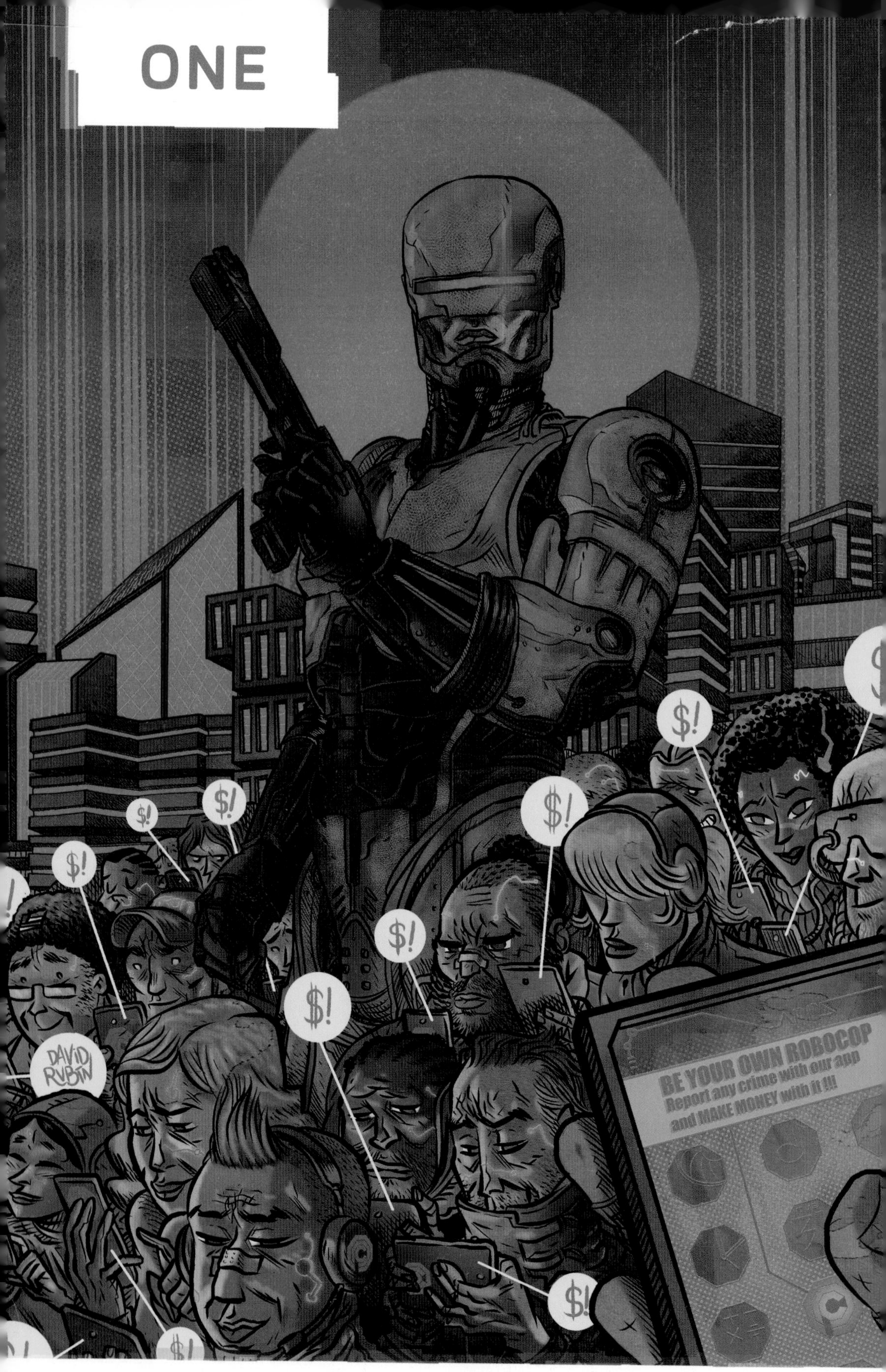
$!
$!
$!
$!
$!
$!
$!
$!
$!
DAVID RUBÍN
BE YOUR OWN ROBOCOP
Report any crime with our app
and MAKE MONEY with it !!!

ISSUE 01 COVER **DAVID RUBÍN**

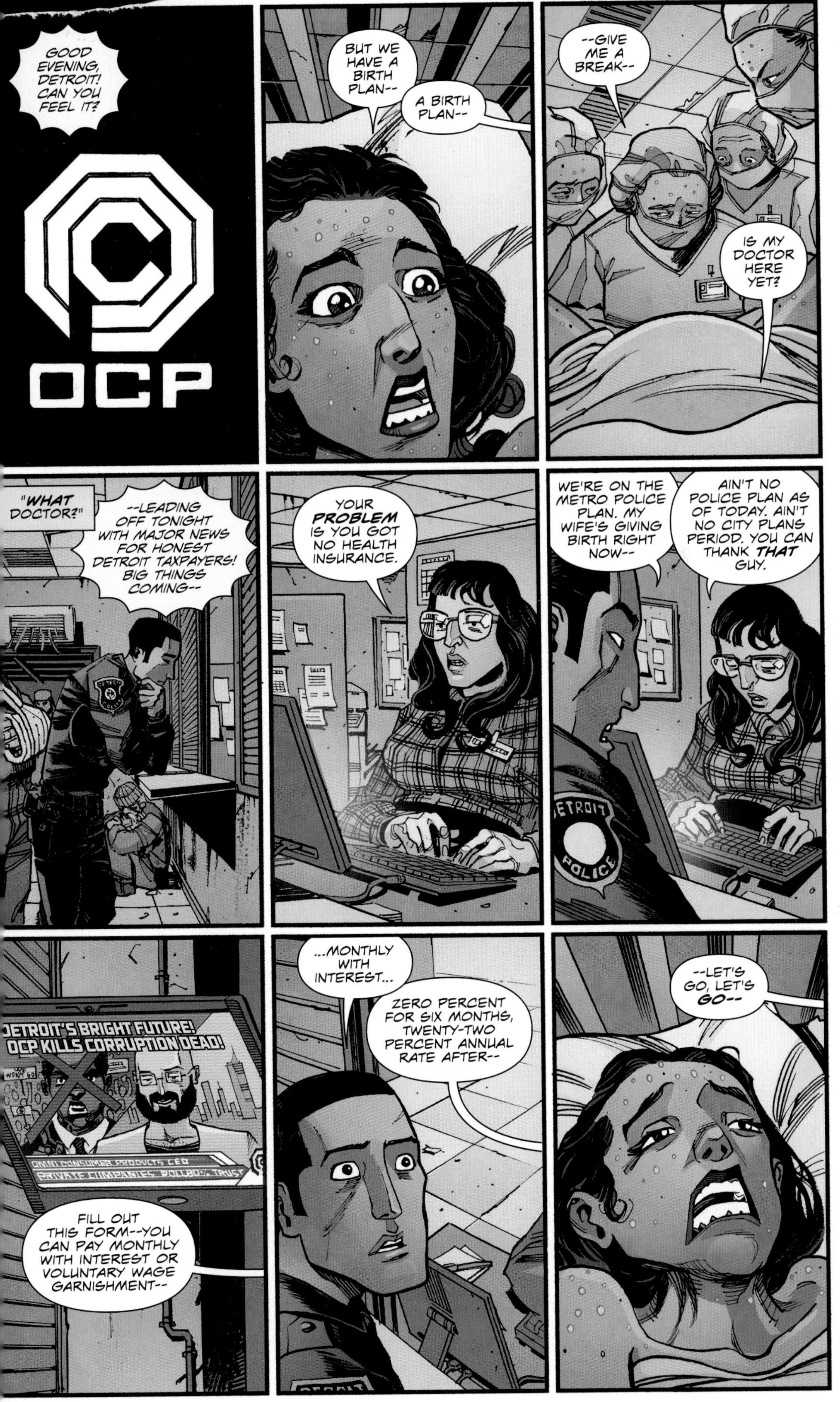
GOOD EVENING, DETROIT! CAN YOU FEEL IT?
OCP
BUT WE HAVE A BIRTH PLAN--
A BIRTH PLAN--
--GIVE ME A BREAK--
IS MY DOCTOR HERE YET?
"WHAT DOCTOR?"
--LEADING OFF TONIGHT WITH MAJOR NEWS FOR HONEST DETROIT TAXPAYERS! BIG THINGS COMING--
YOUR PROBLEM IS YOU GOT NO HEALTH INSURANCE.
WE'RE ON THE METRO POLICE PLAN. MY WIFE'S GIVING BIRTH RIGHT NOW--
AIN'T NO POLICE PLAN AS OF TODAY. AIN'T NO CITY PLANS PERIOD. YOU CAN THANK THAT GUY.
DETROIT POLICE
DETROIT'S BRIGHT FUTURE! OCP KILLS CORRUPTION DEAD!
OMNI CONSUMER PRODUCTS CEO
FILL OUT THIS FORM--YOU CAN PAY MONTHLY WITH INTEREST OR VOLUNTARY WAGE GARNISHMENT--
...MONTHLY WITH INTEREST...
ZERO PERCENT FOR SIX MONTHS, TWENTY-TWO PERCENT ANNUAL RATE AFTER--
--LET'S GO, LET'S GO--

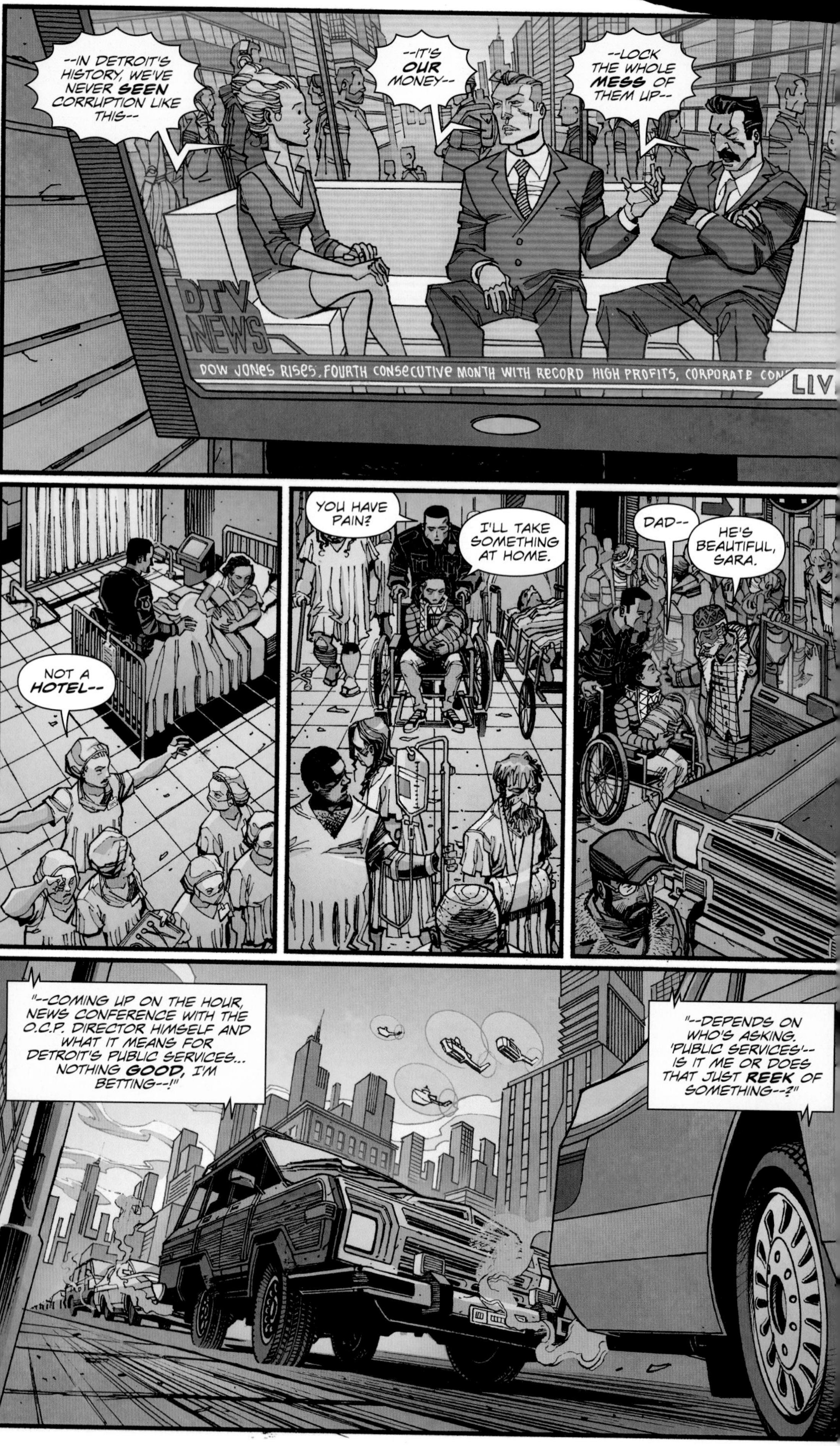
--IN DETROIT'S HISTORY, WE'VE NEVER SEEN CORRUPTION LIKE THIS--
--IT'S OUR MONEY--
--LOCK THE WHOLE MESS OF THEM UP--
DTV NEWS
DOW JONES RISES. FOURTH CONSECUTIVE MONTH WITH RECORD HIGH PROFITS. CORPORATE CON
LIV
NOT A HOTEL--
YOU HAVE PAIN?
I'LL TAKE SOMETHING AT HOME.
DAD--
HE'S BEAUTIFUL, SARA.
"--COMING UP ON THE HOUR, NEWS CONFERENCE WITH THE O.C.P. DIRECTOR HIMSELF AND WHAT IT MEANS FOR DETROIT'S PUBLIC SERVICES... NOTHING GOOD, I'M BETTING--!"
"--DEPENDS ON WHO'S ASKING. 'PUBLIC SERVICES'-- IS IT ME OR DOES THAT JUST REEK OF SOMETHING--?"

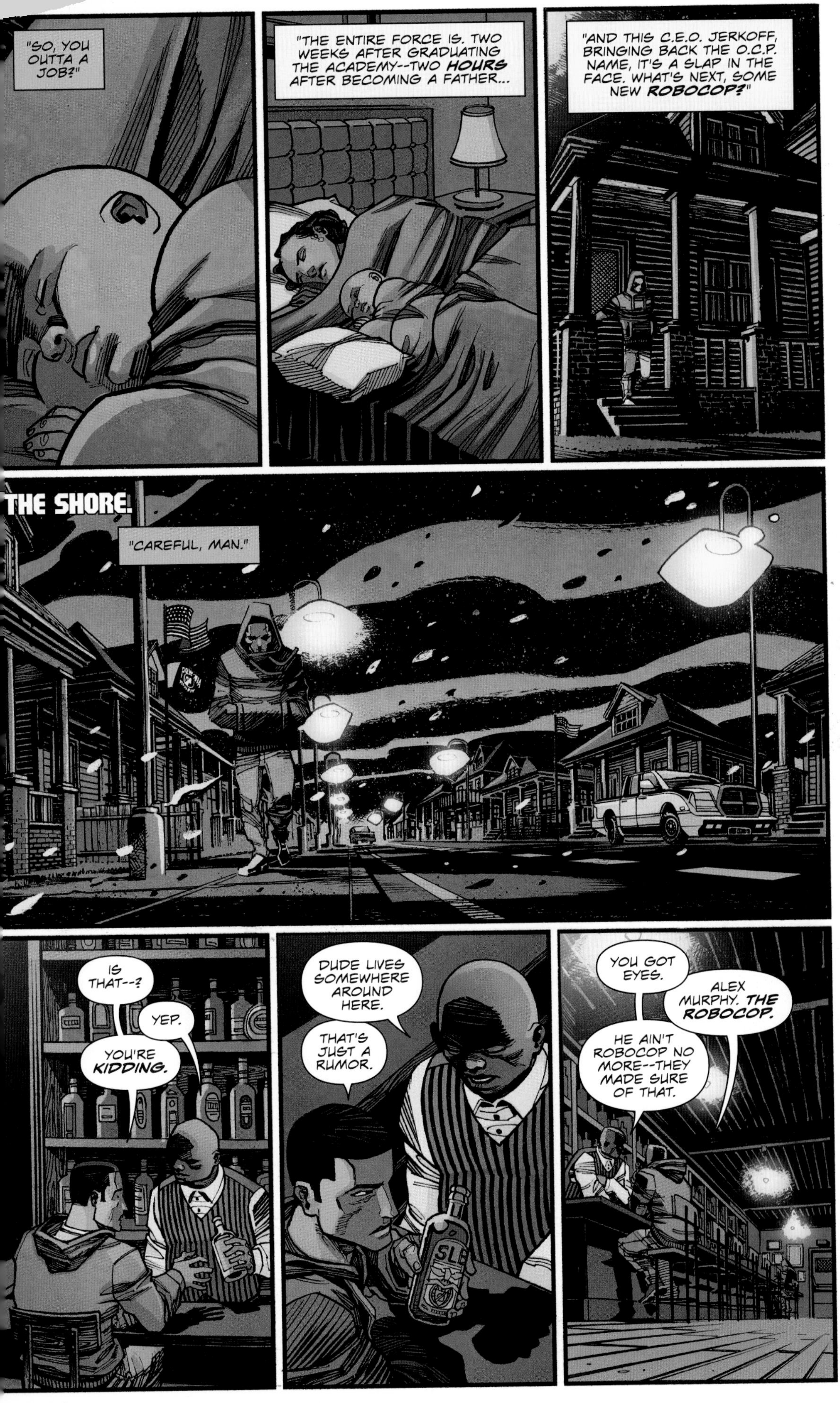
"SO, YOU OUTTA A JOB?"
"THE ENTIRE FORCE IS. TWO WEEKS AFTER GRADUATING THE *ACADEMY*--TWO ***HOURS*** AFTER BECOMING A FATHER...
"AND THIS C.E.O. JERKOFF, BRINGING BACK THE O.C.P. NAME, IT'S A SLAP IN THE FACE. WHAT'S NEXT, SOME NEW ***ROBOCOP?***"
THE SHORE.
"CAREFUL, MAN."
IS THAT--?
YEP.
YOU'RE ***KIDDING.***
DUDE LIVES SOMEWHERE AROUND HERE.
THAT'S JUST A RUMOR.
YOU GOT EYES.
ALEX MURPHY. ***THE ROBOCOP.***
HE AIN'T ROBOCOP NO MORE--THEY MADE SURE OF THAT.

"IT WAS NOT SO LONG AGO THAT DETROIT FOUND ITSELF IN AN EERILY SIMILAR PLACE TO WHERE IT IS NOW. OMNI CONSUMER PRODUCTS--O.C.P.-- HOODWINKED CITY HALL INTO AUTHORIZING AN AGGRESSIVE PRIVATIZATION OF THE POLICE."

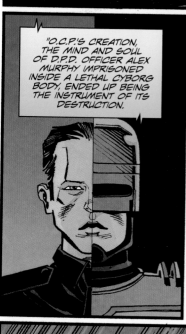

"O.C.P.'S CREATION, THE MIND AND SOUL OF D.P.D. OFFICER ALEX MURPHY IMPRISONED INSIDE A LETHAL CYBORG BODY, ENDED UP BEING THE INSTRUMENT OF ITS DESTRUCTION.

"THE ACTORS HAVE CHANGED, BUT, INCREDIBLY, THE NAMES HAVE NOT, AND YET WE'RE STILL FALLING FOR IT."

WAKE **UP,** DETROIT. WE **HAD** A HERO.

NOW ALL WE GOT ARE PRETENDERS TO THE THRONE.

IVE YEARS LATER.
RCOP
FLAG
REPORT

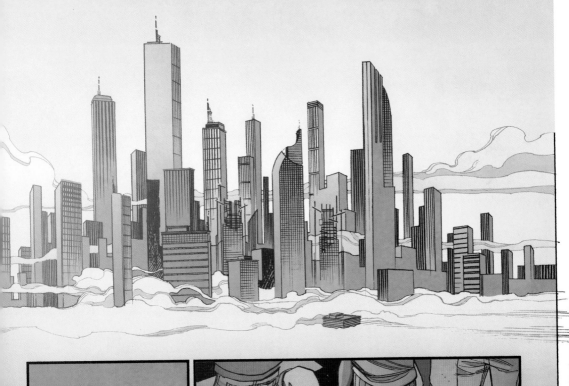

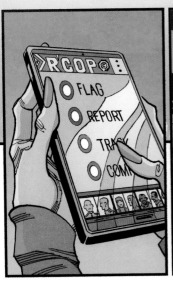

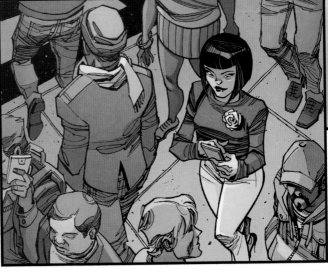

ROBOCOP™

CITIZENS ARREST

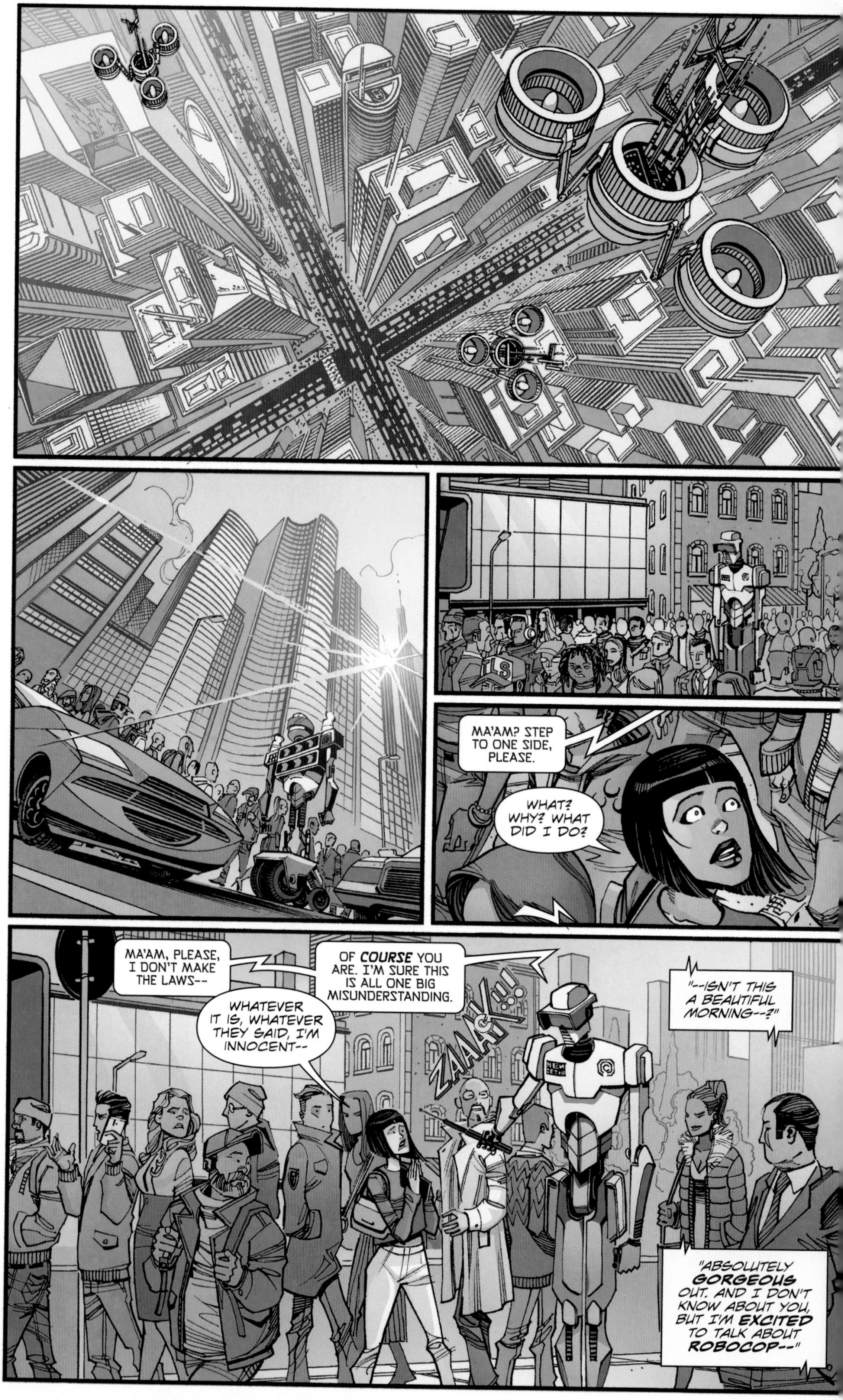
MA'AM? STEP TO ONE SIDE, PLEASE.
WHAT? WHY? WHAT DID I DO?
MA'AM, PLEASE, I DON'T MAKE THE LAWS--
WHATEVER IT IS, WHATEVER THEY SAID, I'M INNOCENT--
OF **COURSE** YOU ARE. I'M SURE THIS IS ALL ONE BIG MISUNDERSTANDING.
ZAAAK!!!
"--ISN'T THIS A BEAUTIFUL MORNING--?"
"ABSOLUTELY **GORGEOUS** OUT. AND I DON'T KNOW ABOUT YOU, BUT I'M **EXCITED** TO TALK ABOUT **ROBOCOP**--"

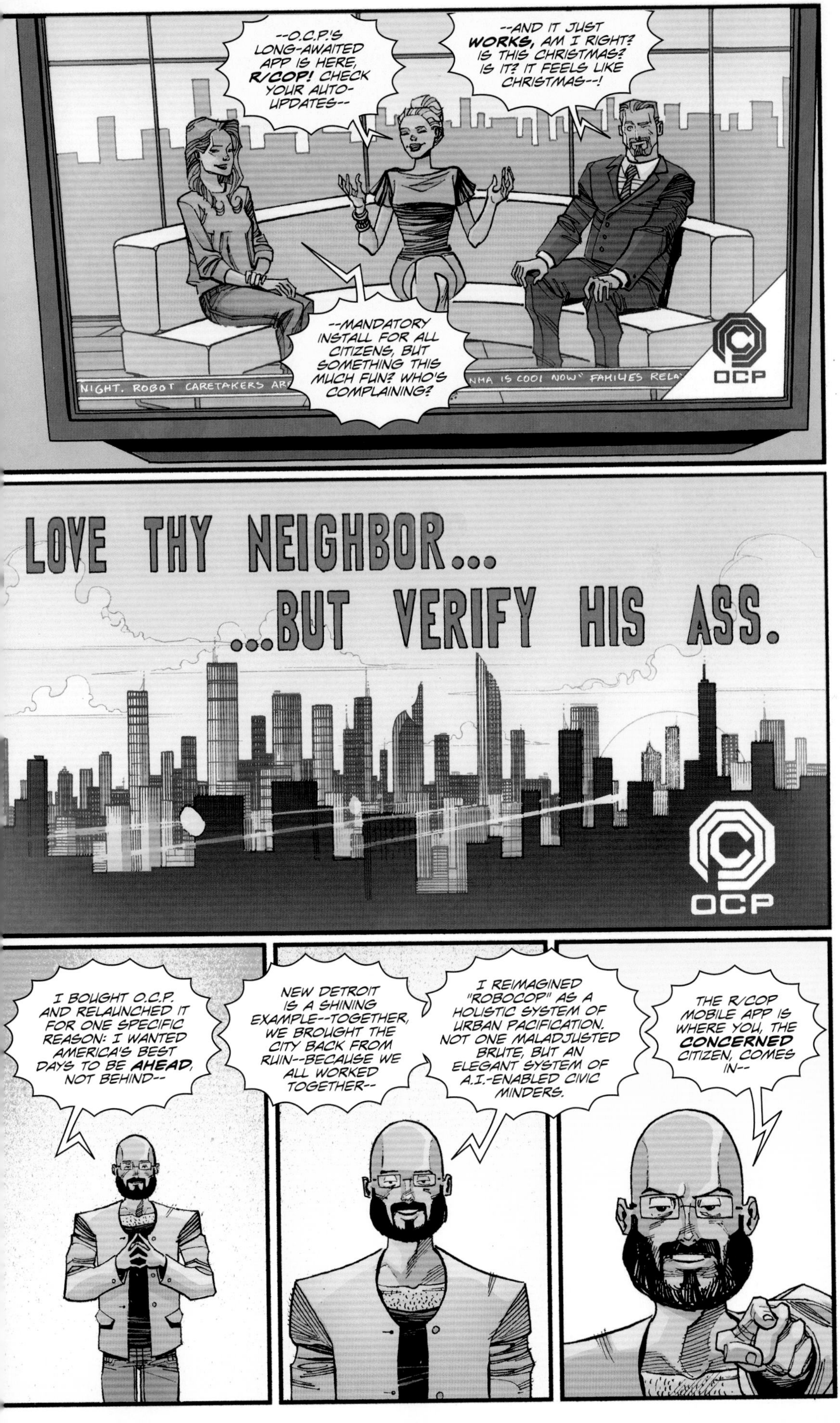
--O.C.P.'S LONG-AWAITED APP IS HERE, R/COP! CHECK YOUR AUTO-UPDATES--
--AND IT JUST WORKS, AM I RIGHT? IS THIS CHRISTMAS? IS IT? IT FEELS LIKE CHRISTMAS--!
--MANDATORY INSTALL FOR ALL CITIZENS, BUT SOMETHING THIS MUCH FUN? WHO'S COMPLAINING?
NIGHT. ROBOT CARETAKERS ARE
NNA IS COOL NOW" FAMILIES RELA
OCP
LOVE THY NEIGHBOR...
...BUT VERIFY HIS ASS.
OCP
I BOUGHT O.C.P. AND RELAUNCHED IT FOR ONE SPECIFIC REASON: I WANTED AMERICA'S BEST DAYS TO BE AHEAD, NOT BEHIND--
NEW DETROIT IS A SHINING EXAMPLE--TOGETHER, WE BROUGHT THE CITY BACK FROM RUIN--BECAUSE WE ALL WORKED TOGETHER--
I REIMAGINED "ROBOCOP" AS A HOLISTIC SYSTEM OF URBAN PACIFICATION. NOT ONE MALADJUSTED BRUTE, BUT AN ELEGANT SYSTEM OF A.I.-ENABLED CIVIC MINDERS.
THE R/COP MOBILE APP IS WHERE YOU, THE CONCERNED CITIZEN, COMES IN--

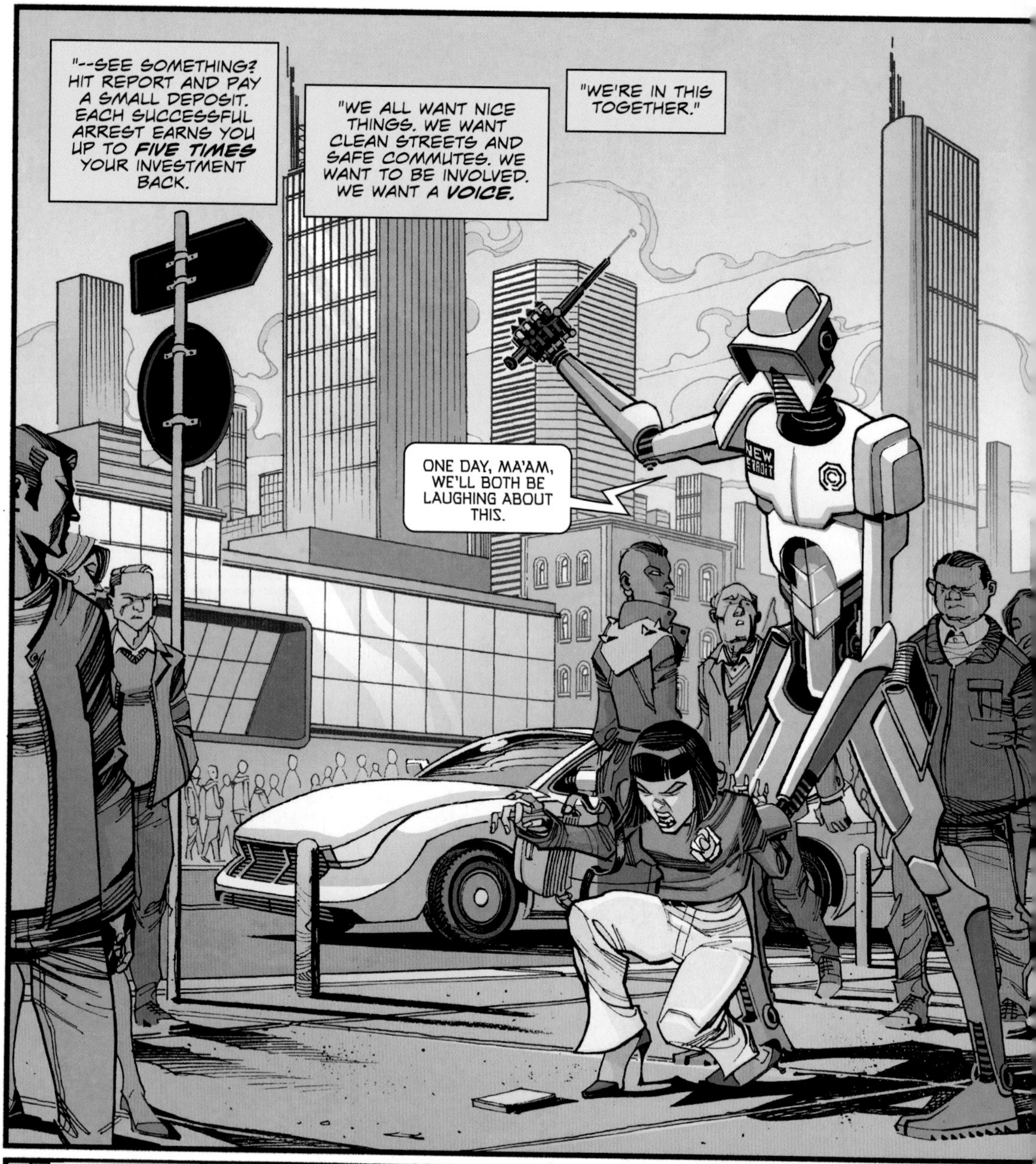
"--SEE SOMETHING? HIT REPORT AND PAY A SMALL DEPOSIT. EACH SUCCESSFUL ARREST EARNS YOU UP TO FIVE TIMES YOUR INVESTMENT BACK.
"WE ALL WANT NICE THINGS. WE WANT CLEAN STREETS AND SAFE COMMUTES. WE WANT TO BE INVOLVED. WE WANT A VOICE.
"WE'RE IN THIS TOGETHER."
NEW DETROIT
ONE DAY, MA'AM, WE'LL BOTH BE LAUGHING ABOUT THIS.

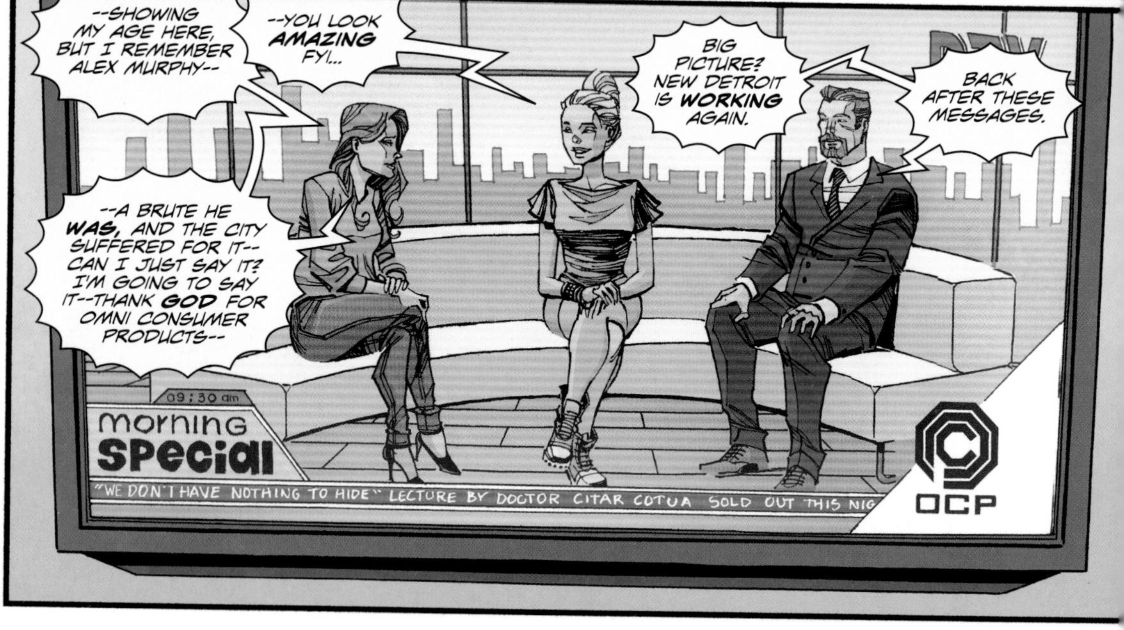
--SHOWING MY AGE HERE, BUT I REMEMBER ALEX MURPHY--
--YOU LOOK AMAZING FYI...
BIG PICTURE? NEW DETROIT IS WORKING AGAIN.
BACK AFTER THESE MESSAGES.
--A BRUTE HE WAS, AND THE CITY SUFFERED FOR IT--CAN I JUST SAY IT? I'M GOING TO SAY IT--THANK GOD FOR OMNI CONSUMER PRODUCTS--
09:30 am
morning Special
"WE DON'T HAVE NOTHING TO HIDE" LECTURE BY DOCTOR CITAR COTUA SOLD OUT THIS NIG
OCP

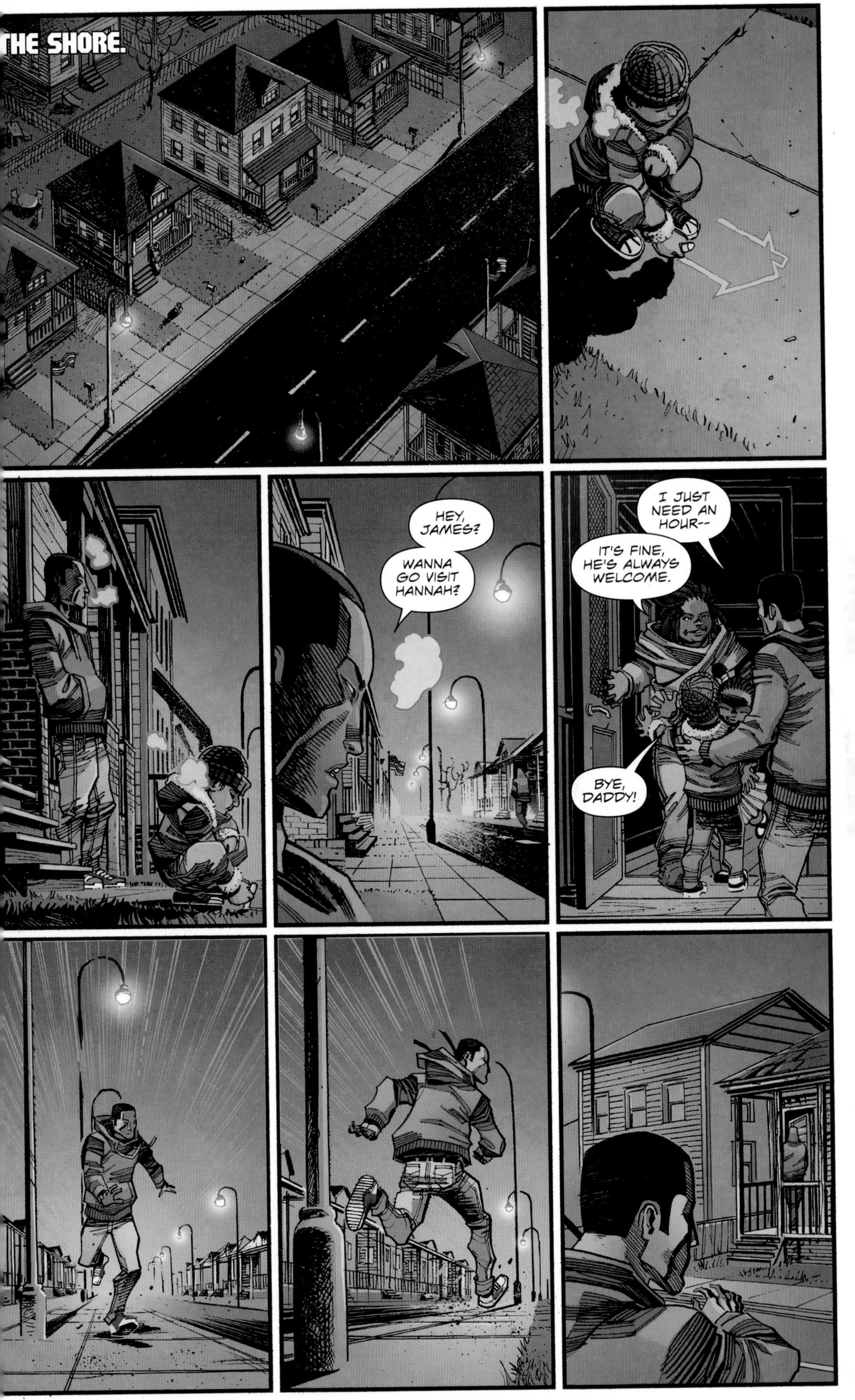
THE SHORE.
HEY, JAMES?
WANNA GO VISIT HANNAH?
I JUST NEED AN HOUR--
IT'S FINE, HE'S ALWAYS WELCOME.
BYE, DADDY!

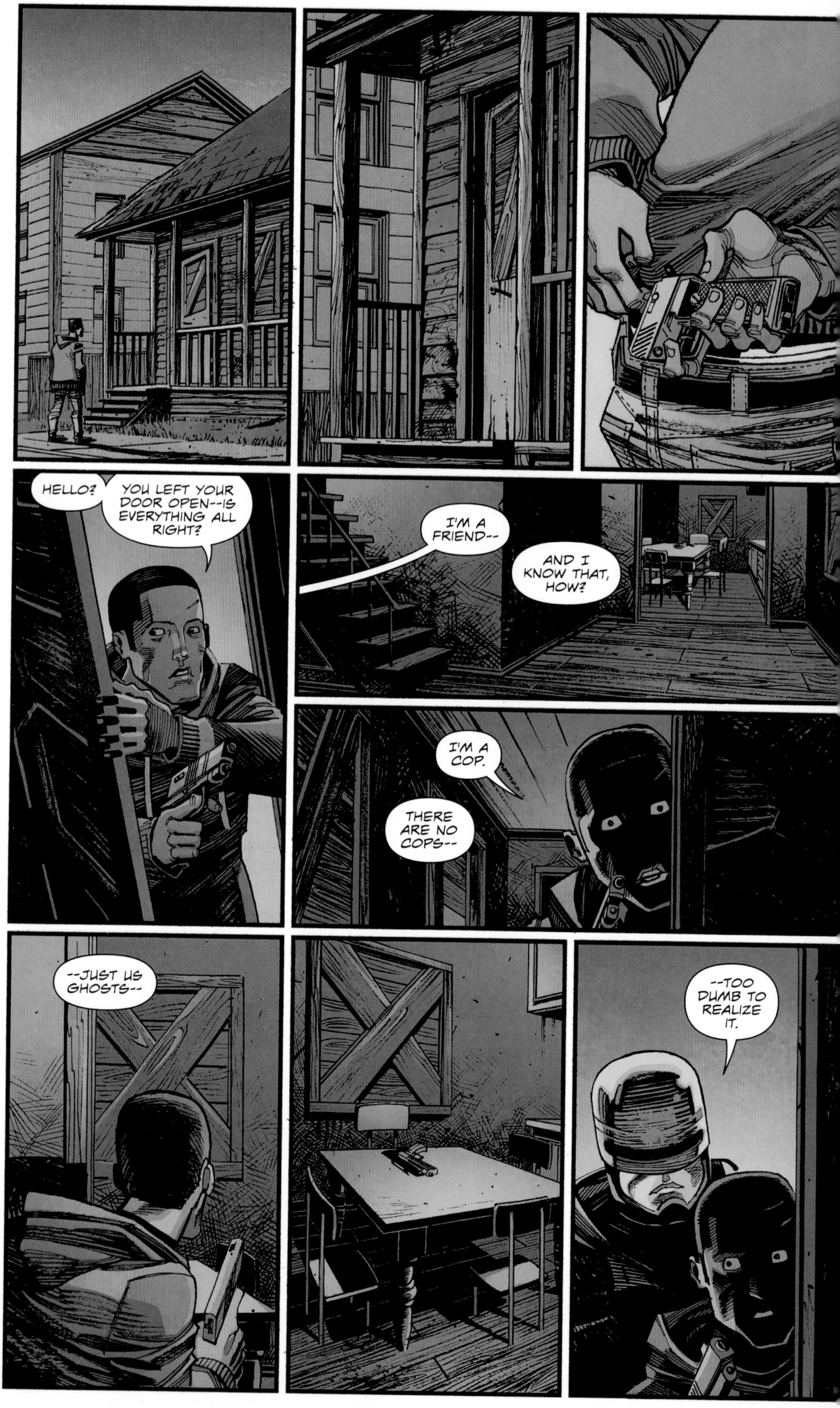
HELLO?
YOU LEFT YOUR DOOR OPEN--IS EVERYTHING ALL RIGHT?
I'M A FRIEND--
AND I KNOW THAT, HOW?
I'M A COP.
THERE ARE NO COPS--
--JUST US GHOSTS--
--TOO DUMB TO REALIZE IT.

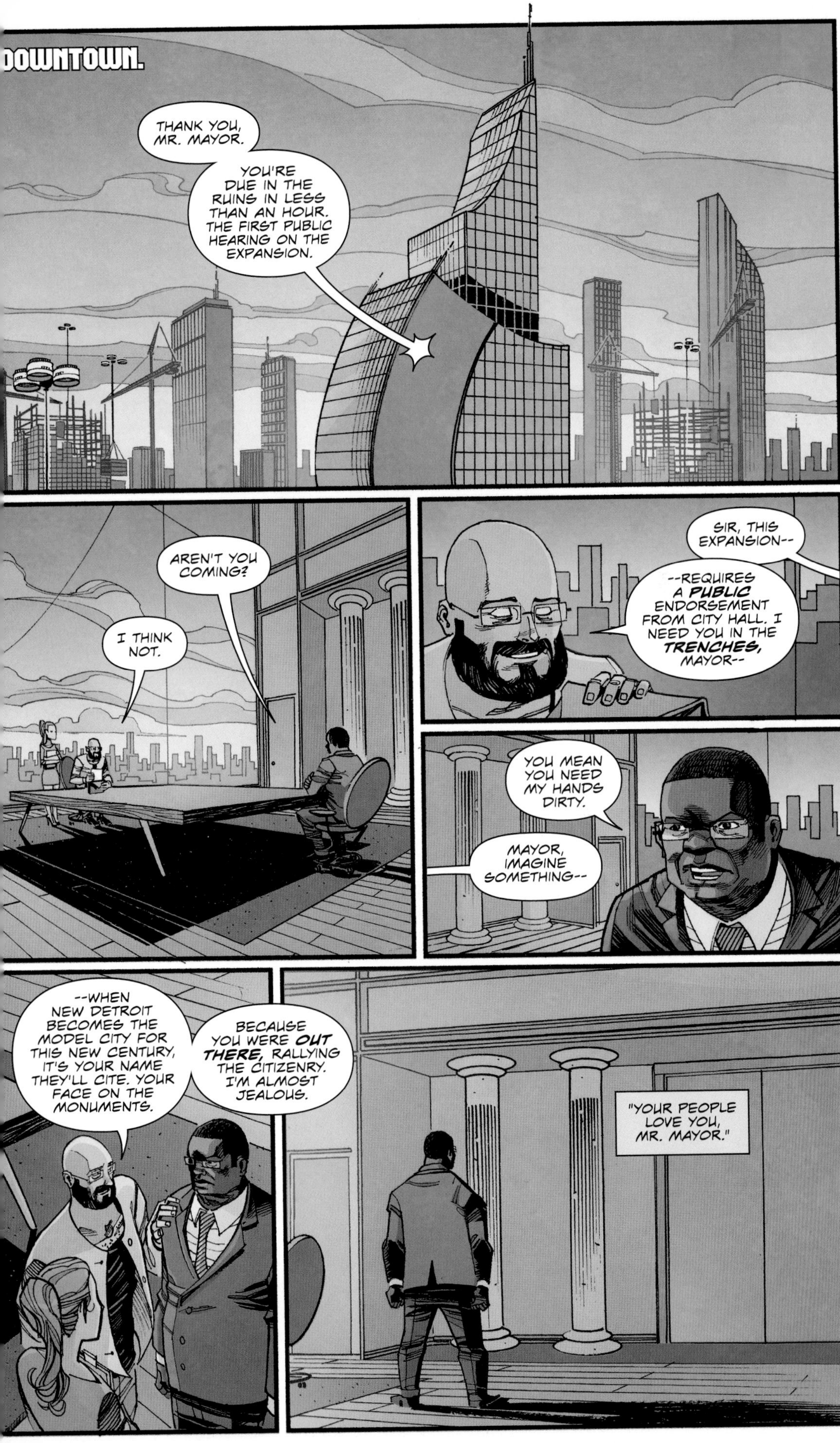
DOWNTOWN.
THANK YOU, MR. MAYOR.
YOU'RE DUE IN THE RUINS IN LESS THAN AN HOUR. THE FIRST PUBLIC HEARING ON THE EXPANSION.
AREN'T YOU COMING?
I THINK NOT.
SIR, THIS EXPANSION--
--REQUIRES A PUBLIC ENDORSEMENT FROM CITY HALL. I NEED YOU IN THE TRENCHES, MAYOR--
YOU MEAN YOU NEED MY HANDS DIRTY.
MAYOR, IMAGINE SOMETHING--
--WHEN NEW DETROIT BECOMES THE MODEL CITY FOR THIS NEW CENTURY, IT'S YOUR NAME THEY'LL CITE. YOUR FACE ON THE MONUMENTS.
BECAUSE YOU WERE OUT THERE, RALLYING THE CITIZENRY. I'M ALMOST JEALOUS.
"YOUR PEOPLE LOVE YOU, MR. MAYOR."

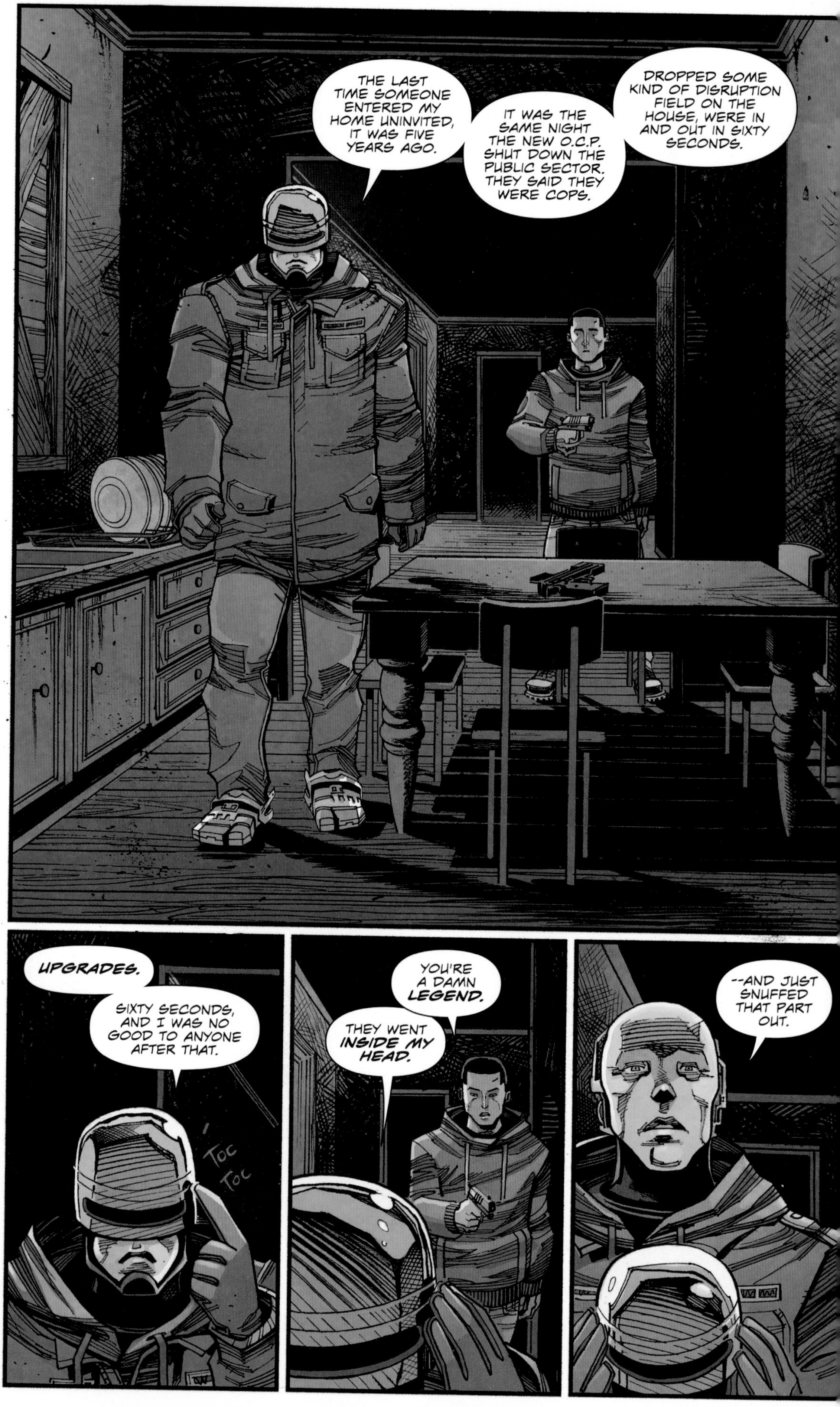
THE LAST TIME SOMEONE ENTERED MY HOME UNINVITED, IT WAS FIVE YEARS AGO.
IT WAS THE SAME NIGHT THE NEW O.C.P. SHUT DOWN THE PUBLIC SECTOR. THEY SAID THEY WERE COPS.
DROPPED SOME KIND OF DISRUPTION FIELD ON THE HOUSE, WERE IN AND OUT IN SIXTY SECONDS.
UPGRADES.
SIXTY SECONDS, AND I WAS NO GOOD TO ANYONE AFTER THAT.
TOC TOC
YOU'RE A DAMN LEGEND.
THEY WENT INSIDE MY HEAD.
--AND JUST SNUFFED THAT PART OUT.

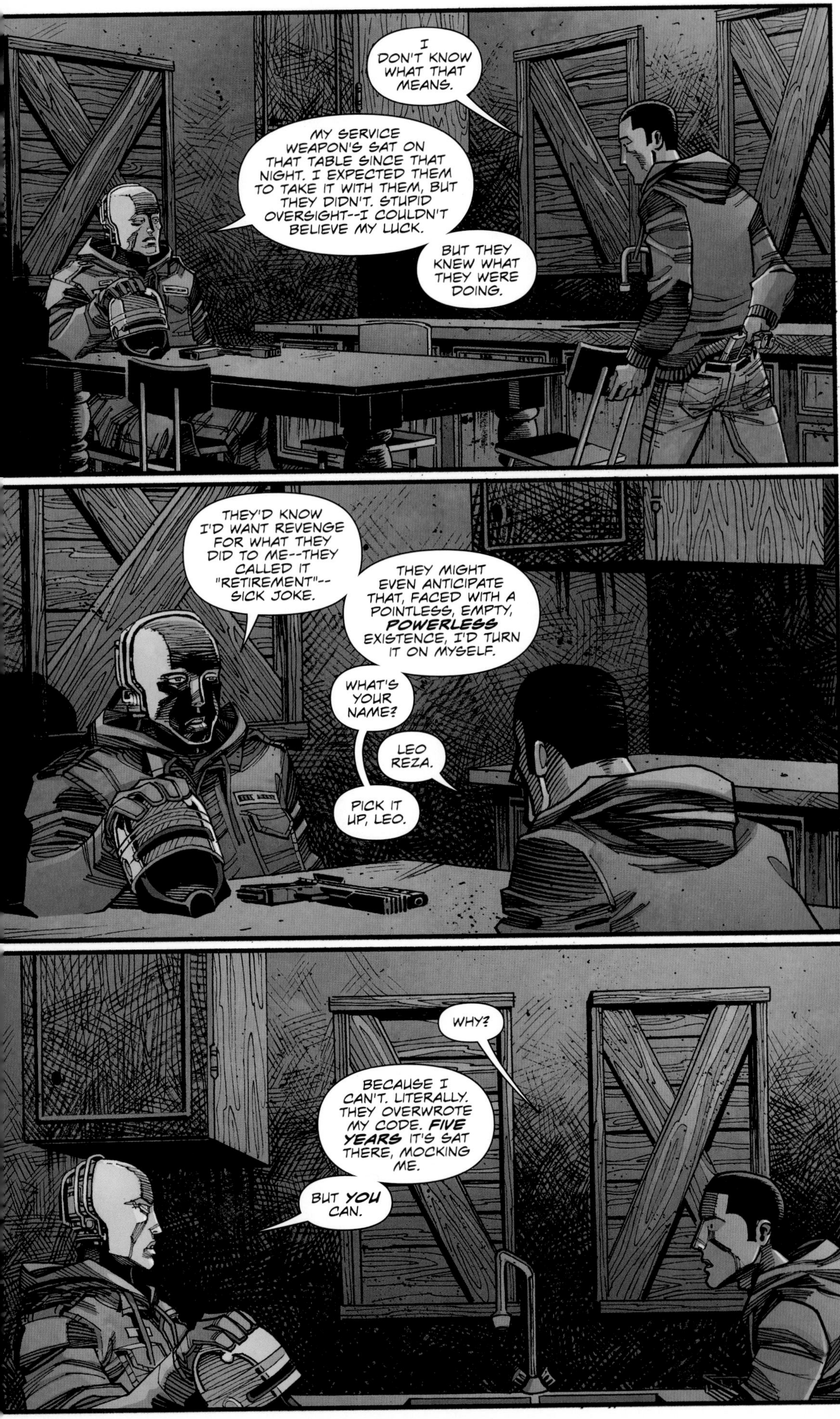
I DON'T KNOW WHAT THAT MEANS.
MY SERVICE WEAPON'S SAT ON THAT TABLE SINCE THAT NIGHT. I EXPECTED THEM TO TAKE IT WITH THEM, BUT THEY DIDN'T. STUPID OVERSIGHT--I COULDN'T BELIEVE MY LUCK.
BUT THEY KNEW WHAT THEY WERE DOING.
THEY'D KNOW I'D WANT REVENGE FOR WHAT THEY DID TO ME--THEY CALLED IT "RETIREMENT"--SICK JOKE.
THEY MIGHT EVEN ANTICIPATE THAT, FACED WITH A POINTLESS, EMPTY, **POWERLESS** EXISTENCE, I'D TURN IT ON MYSELF.
WHAT'S YOUR NAME?
LEO REZA.
PICK IT UP, LEO.
WHY?
BECAUSE I CAN'T. LITERALLY. THEY OVERWROTE MY CODE. ***FIVE YEARS*** IT'S SAT THERE, MOCKING ME.
BUT ***YOU*** CAN.

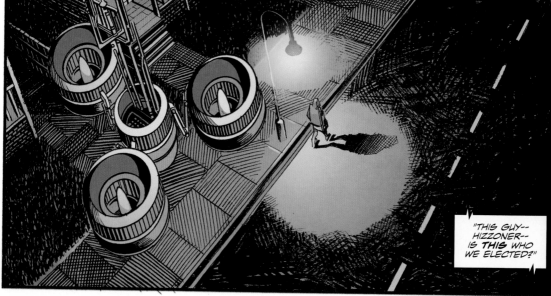

"THIS GUY-- HIZZONER-- IS **THIS** WHO WE ELECTED?"

A PUBLIC HEARING-- PUH-LEEZE. "BUT IT'S DEMOCRACY IN ACTION!", THEY SAY.

DEMOCRACY IS **DEAD.** YOU KNOW WHAT KILLED IT? THE FREE MARKET. INNOVATION. PROSPERITY. OH, BOO HOO HOO, HOW **TERRIBLE.**

YOU WANT TO KNOW WHAT **SURRENDER** LOOKS LIKE? THE MAYOR OF DETROIT HEADING DOWN TO THE **RUINS** TO GIVE THOSE FILTHY ANIMALS THE PRIVILEGE OF A VOICE.

MEANWHILE, **I** HAVE TO GO TO **REHAB** FOR **PILLS.**

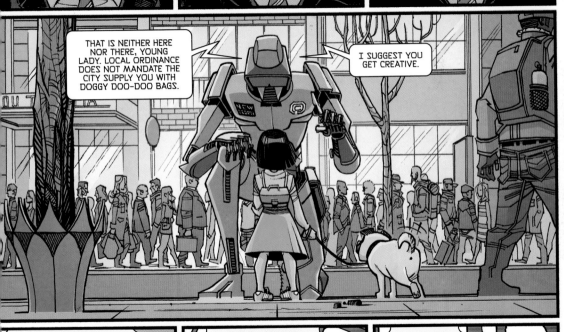

THAT IS NEITHER HERE NOR THERE, YOUNG LADY. LOCAL ORDINANCE DOES NOT MANDATE THE CITY SUPPLY YOU WITH DOGGY DOO-DOO BAGS.

I SUGGEST YOU GET CREATIVE.

AT FIRST, I DIDN'T LIKE HOW WE HAD TO **PAY** TO REPORT A CRIME ON R/COP. BUT IT COMES RIGHT OUT OF YOUR BANK ACCOUNT! SO EASY! YOU BARELY NOTICE IT!

THEN, IT BECOMES LIKE A **GAME.** BECAUSE IF YOU'RE **RIGHT** AND YOU DID SPOT A CRIME, YOU WIN A JACKPOT! ACTUAL MONEY!

ALL I **DO** NOW IS LOOK FOR THINGS TO REPORT.

THAT SMUG BITCH AT WORK BEST WATCH HER ASS.

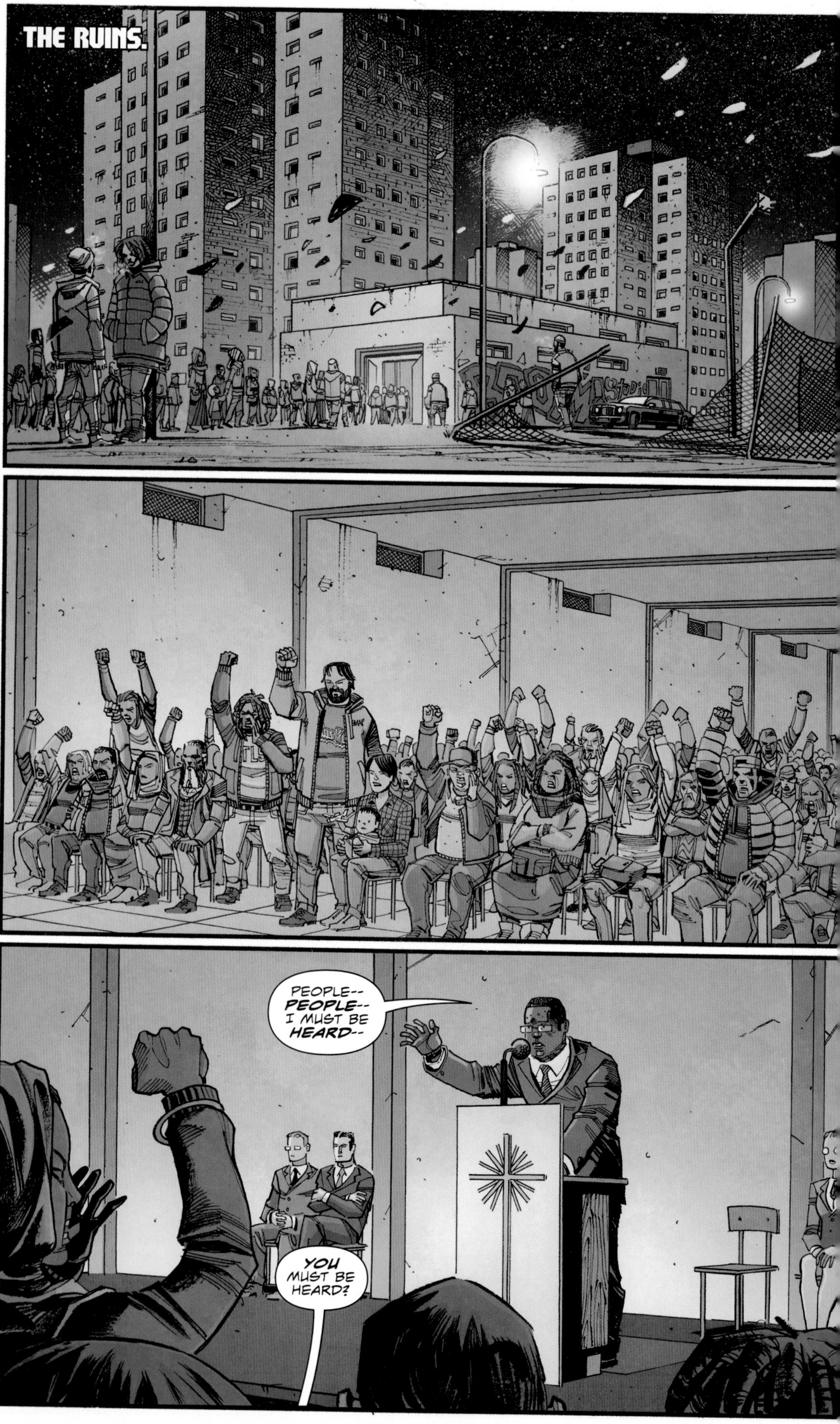
THE RUINS.
PEOPLE-- PEOPLE-- I MUST BE HEARD--
YOU MUST BE HEARD?

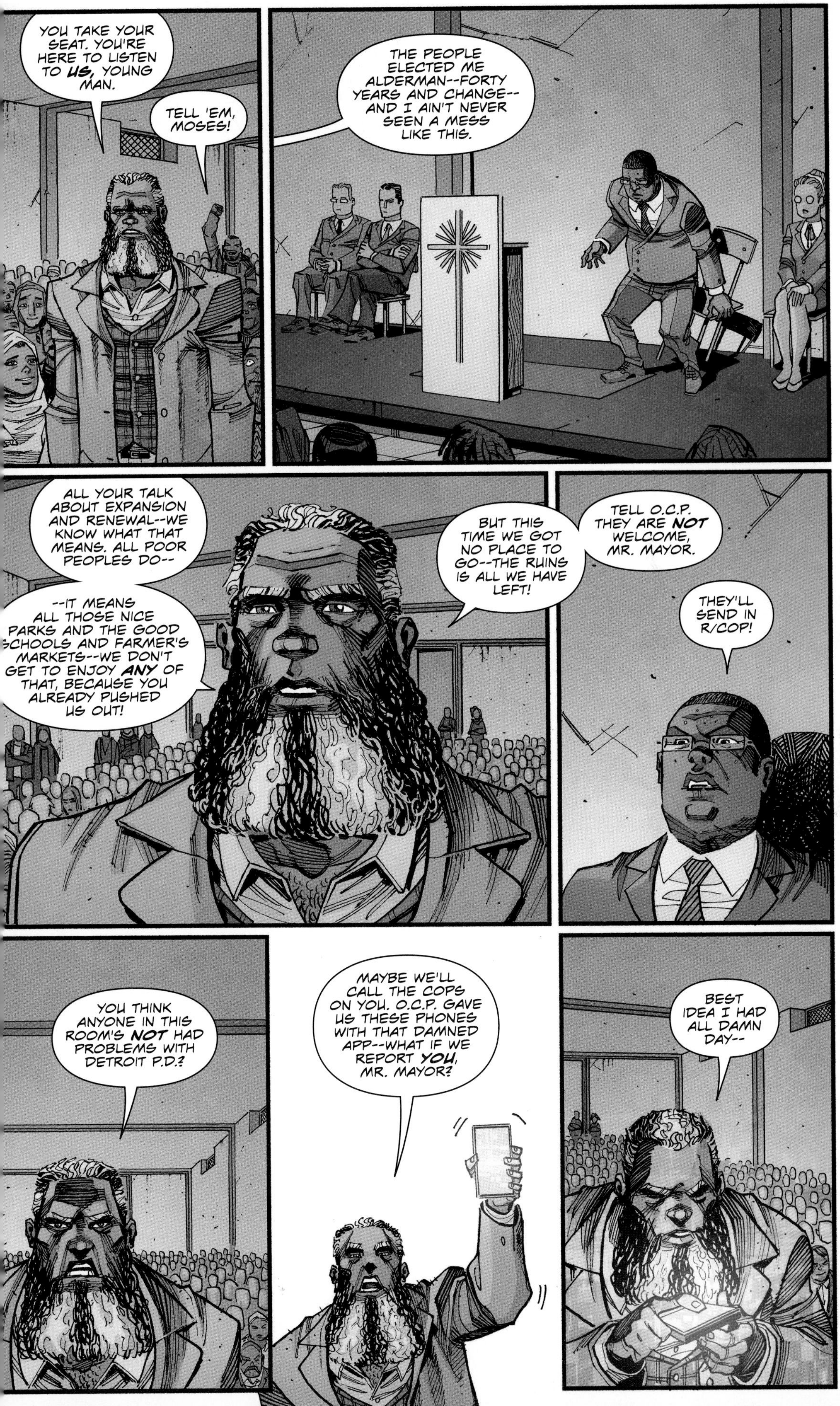

YOU TAKE YOUR SEAT. YOU'RE HERE TO LISTEN TO US, YOUNG MAN.
TELL 'EM, MOSES!
THE PEOPLE ELECTED ME ALDERMAN--FORTY YEARS AND CHANGE--AND I AIN'T NEVER SEEN A MESS LIKE THIS.
ALL YOUR TALK ABOUT EXPANSION AND RENEWAL--WE KNOW WHAT THAT MEANS. ALL POOR PEOPLES DO--
--IT MEANS ALL THOSE NICE PARKS AND THE GOOD SCHOOLS AND FARMER'S MARKETS--WE DON'T GET TO ENJOY ANY OF THAT, BECAUSE YOU ALREADY PUSHED US OUT!
BUT THIS TIME WE GOT NO PLACE TO GO--THE RUINS IS ALL WE HAVE LEFT!
TELL O.C.P. THEY ARE NOT WELCOME, MR. MAYOR.
THEY'LL SEND IN R/COP!
YOU THINK ANYONE IN THIS ROOM'S NOT HAD PROBLEMS WITH DETROIT P.D.?
MAYBE WE'LL CALL THE COPS ON YOU. O.C.P. GAVE US THESE PHONES WITH THAT DAMNED APP--WHAT IF WE REPORT YOU, MR. MAYOR?
BEST IDEA I HAD ALL DAMN DAY--

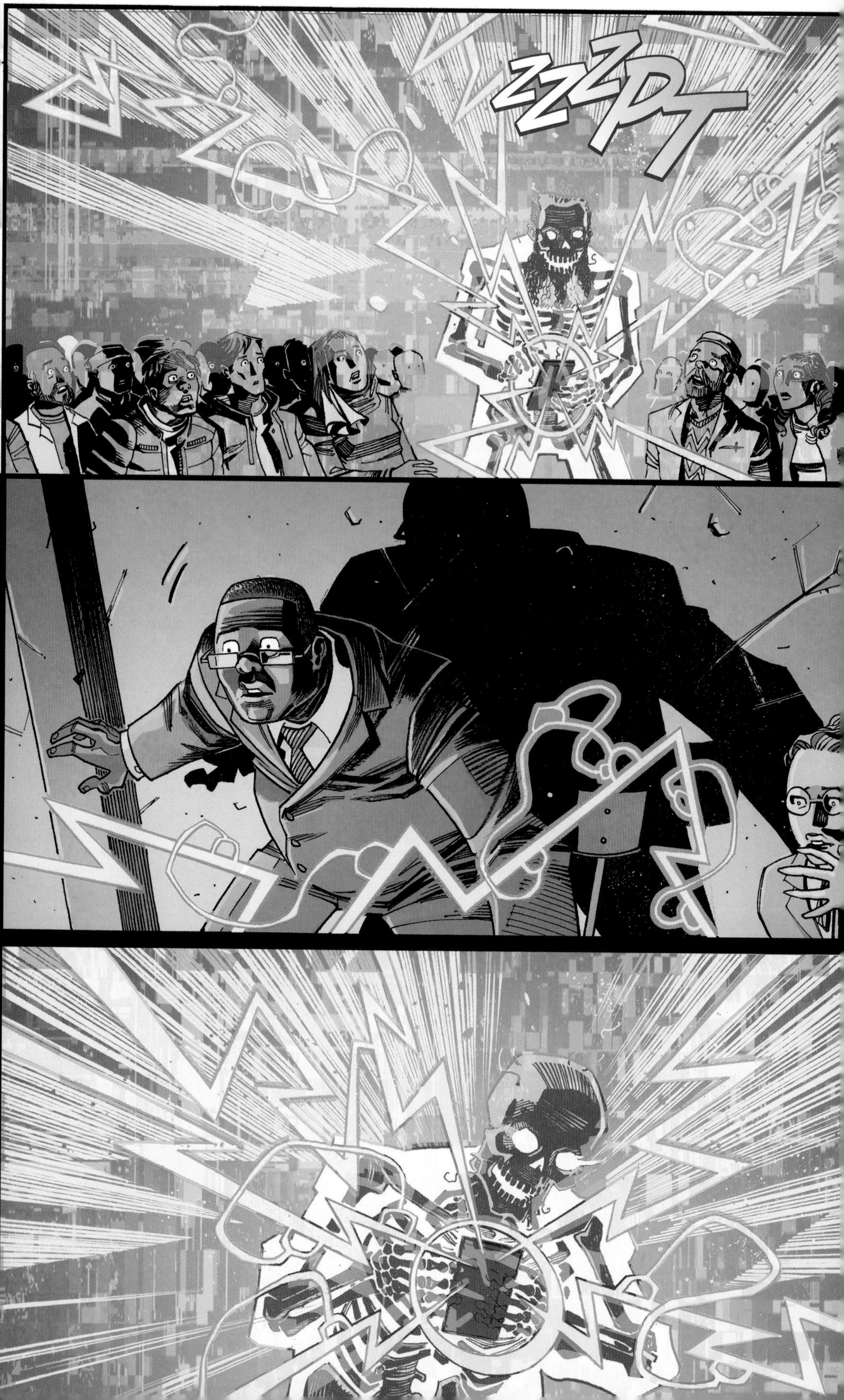
ZZZPT

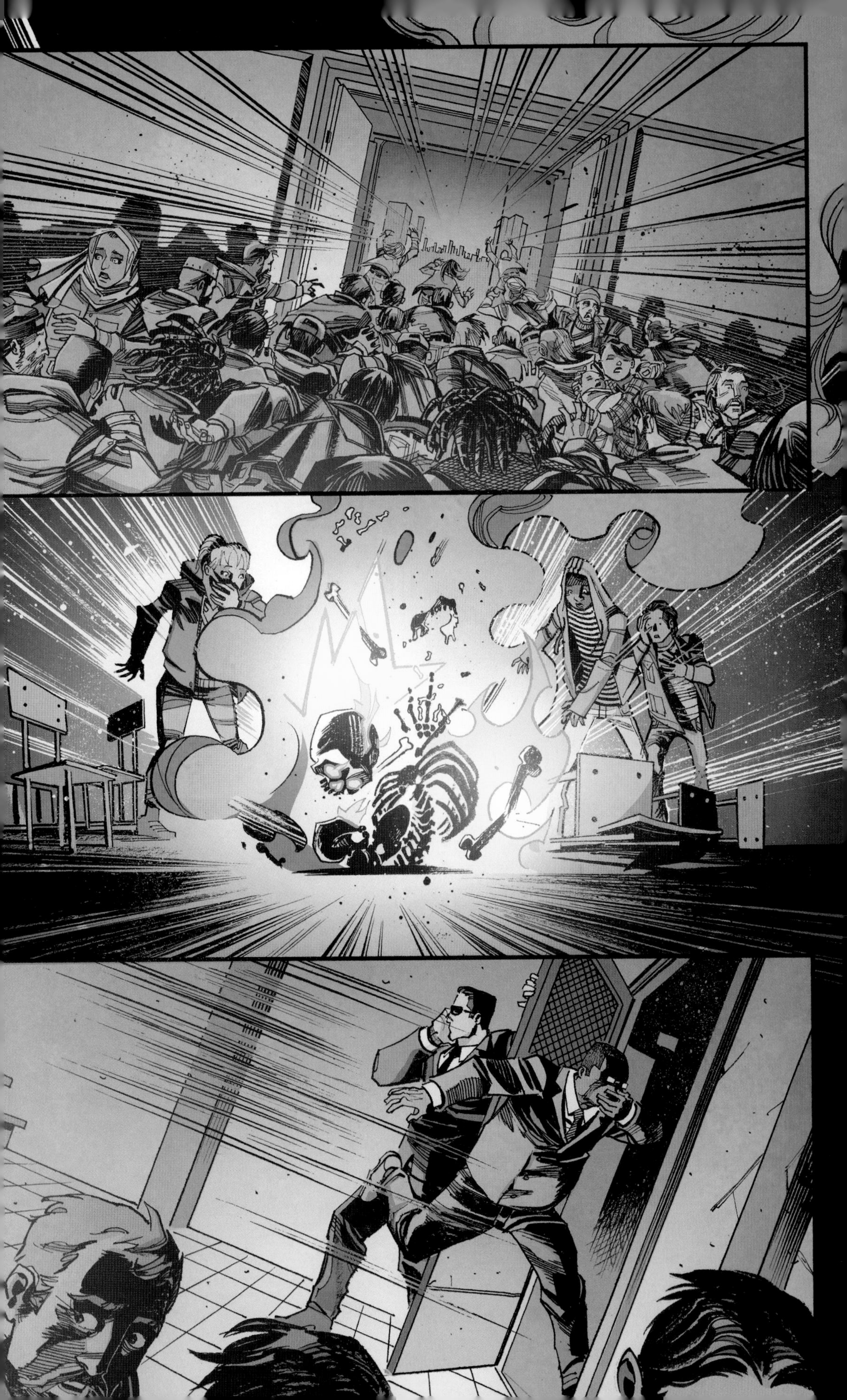

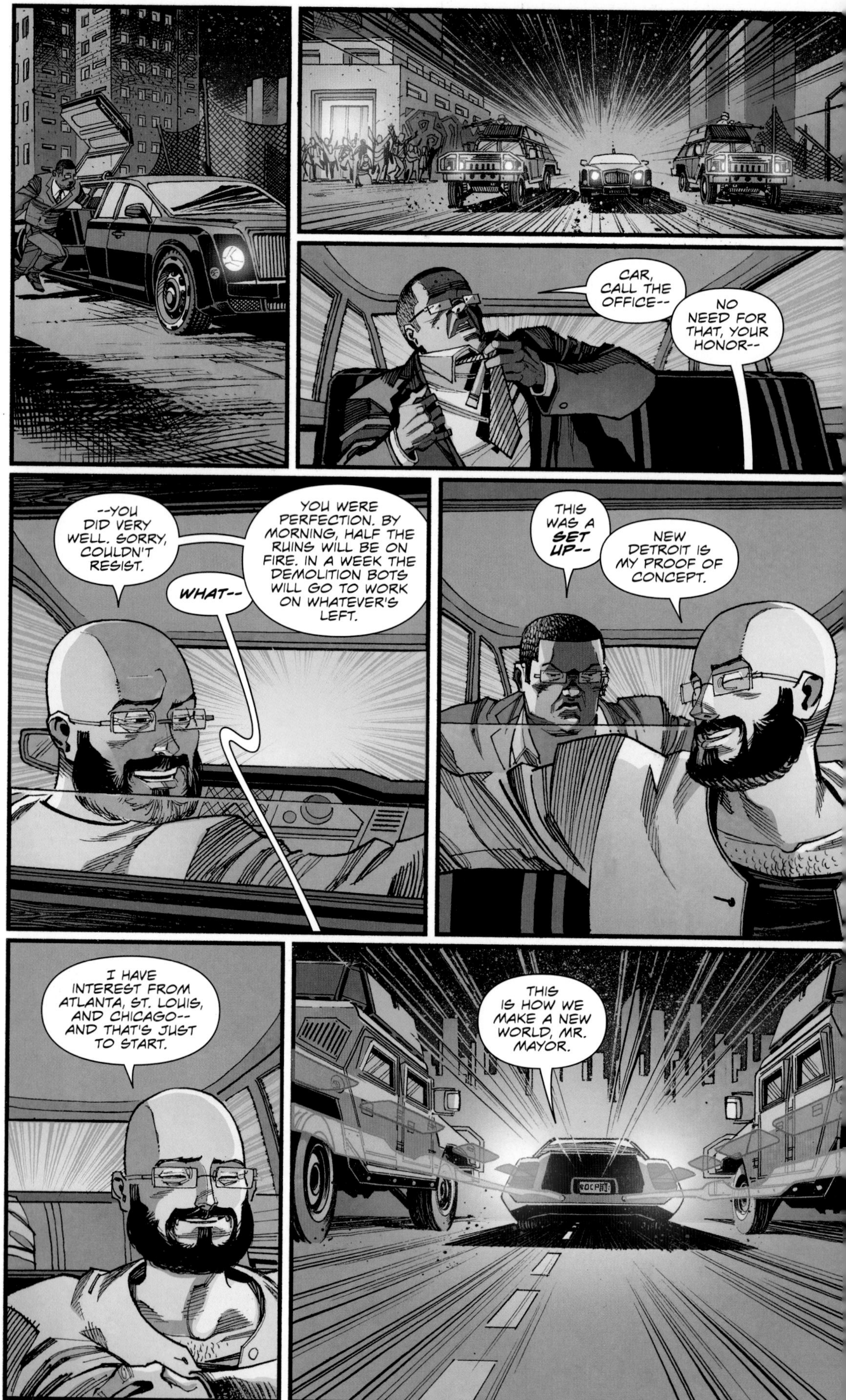
CAR, CALL THE OFFICE--
NO NEED FOR THAT, YOUR HONOR--
--YOU DID VERY WELL. SORRY, COULDN'T RESIST.
WHAT--
YOU WERE PERFECTION. BY MORNING, HALF THE RUINS WILL BE ON FIRE. IN A WEEK THE DEMOLITION BOTS WILL GO TO WORK ON WHATEVER'S LEFT.
THIS WAS A SET UP--
NEW DETROIT IS MY PROOF OF CONCEPT.
I HAVE INTEREST FROM ATLANTA, ST. LOUIS, AND CHICAGO-- AND THAT'S JUST TO START.
THIS IS HOW WE MAKE A NEW WORLD, MR. MAYOR.

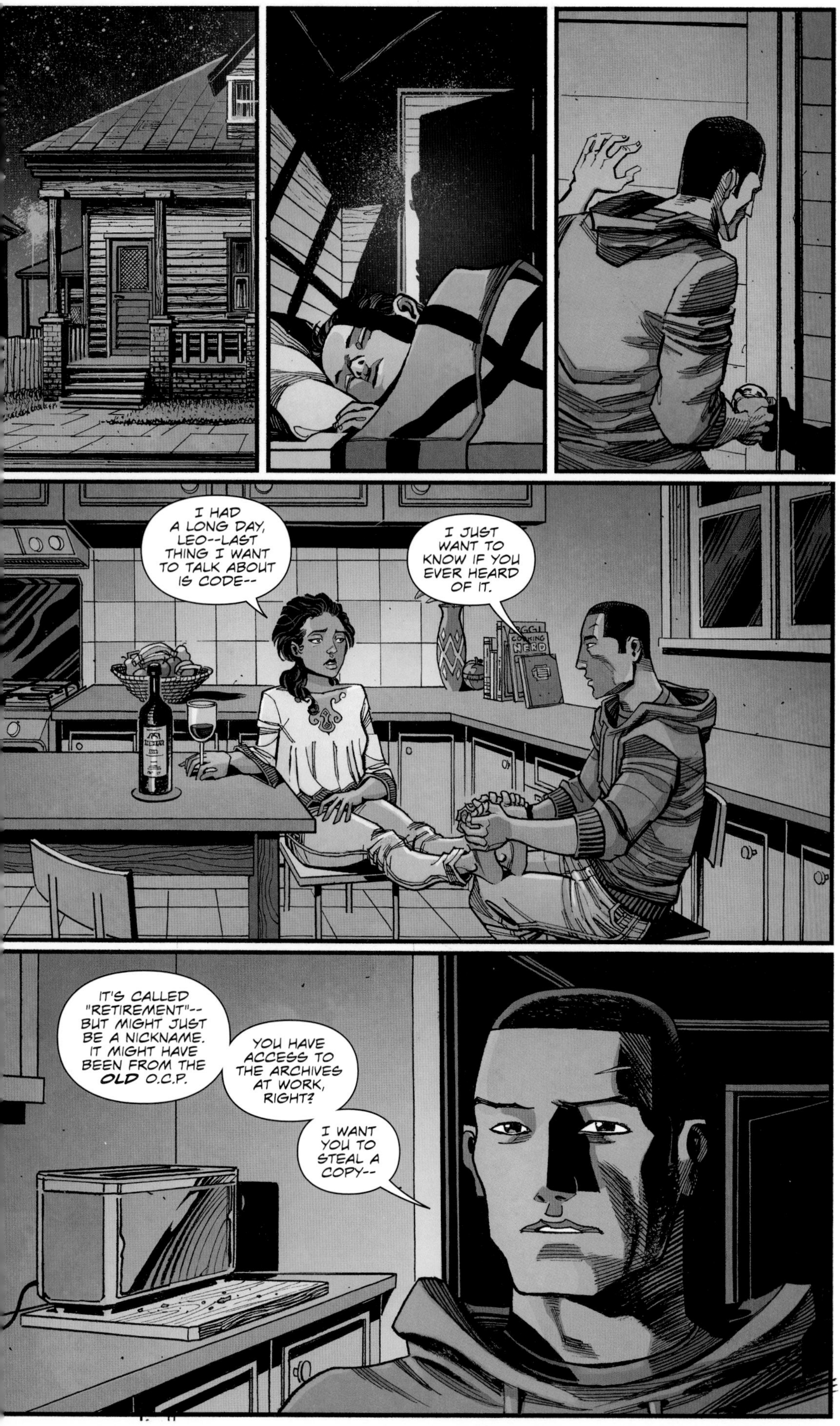

I HAD A LONG DAY, LEO--LAST THING I WANT TO TALK ABOUT IS CODE--
I JUST WANT TO KNOW IF YOU EVER HEARD OF IT.
COOKING NERD
IT'S CALLED "RETIREMENT"--BUT MIGHT JUST BE A NICKNAME. IT MIGHT HAVE BEEN FROM THE OLD O.C.P.
YOU HAVE ACCESS TO THE ARCHIVES AT WORK, RIGHT?
I WANT YOU TO STEAL A COPY--

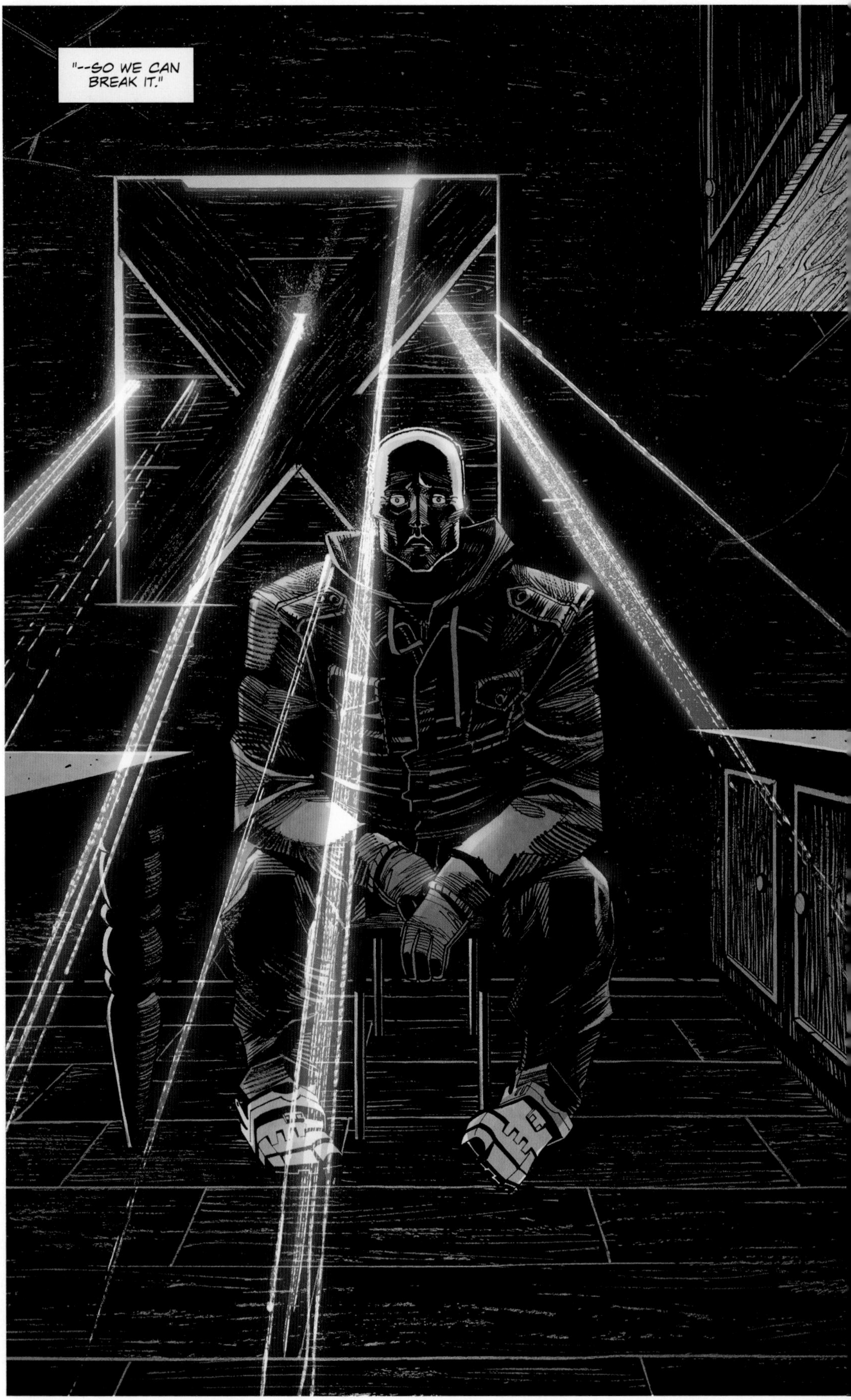
"--SO WE CAN BREAK IT."

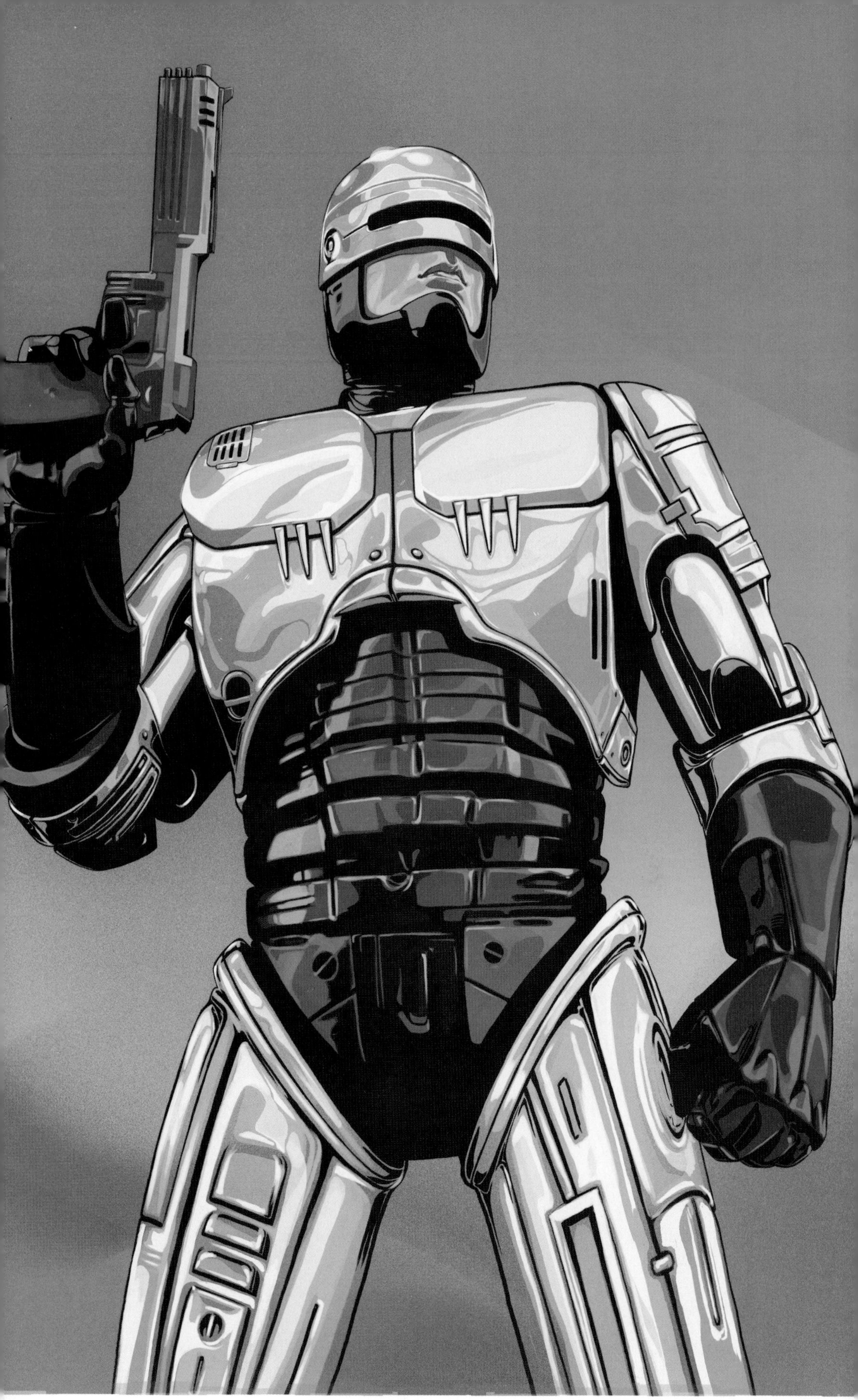

ISSUE 01 COVER NIMIT MALAVIA

TWO

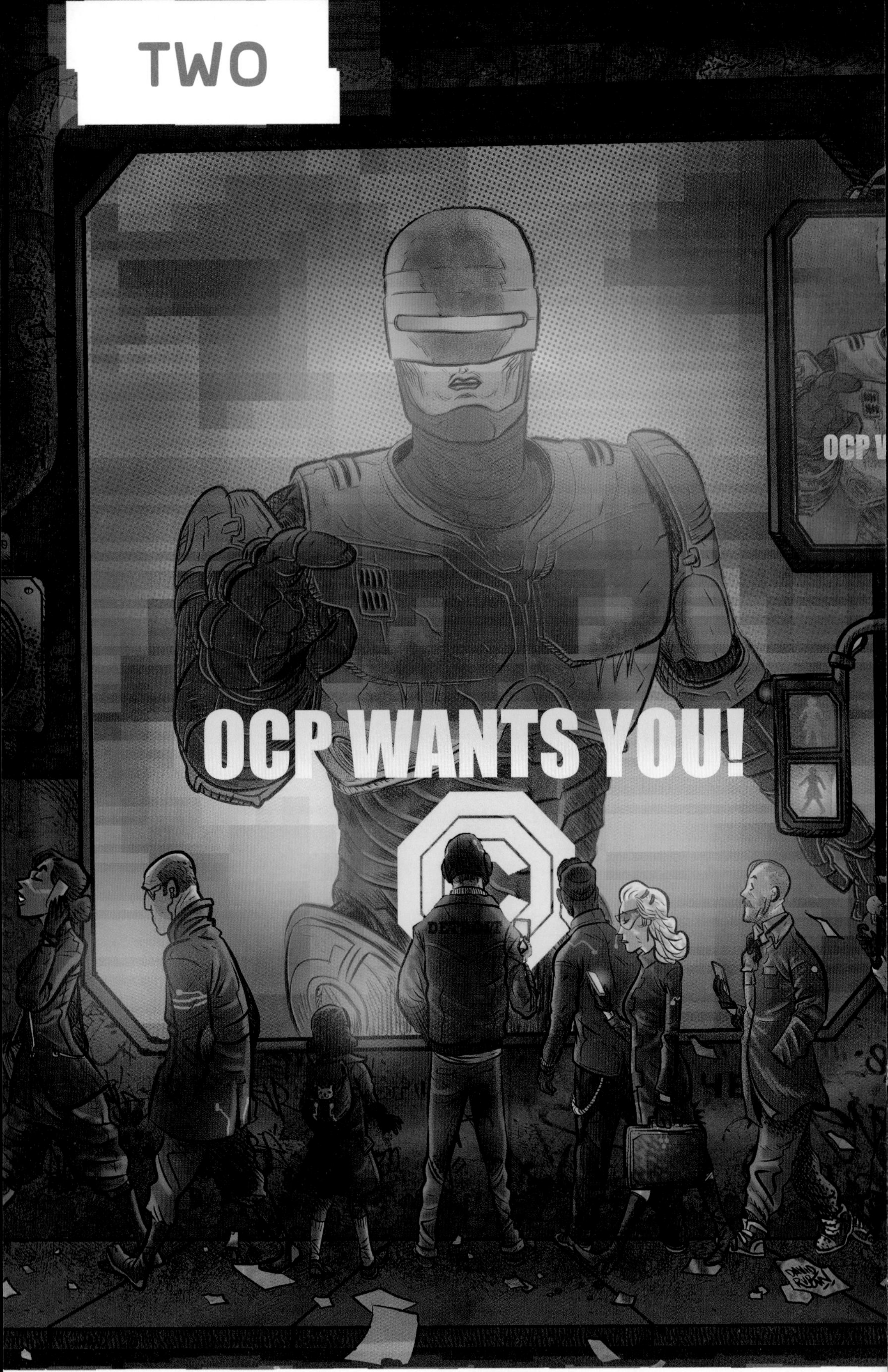
OCP WANTS YOU!

ISSUE 02 COVER DAVID RUBÍN

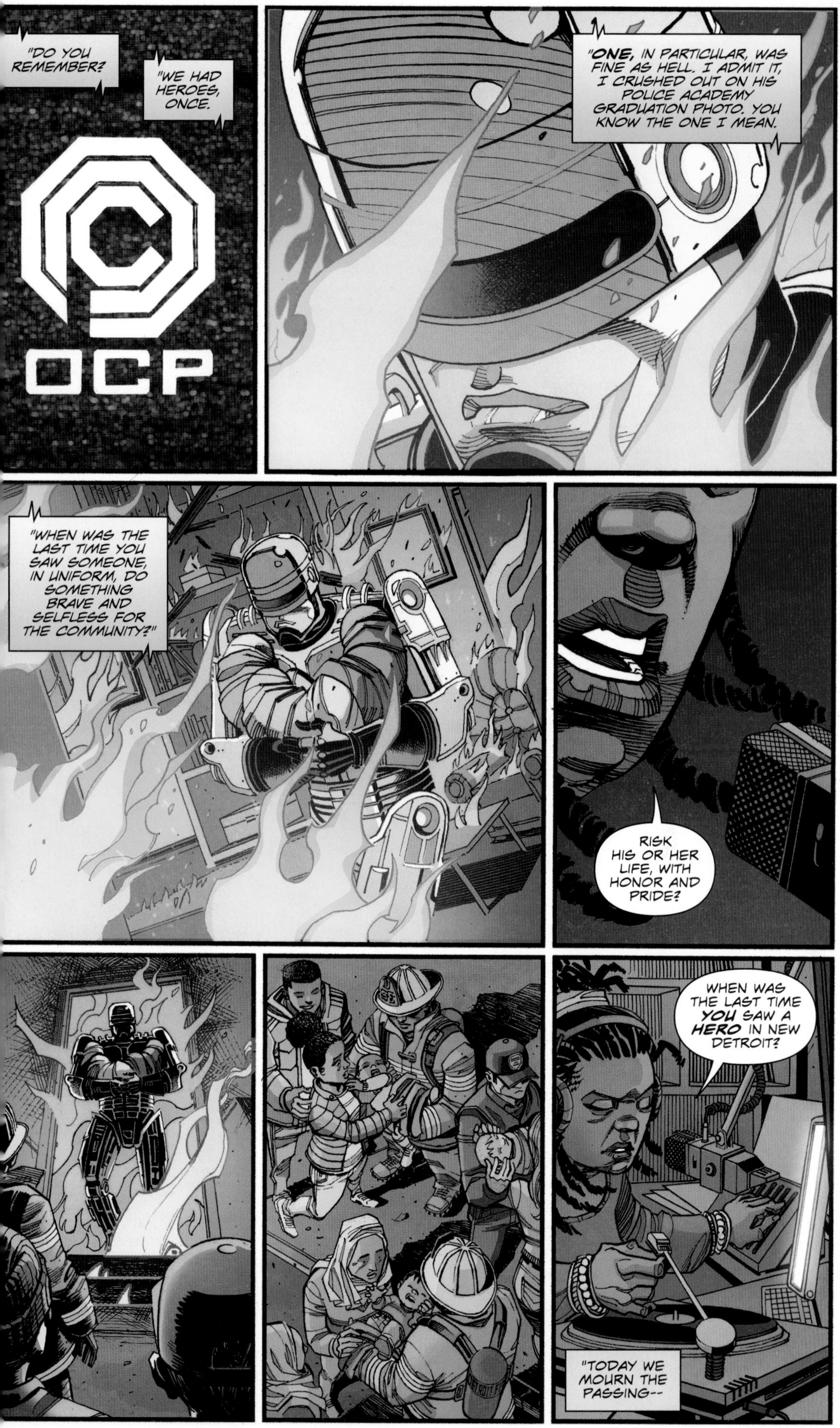
"DO YOU REMEMBER?
"WE HAD HEROES, ONCE.
OCP
"ONE, IN PARTICULAR, WAS FINE AS HELL. I ADMIT IT, I CRUSHED OUT ON HIS POLICE ACADEMY GRADUATION PHOTO. YOU KNOW THE ONE I MEAN.
"WHEN WAS THE LAST TIME YOU SAW SOMEONE, IN UNIFORM, DO SOMETHING BRAVE AND SELFLESS FOR THE COMMUNITY?"
RISK HIS OR HER LIFE, WITH HONOR AND PRIDE?
WHEN WAS THE LAST TIME YOU SAW A HERO IN NEW DETROIT?
"TODAY WE MOURN THE PASSING--

"--ALDERMAN *MOSES DESULMA*, WHO SPENT NEARLY HIS ENTIRE LIFE IN SERVICE TO THIS CITY.

"AS WE COME TOGETHER TO REMEMBER MOSES, LET US ALSO UNITE OUR SPIRITS TOWARDS ANOTHER COMMON PURPOSE--

"--MAKING *ALL* OF DETROIT A *NEW* DETROIT, SAFE AND CLEAN AND HONEST. LET'S MAKE MOSES *PROUD.*"

THE RUINS

Brighthill

INTRODUCING O.C.P.'S NEWEST EXPANSION!

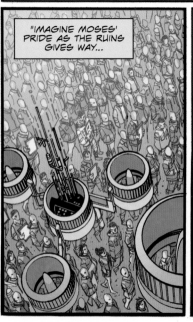

"IMAGINE MOSES' PRIDE AS THE RUINS GIVES WAY...

"...TO A GLEAMING NEW NEIGHBORHOOD WITH A NAME TO MATCH.

"CHECK YOUR PHONES--OPEN YOUR R/COP APP AND ENTER THE LOTTERY TO BE ONE OF THE FIRST CITIZENS--

"--TO WIN *LUXURY APARTMENTS* IN THE BEAUTIFUL TOWERS WE'LL SOON BUILD IN BRIGHTHILL!"

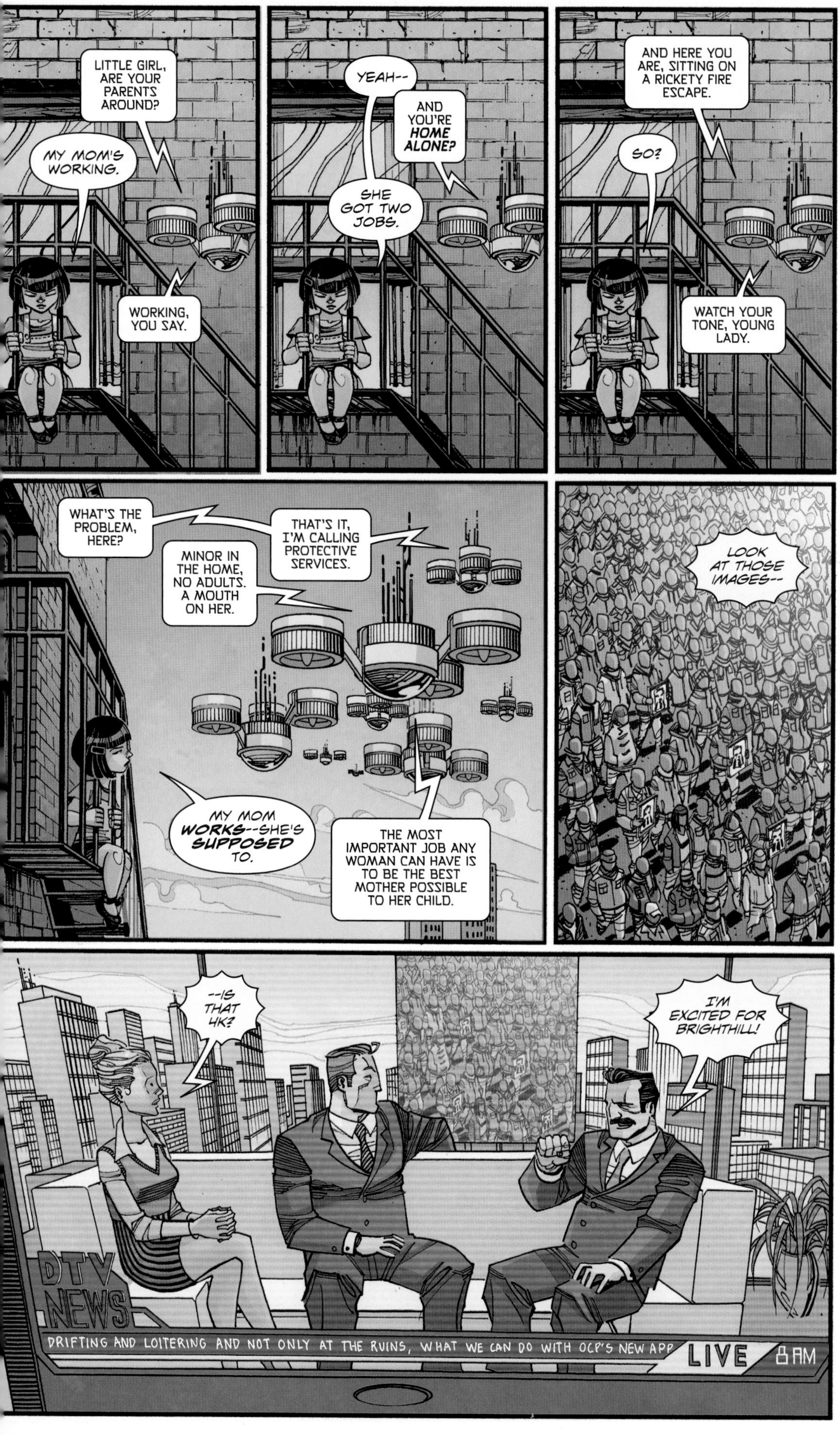
LITTLE GIRL, ARE YOUR PARENTS AROUND?
MY MOM'S WORKING.
WORKING, YOU SAY.
YEAH--
SHE GOT TWO JOBS.
AND YOU'RE HOME ALONE?
AND HERE YOU ARE, SITTING ON A RICKETY FIRE ESCAPE.
SO?
WATCH YOUR TONE, YOUNG LADY.
WHAT'S THE PROBLEM, HERE?
MINOR IN THE HOME, NO ADULTS. A MOUTH ON HER.
THAT'S IT, I'M CALLING PROTECTIVE SERVICES.
MY MOM WORKS--SHE'S SUPPOSED TO.
THE MOST IMPORTANT JOB ANY WOMAN CAN HAVE IS TO BE THE BEST MOTHER POSSIBLE TO HER CHILD.
LOOK AT THOSE IMAGES--
--IS THAT 4K?
I'M EXCITED FOR BRIGHTHILL!
DTV NEWS
DRIFTING AND LOITERING AND NOT ONLY AT THE RUINS, WHAT WE CAN DO WITH OCP'S NEW APP
LIVE
8 AM

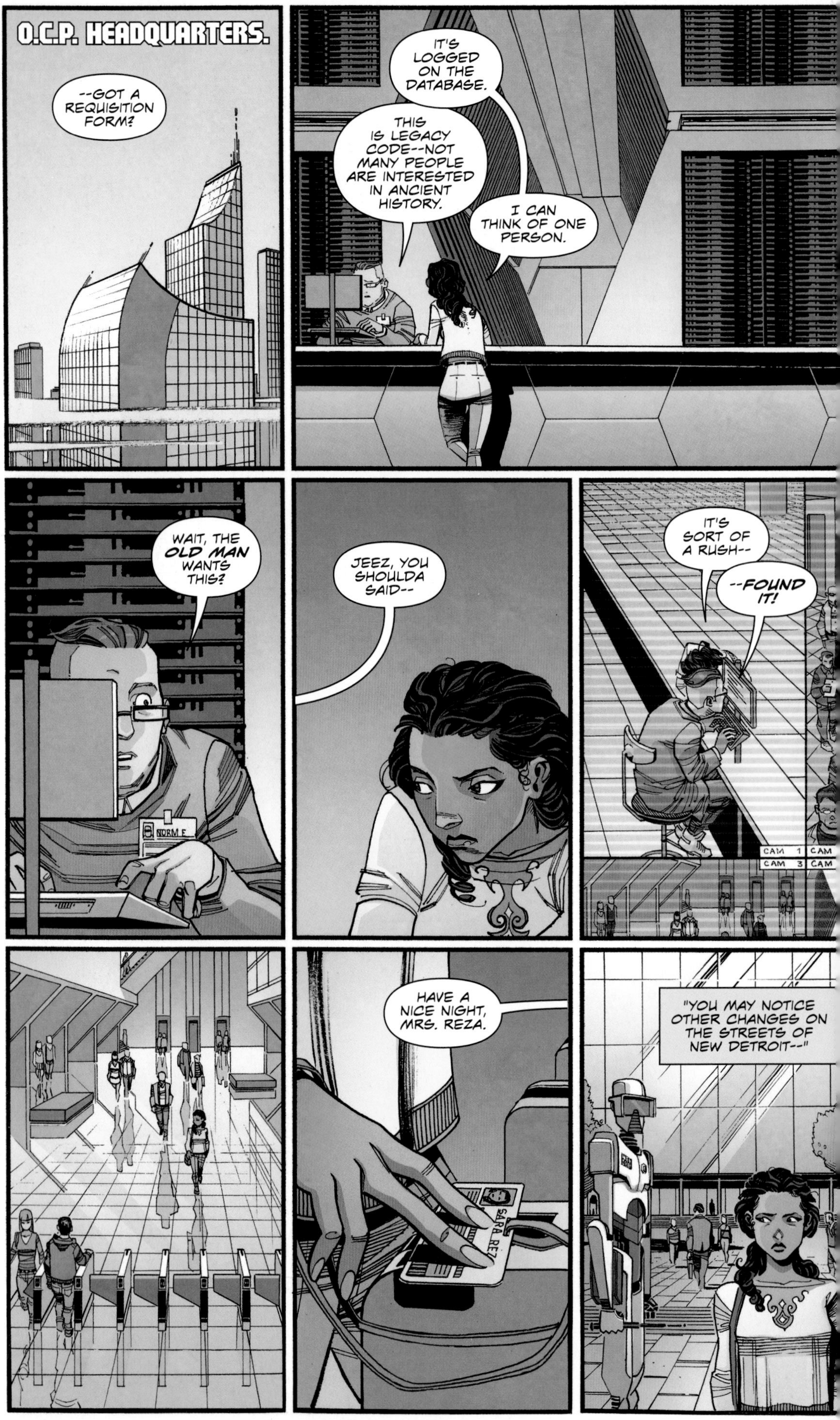
O.C.P. HEADQUARTERS.
--GOT A REQUISITION FORM?
IT'S LOGGED ON THE DATABASE.
THIS IS LEGACY CODE--NOT MANY PEOPLE ARE INTERESTED IN ANCIENT HISTORY.
I CAN THINK OF ONE PERSON.
WAIT, THE OLD MAN WANTS THIS?
NORM F.
JEEZ, YOU SHOULDA SAID--
IT'S SORT OF A RUSH--
--FOUND IT!
CAM 1
CAM
CAM 3
CAM
HAVE A NICE NIGHT, MRS. REZA.
SARA REZ
"YOU MAY NOTICE OTHER CHANGES ON THE STREETS OF NEW DETROIT--"

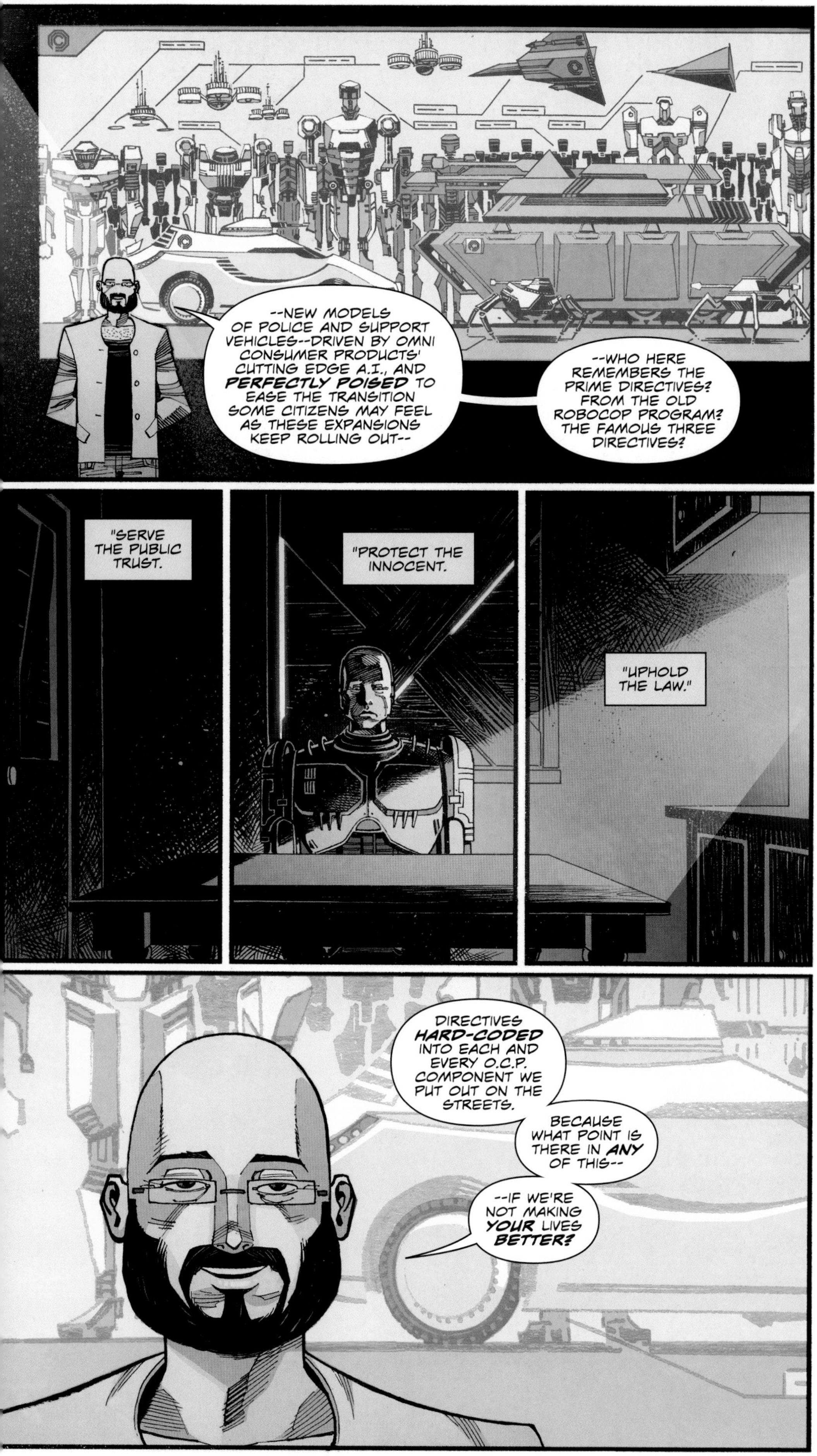
--NEW MODELS OF POLICE AND SUPPORT VEHICLES--DRIVEN BY OMNI CONSUMER PRODUCTS' CUTTING EDGE A.I., AND PERFECTLY POISED TO EASE THE TRANSITION SOME CITIZENS MAY FEEL AS THESE EXPANSIONS KEEP ROLLING OUT--
--WHO HERE REMEMBERS THE PRIME DIRECTIVES? FROM THE OLD ROBOCOP PROGRAM? THE FAMOUS THREE DIRECTIVES?
"SERVE THE PUBLIC TRUST.
"PROTECT THE INNOCENT.
"UPHOLD THE LAW."
DIRECTIVES HARD-CODED INTO EACH AND EVERY O.C.P. COMPONENT WE PUT OUT ON THE STREETS.
BECAUSE WHAT POINT IS THERE IN ANY OF THIS--
--IF WE'RE NOT MAKING YOUR LIVES BETTER?

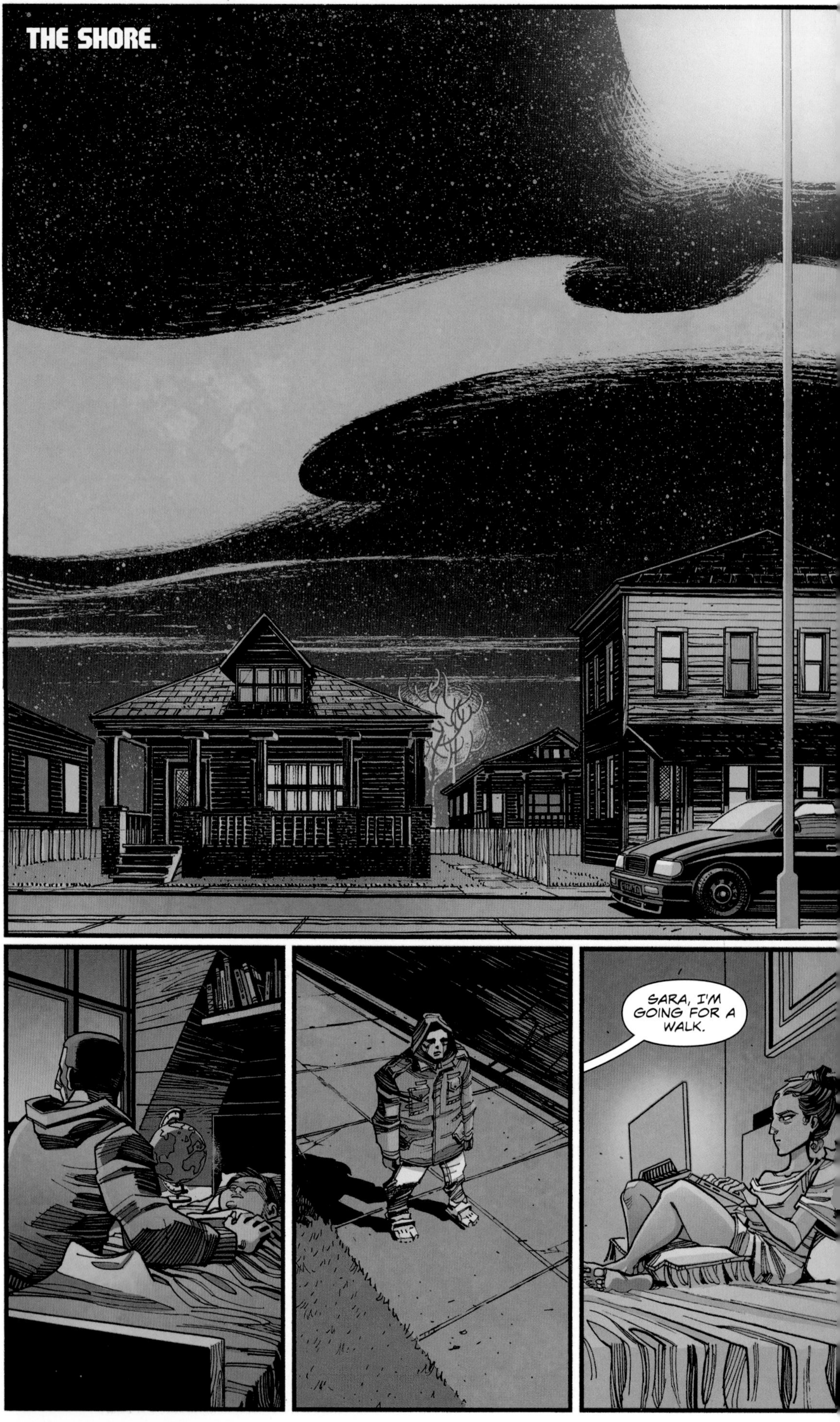
THE SHORE.
SARA, I'M GOING FOR A WALK.

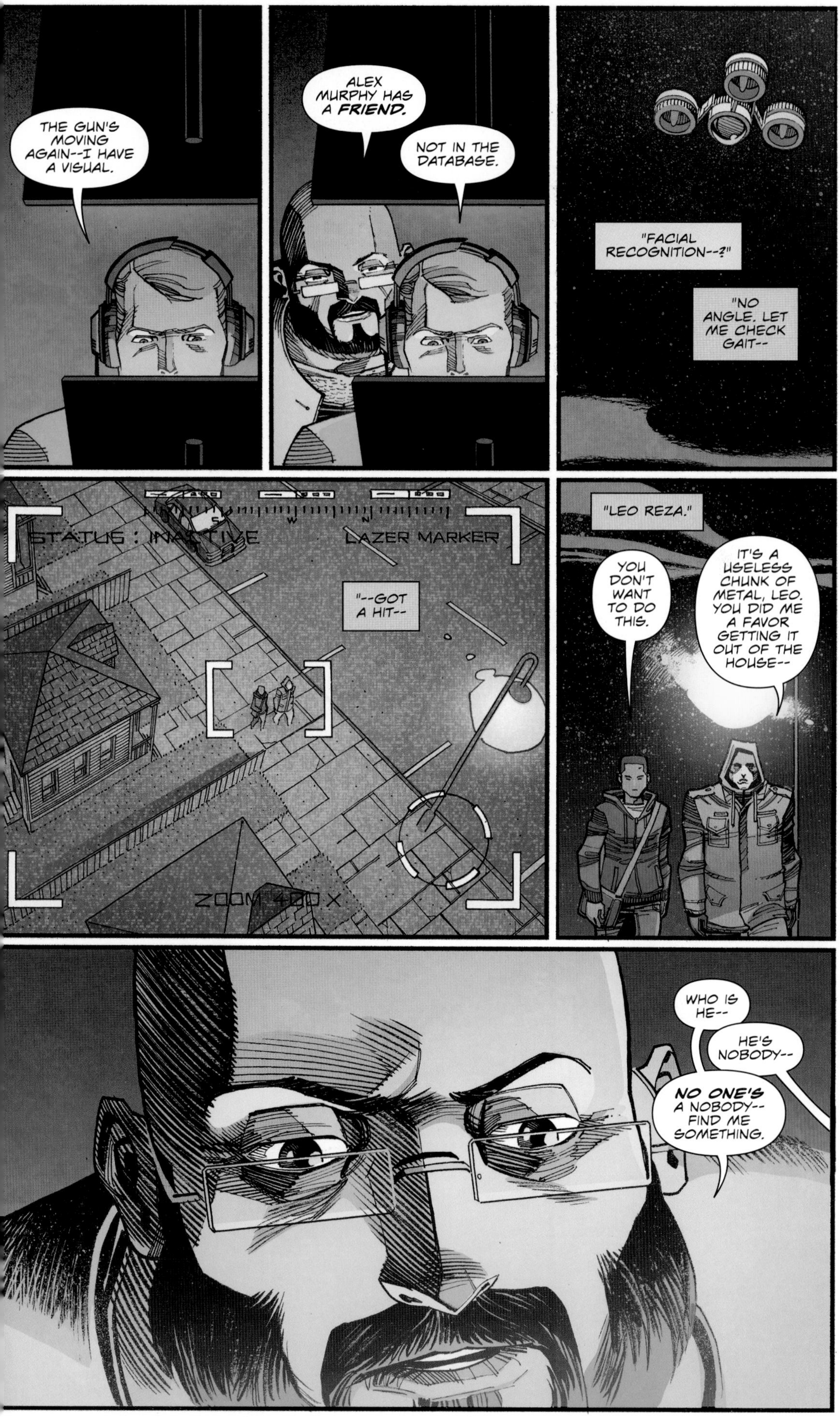
THE GUN'S MOVING AGAIN--I HAVE A VISUAL.
ALEX MURPHY HAS A **FRIEND.**
NOT IN THE DATABASE.
"FACIAL RECOGNITION--?"
"NO ANGLE. LET ME CHECK GAIT--
STATUS : INACTIVE
LAZER MARKER
"--GOT A HIT--
ZOOM 400 X
"LEO REZA."
YOU DON'T WANT TO DO THIS.
IT'S A USELESS CHUNK OF METAL, LEO. YOU DID ME A FAVOR GETTING IT OUT OF THE HOUSE--
WHO IS HE--
HE'S NOBODY--
NO ONE'S A NOBODY--FIND ME SOMETHING.

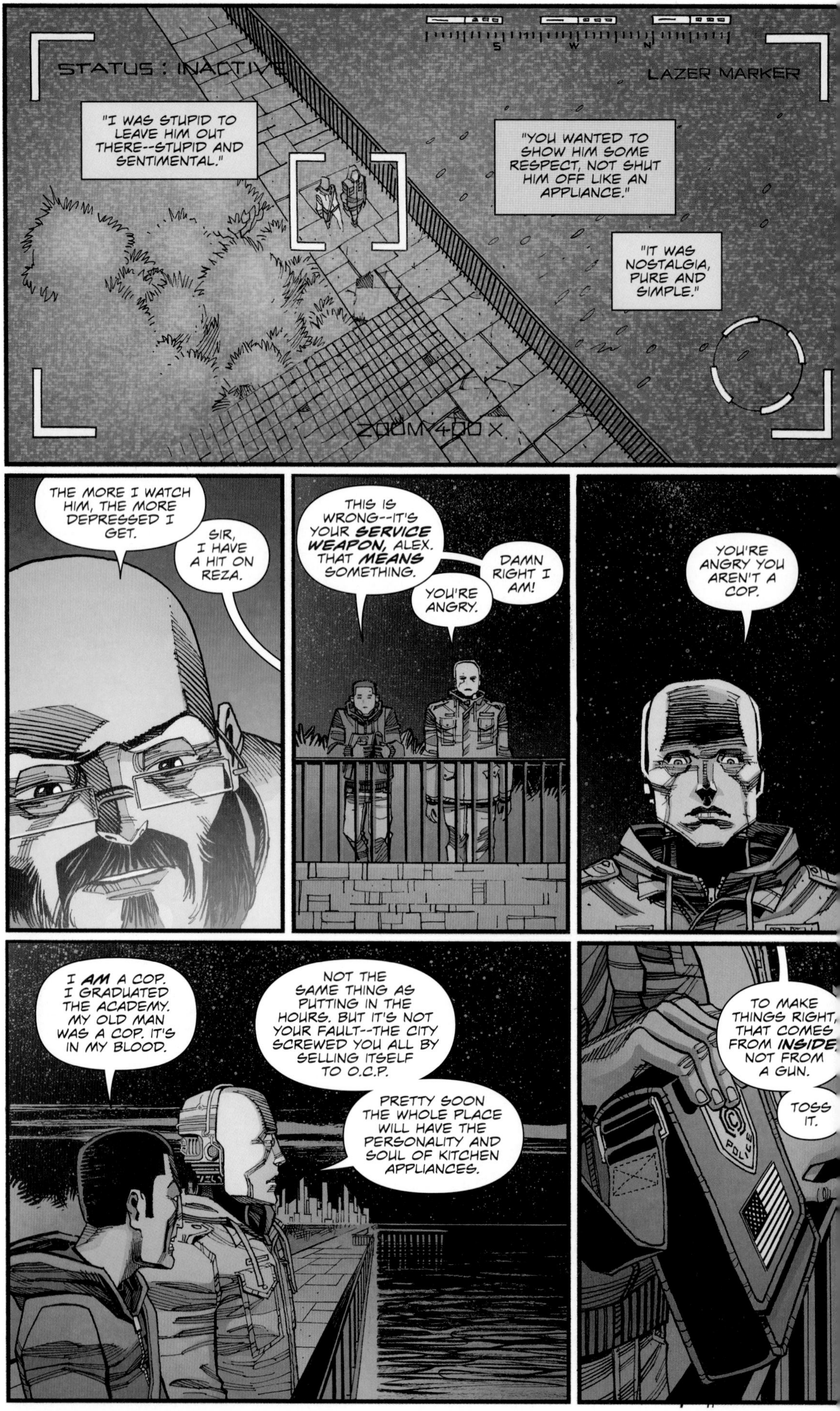
STATUS : INACTIVE
LAZER MARKER
"I WAS STUPID TO LEAVE HIM OUT THERE--STUPID AND SENTIMENTAL."
"YOU WANTED TO SHOW HIM SOME RESPECT, NOT SHUT HIM OFF LIKE AN APPLIANCE."
"IT WAS NOSTALGIA, PURE AND SIMPLE."
ZOOM 400 X
THE MORE I WATCH HIM, THE MORE DEPRESSED I GET.
SIR, I HAVE A HIT ON REZA.
THIS IS WRONG--IT'S YOUR SERVICE WEAPON, ALEX. THAT MEANS SOMETHING.
YOU'RE ANGRY.
DAMN RIGHT I AM!
YOU'RE ANGRY YOU AREN'T A COP.
I AM A COP. I GRADUATED THE ACADEMY. MY OLD MAN WAS A COP. IT'S IN MY BLOOD.
NOT THE SAME THING AS PUTTING IN THE HOURS. BUT IT'S NOT YOUR FAULT--THE CITY SCREWED YOU ALL BY SELLING ITSELF TO O.C.P.
PRETTY SOON THE WHOLE PLACE WILL HAVE THE PERSONALITY AND SOUL OF KITCHEN APPLIANCES.
TO MAKE THINGS RIGHT, THAT COMES FROM INSIDE. NOT FROM A GUN.
TOSS IT.
POLICE

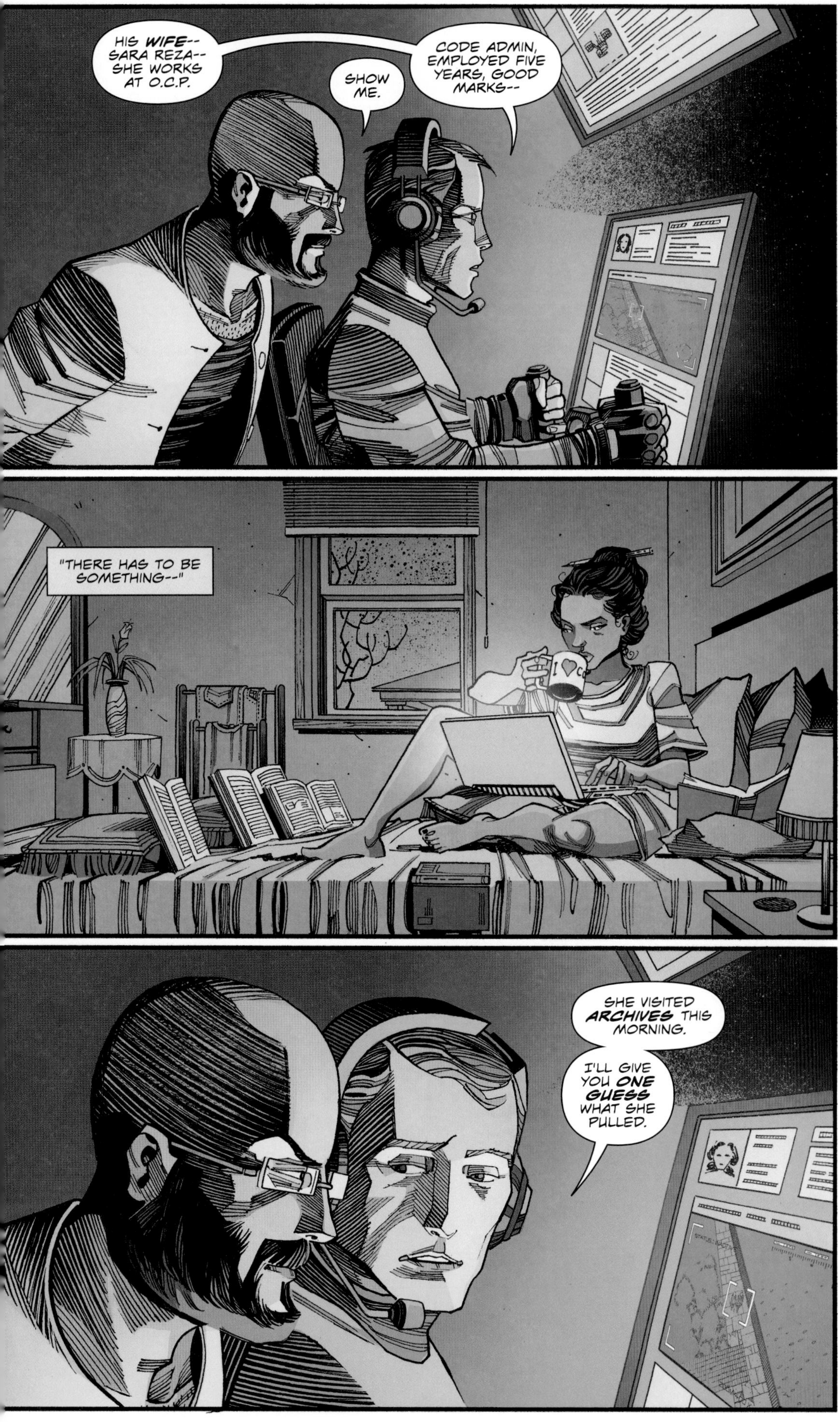
HIS WIFE-- SARA REZA-- SHE WORKS AT O.C.P.
CODE ADMIN, EMPLOYED FIVE YEARS, GOOD MARKS--
SHOW ME.
"THERE HAS TO BE SOMETHING--"
SHE VISITED ARCHIVES THIS MORNING.
I'LL GIVE YOU ONE GUESS WHAT SHE PULLED.

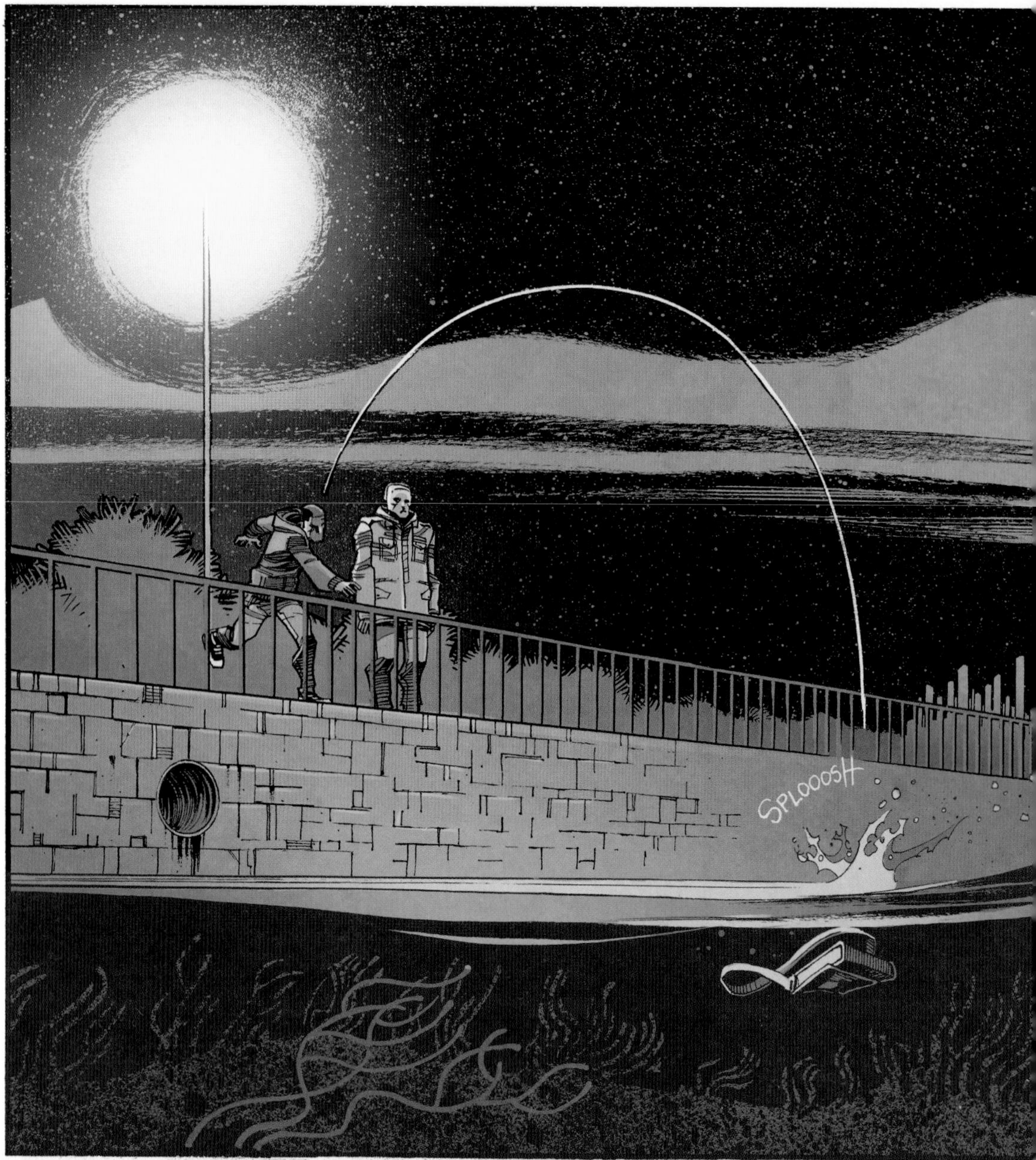
SPLOOOSH

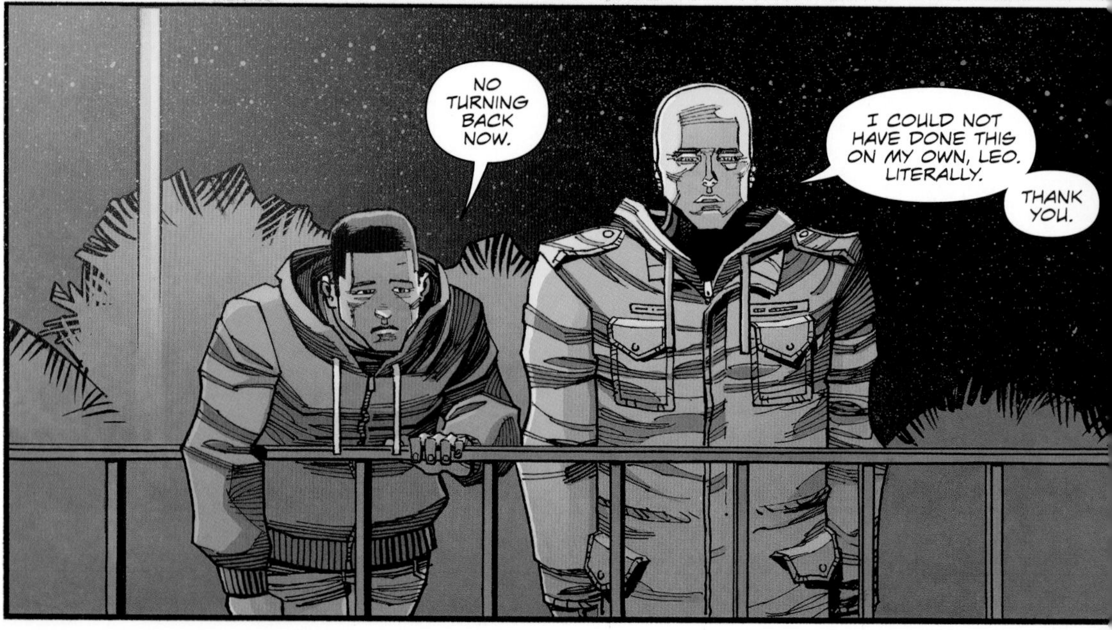
NO TURNING BACK NOW.
I COULD NOT HAVE DONE THIS ON MY OWN, LEO. LITERALLY.
THANK YOU.

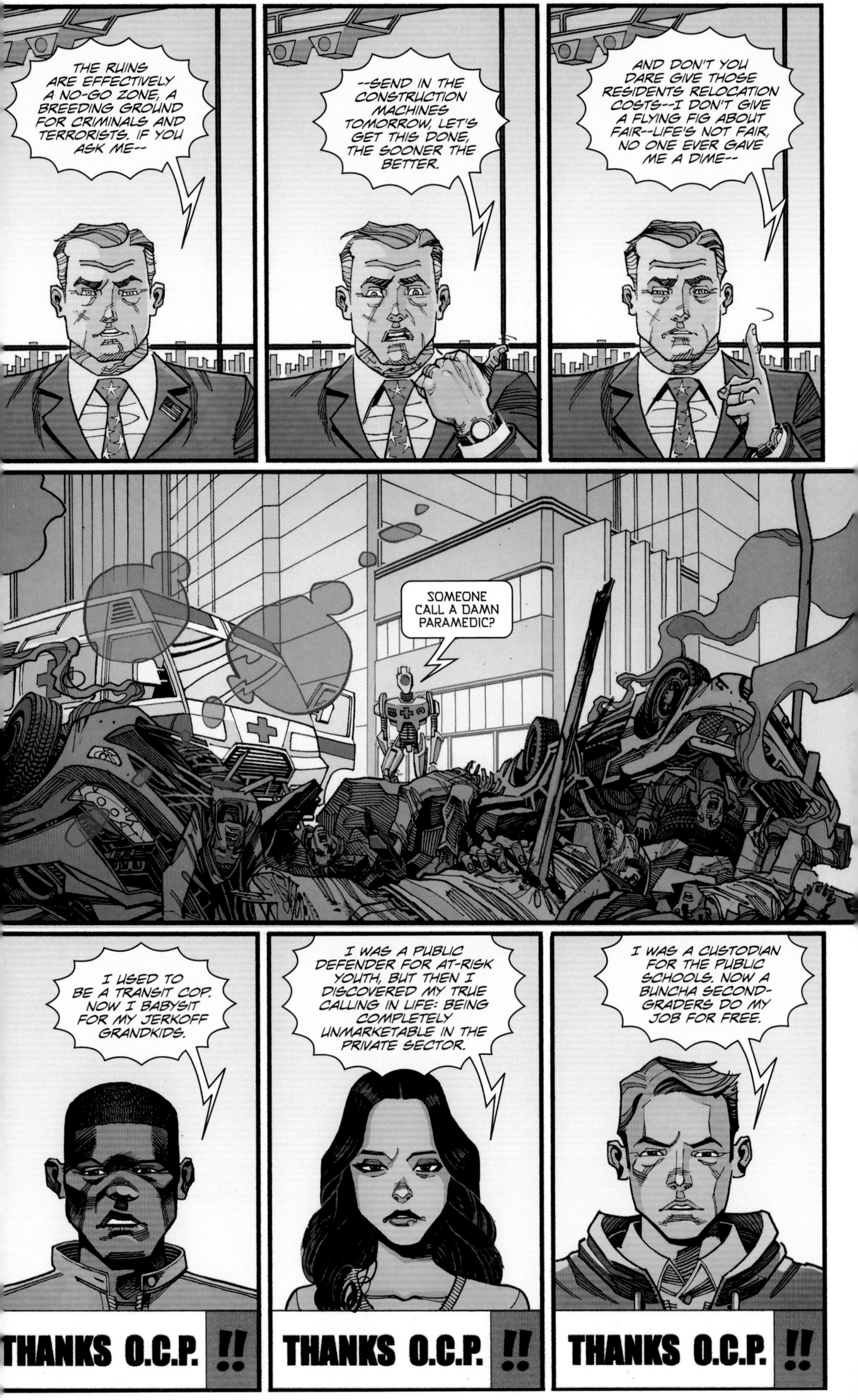
THE RUINS ARE EFFECTIVELY A NO-GO ZONE, A BREEDING GROUND FOR CRIMINALS AND TERRORISTS. IF YOU ASK ME--
--SEND IN THE CONSTRUCTION MACHINES TOMORROW, LET'S GET THIS DONE, THE SOONER THE BETTER.
AND DON'T YOU DARE GIVE THOSE RESIDENTS RELOCATION COSTS--I DON'T GIVE A FLYING FIG ABOUT FAIR--LIFE'S NOT FAIR, NO ONE EVER GAVE ME A DIME--
SOMEONE CALL A DAMN PARAMEDIC?
I USED TO BE A TRANSIT COP. NOW I BABYSIT FOR MY JERKOFF GRANDKIDS.
THANKS O.C.P. !!
I WAS A PUBLIC DEFENDER FOR AT-RISK YOUTH, BUT THEN I DISCOVERED MY TRUE CALLING IN LIFE: BEING COMPLETELY UNMARKETABLE IN THE PRIVATE SECTOR.
THANKS O.C.P. !!
I WAS A CUSTODIAN FOR THE PUBLIC SCHOOLS. NOW A BUNCHA SECOND-GRADERS DO MY JOB FOR FREE.
THANKS O.C.P. !!

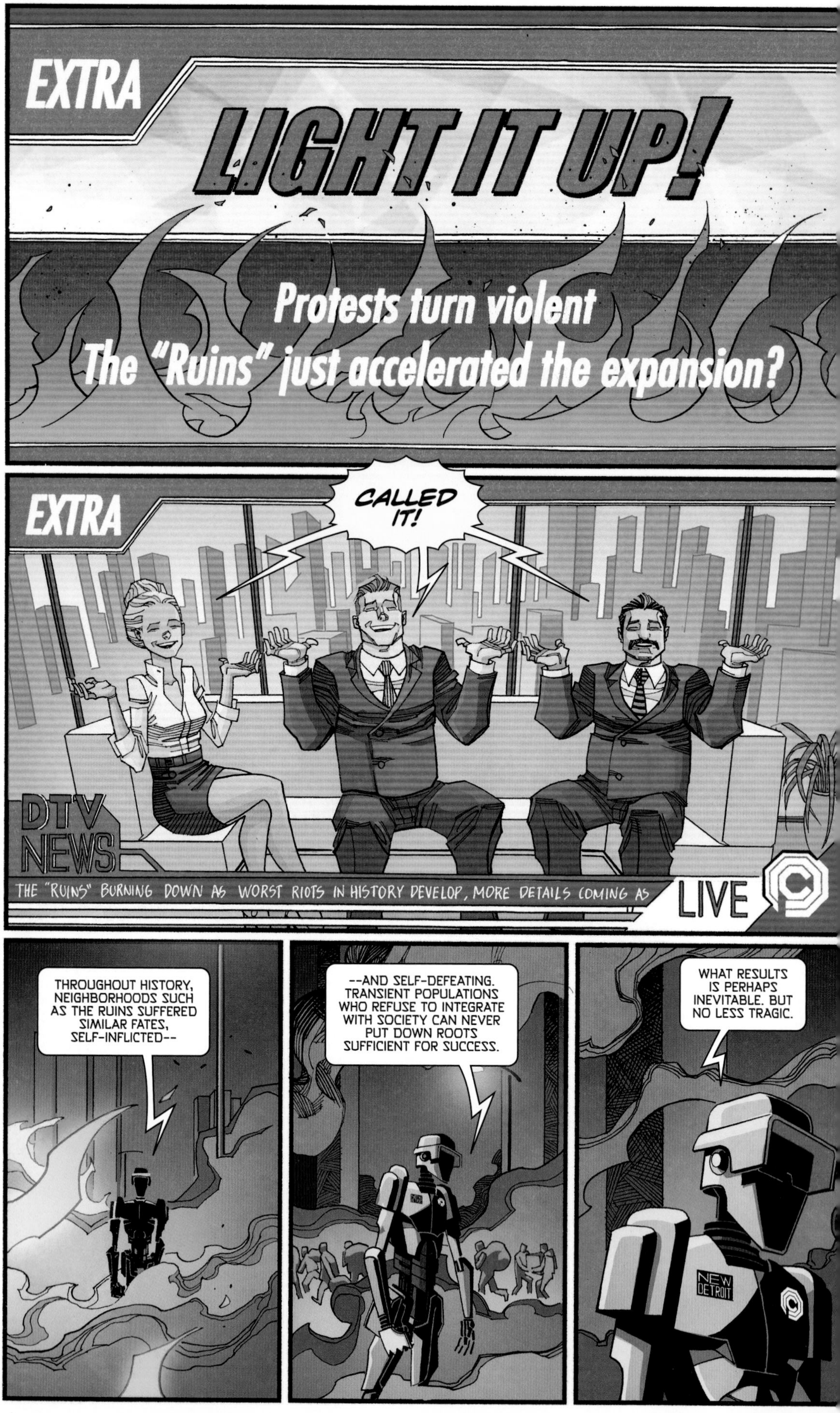
EXTRA
LIGHT IT UP!
Protests turn violent
The "Ruins" just accelerated the expansion?
EXTRA
CALLED IT!
DTV NEWS
THE "RUINS" BURNING DOWN AS WORST RIOTS IN HISTORY DEVELOP, MORE DETAILS COMING AS
LIVE
THROUGHOUT HISTORY, NEIGHBORHOODS SUCH AS THE RUINS SUFFERED SIMILAR FATES, SELF-INFLICTED--
--AND SELF-DEFEATING. TRANSIENT POPULATIONS WHO REFUSE TO INTEGRATE WITH SOCIETY CAN NEVER PUT DOWN ROOTS SUFFICIENT FOR SUCCESS.
WHAT RESULTS IS PERHAPS INEVITABLE. BUT NO LESS TRAGIC.
NEW DETROIT

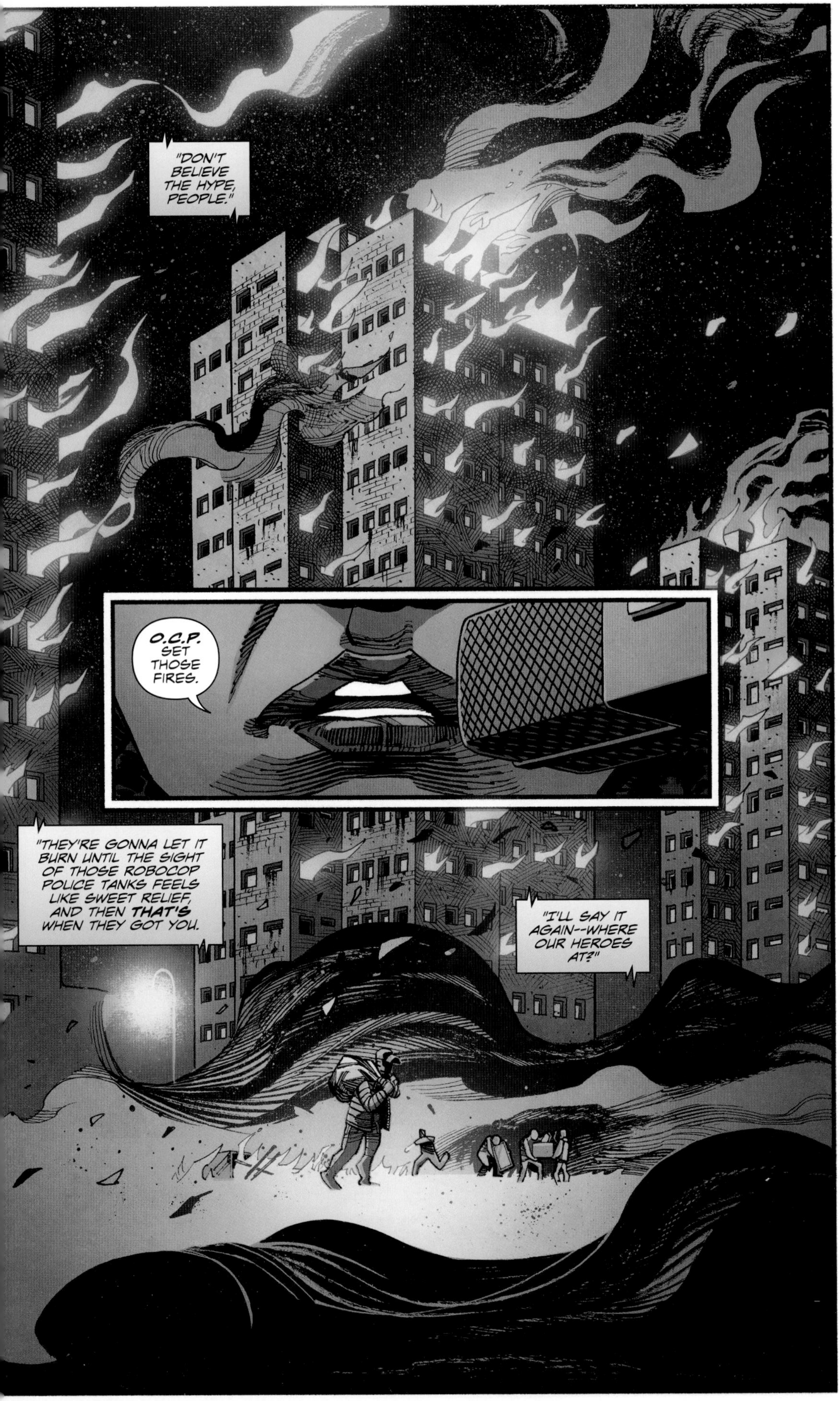
"DON'T BELIEVE THE HYPE, PEOPLE."
O.C.P. SET THOSE FIRES.
"THEY'RE GONNA LET IT BURN UNTIL THE SIGHT OF THOSE ROBOCOP POLICE TANKS FEELS LIKE SWEET RELIEF, AND THEN **THAT'S** WHEN THEY GOT YOU.
"I'LL SAY IT AGAIN--WHERE OUR HEROES AT?"

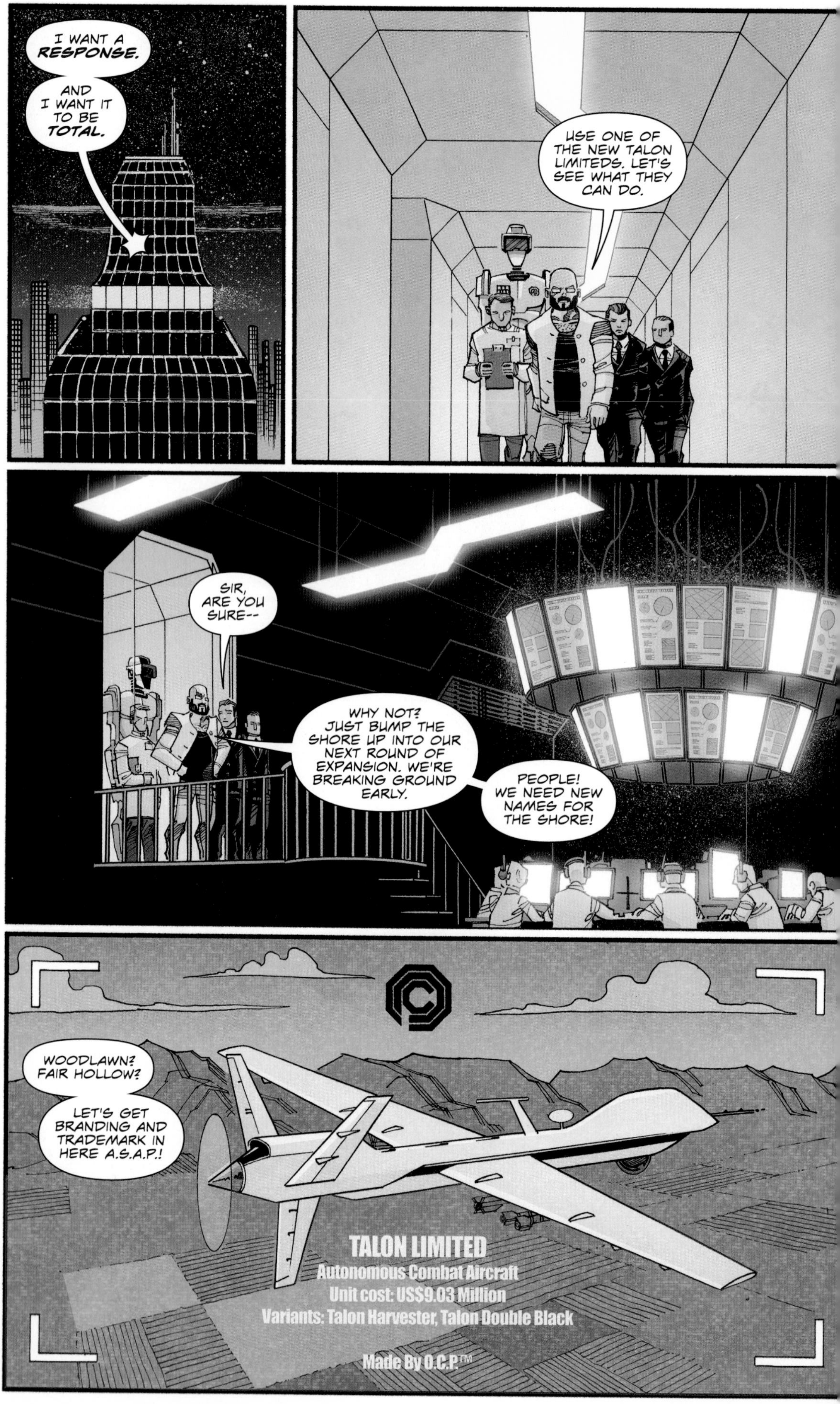
I WANT A RESPONSE.
AND I WANT IT TO BE TOTAL.
USE ONE OF THE NEW TALON LIMITEDS. LET'S SEE WHAT THEY CAN DO.
SIR, ARE YOU SURE--
WHY NOT? JUST BUMP THE SHORE UP INTO OUR NEXT ROUND OF EXPANSION. WE'RE BREAKING GROUND EARLY.
PEOPLE! WE NEED NEW NAMES FOR THE SHORE!
WOODLAWN? FAIR HOLLOW?
LET'S GET BRANDING AND TRADEMARK IN HERE A.S.A.P.!
TALON LIMITED
Autonomous Combat Aircraft
Unit cost: US$9.03 Million
Variants: Talon Harvester, Talon Double Black
Made By O.C.P.™

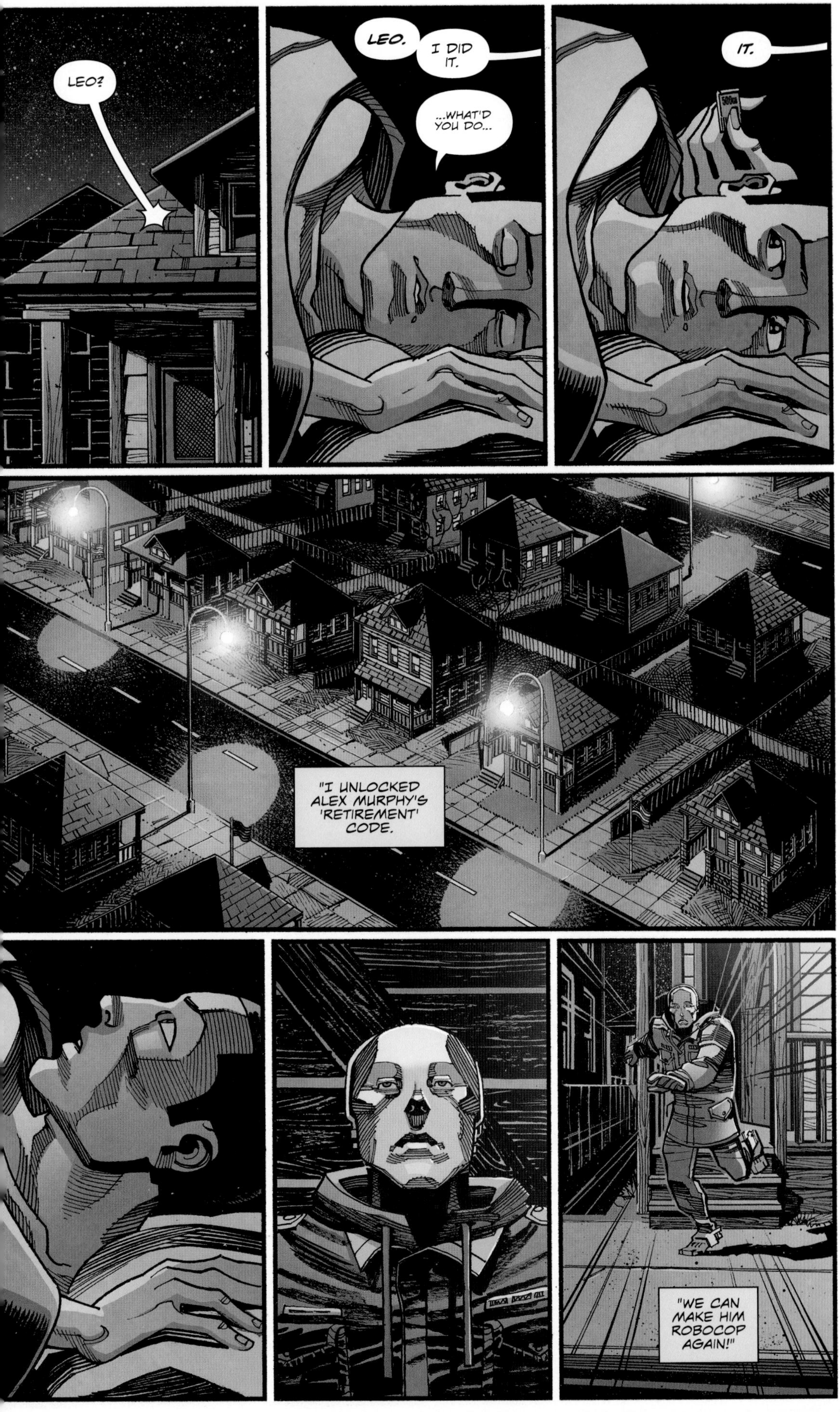
LEO?
LEO.
I DID IT.
...WHAT'D YOU DO...
IT.
500CR
"I UNLOCKED ALEX MURPHY'S 'RETIREMENT' CODE.
"WE CAN MAKE HIM ROBOCOP AGAIN!"

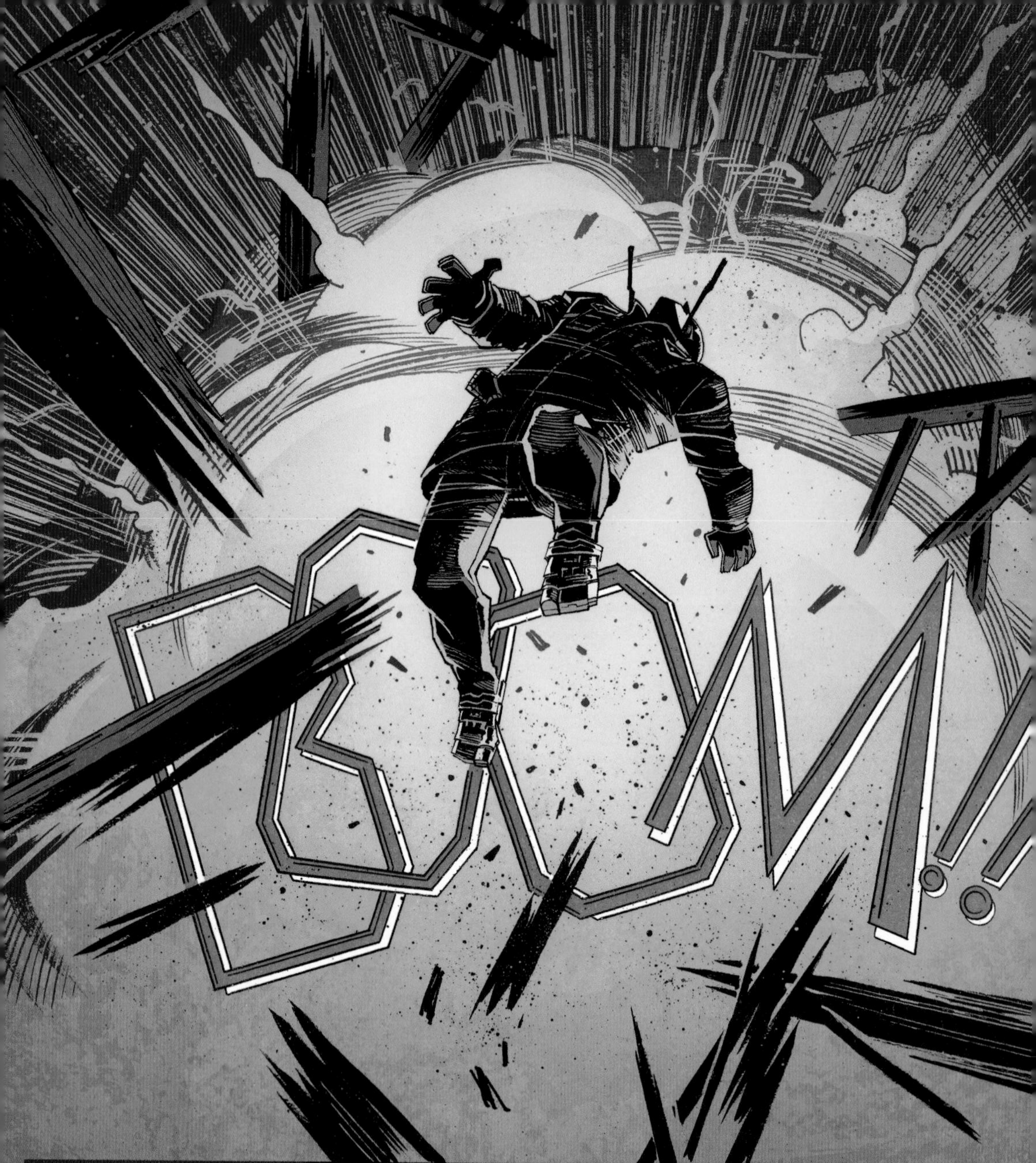
BOOM!!

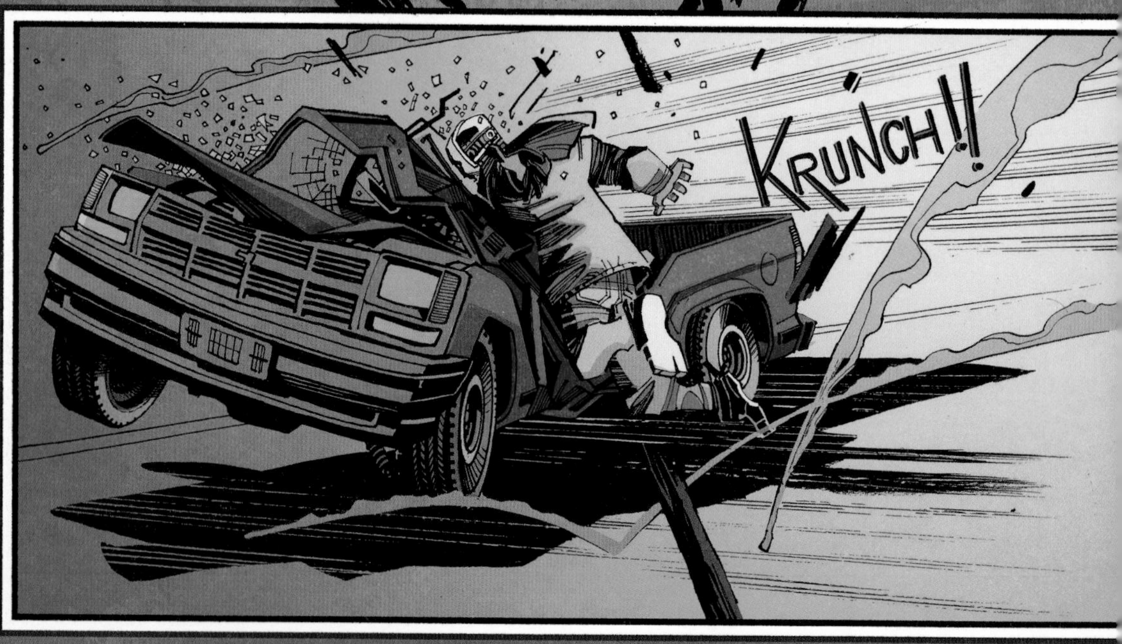
KRUNCH!!

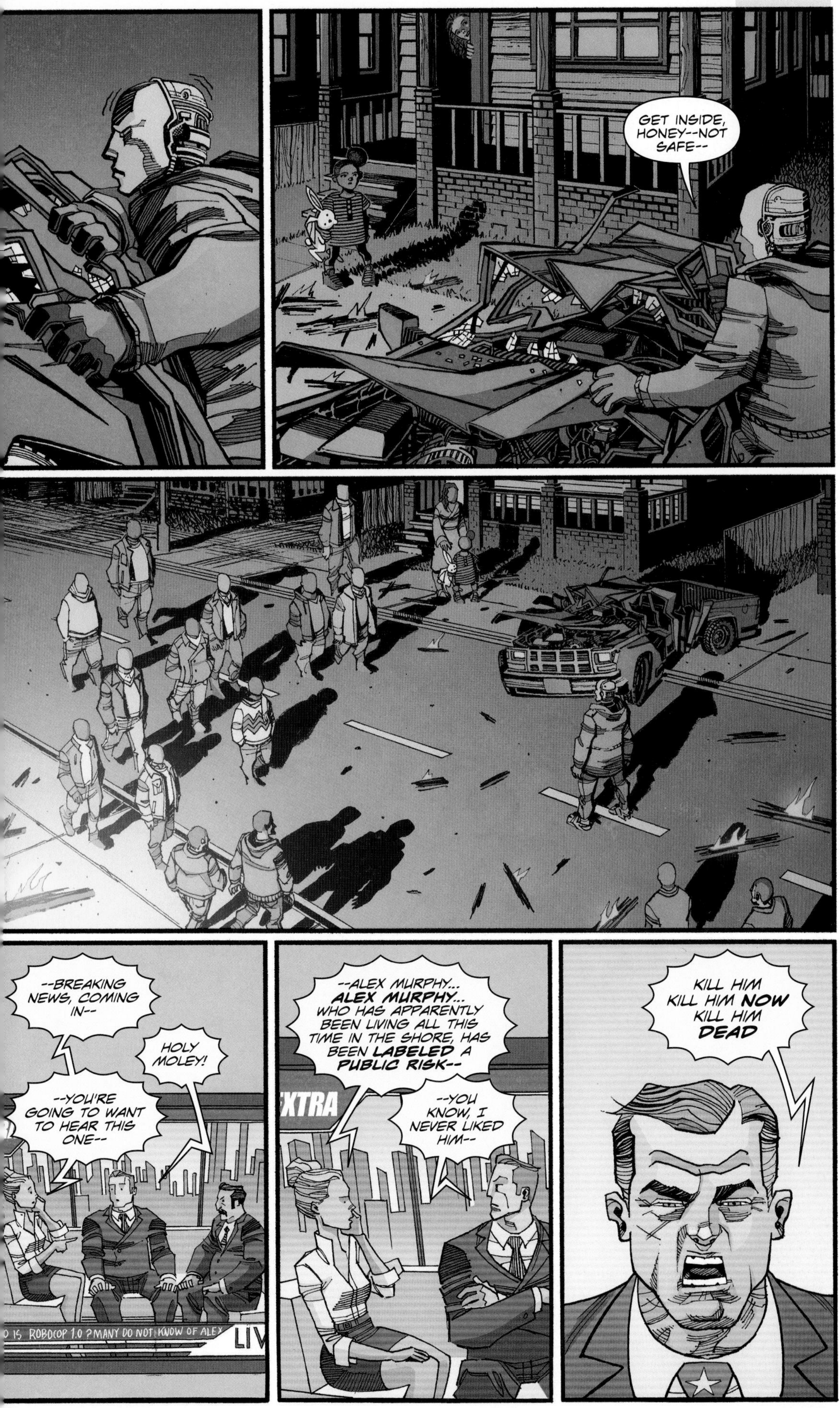
GET INSIDE, HONEY--NOT SAFE--
--BREAKING NEWS, COMING IN--
--YOU'RE GOING TO WANT TO HEAR THIS ONE--
HOLY MOLEY!
O IS ROBOCOP 1.0 ? MANY DO NOT KNOW OF ALEX
LIV
--ALEX MURPHY... ALEX MURPHY... WHO HAS APPARENTLY BEEN LIVING ALL THIS TIME IN THE SHORE, HAS BEEN LABELED A PUBLIC RISK--
EXTRA
--YOU KNOW, I NEVER LIKED HIM--
KILL HIM KILL HIM NOW KILL HIM DEAD

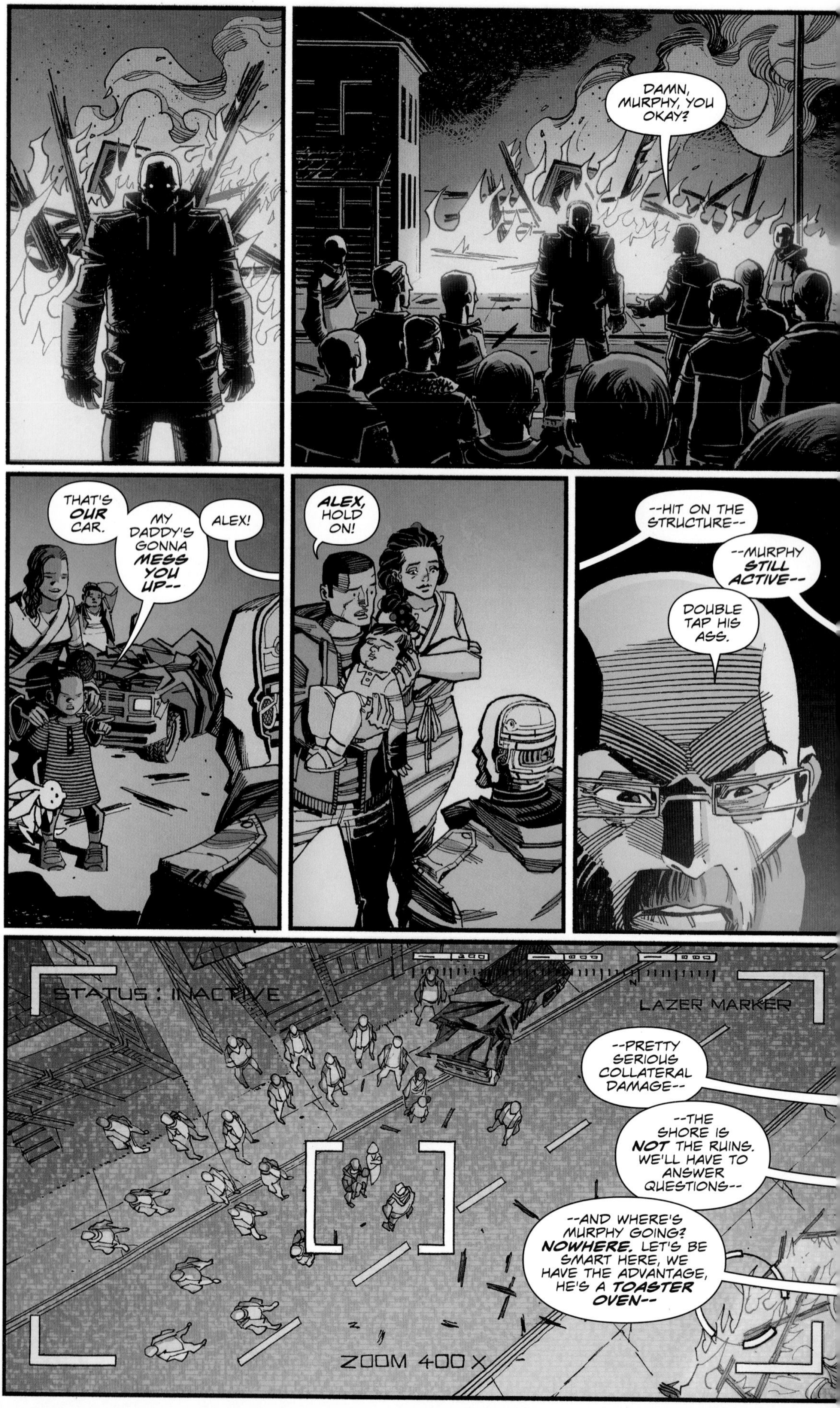
DAMN, MURPHY, YOU OKAY?
THAT'S **OUR** CAR.
MY DADDY'S GONNA **MESS YOU UP--**
ALEX!
ALEX, HOLD ON!
--HIT ON THE STRUCTURE--
--MURPHY **STILL ACTIVE--**
DOUBLE TAP HIS ASS.
STATUS : INACTIVE
LAZER MARKER
--PRETTY SERIOUS COLLATERAL DAMAGE--
--THE SHORE IS **NOT** THE RUINS. WE'LL HAVE TO ANSWER QUESTIONS--
--AND WHERE'S MURPHY GOING? **NOWHERE.** LET'S BE SMART HERE, WE HAVE THE ADVANTAGE, HE'S A **TOASTER OVEN--**
ZOOM 400 X

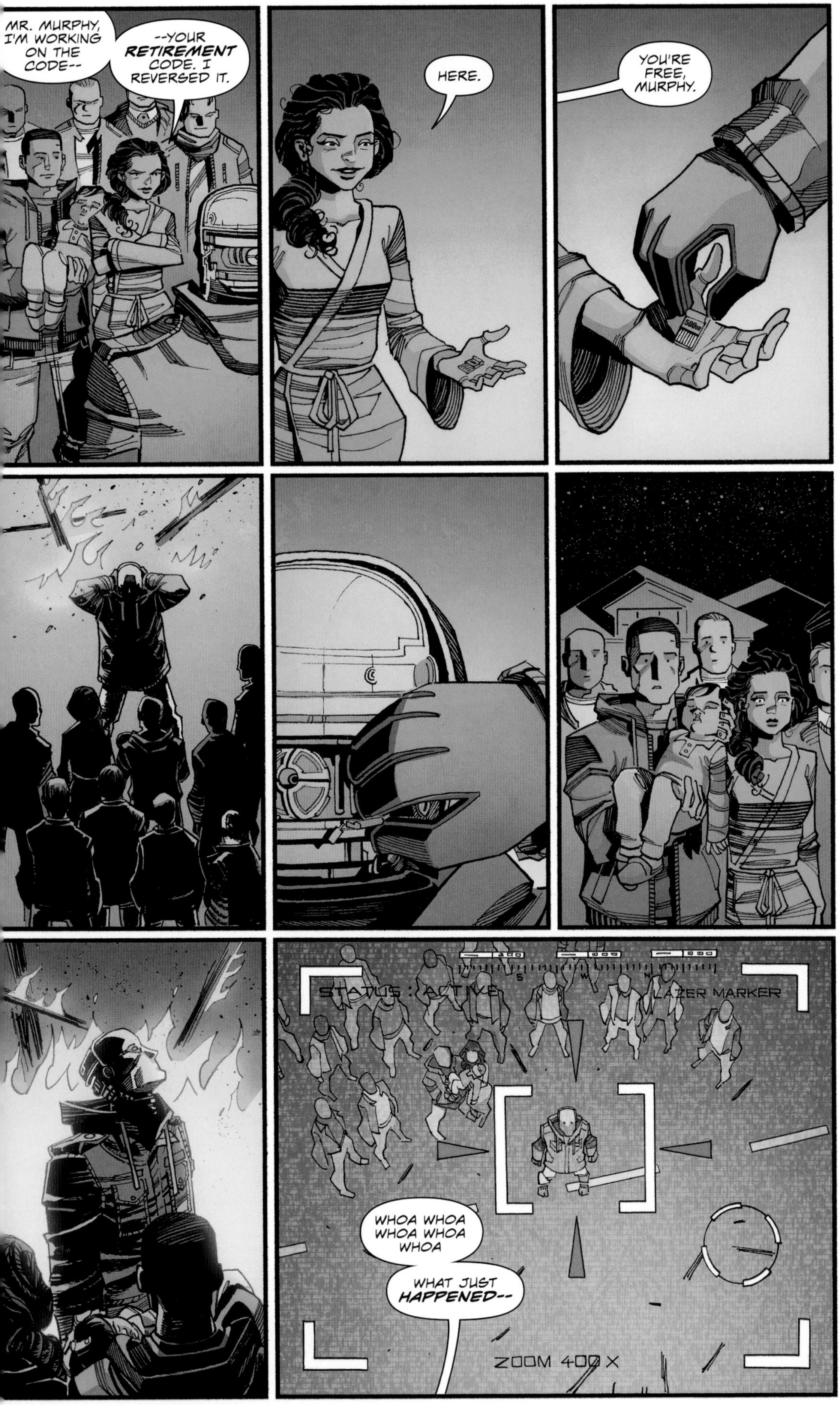
MR. MURPHY, I'M WORKING ON THE CODE--
--YOUR RETIREMENT CODE. I REVERSED IT.
HERE.
YOU'RE FREE, MURPHY.
500GB
STATUS : ACTIVE
LAZER MARKER
WHOA WHOA WHOA WHOA WHOA
WHAT JUST HAPPENED--
ZOOM 400 X

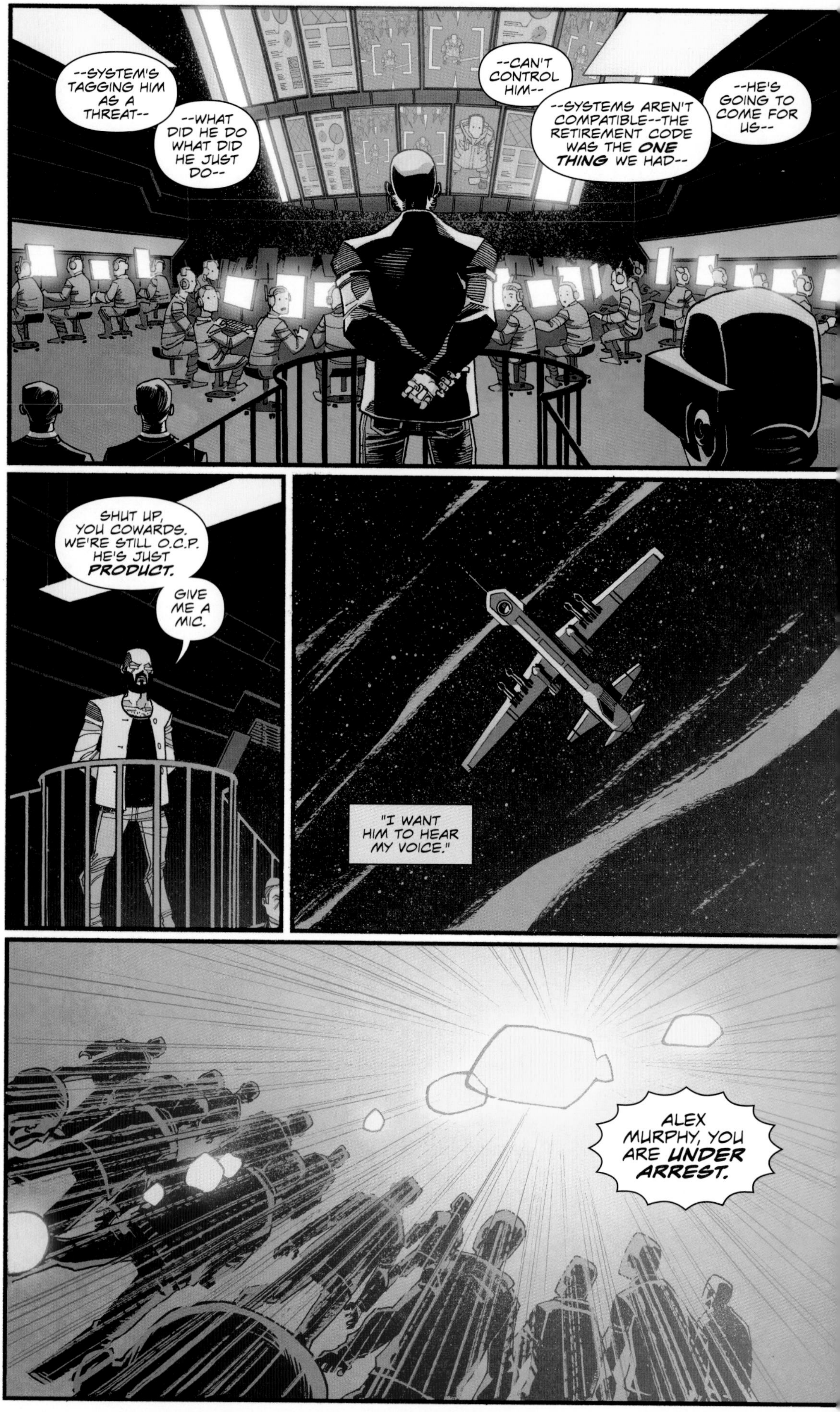
--SYSTEM'S TAGGING HIM AS A THREAT--
--WHAT DID HE DO WHAT DID HE JUST DO--
--CAN'T CONTROL HIM--
--SYSTEMS AREN'T COMPATIBLE--THE RETIREMENT CODE WAS THE ONE THING WE HAD--
--HE'S GOING TO COME FOR US--
SHUT UP, YOU COWARDS. WE'RE STILL O.C.P. HE'S JUST PRODUCT.
GIVE ME A MIC.
"I WANT HIM TO HEAR MY VOICE."
ALEX MURPHY, YOU ARE UNDER ARREST.

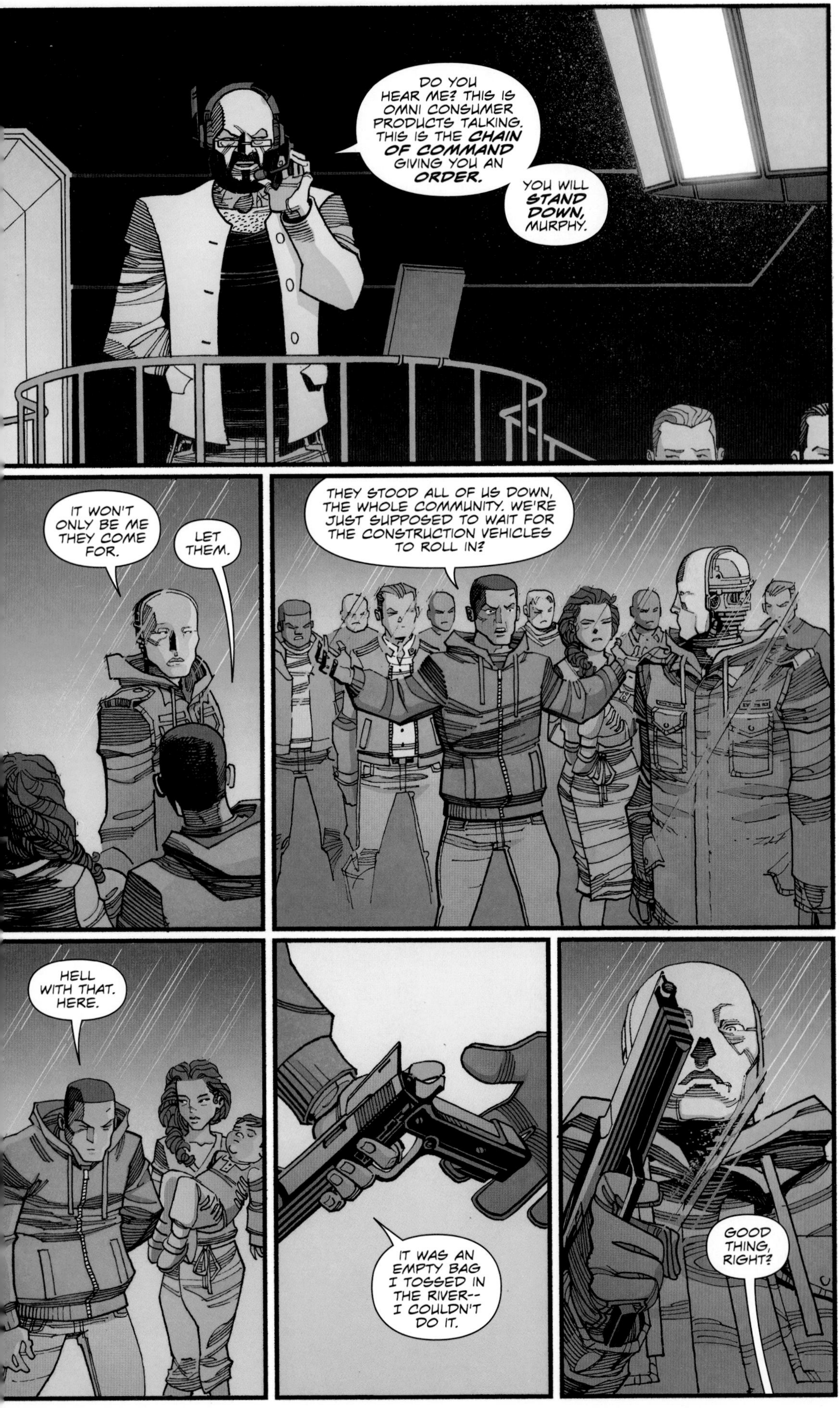
DO YOU HEAR ME? THIS IS OMNI CONSUMER PRODUCTS TALKING. THIS IS THE **CHAIN OF COMMAND** GIVING YOU AN **ORDER.**
YOU WILL **STAND DOWN,** MURPHY.
IT WON'T ONLY BE ME THEY COME FOR.
LET THEM.
THEY STOOD ALL OF US DOWN, THE WHOLE COMMUNITY. WE'RE JUST SUPPOSED TO WAIT FOR THE CONSTRUCTION VEHICLES TO ROLL IN?
HELL WITH THAT. HERE.
IT WAS AN EMPTY BAG I TOSSED IN THE RIVER-- I COULDN'T DO IT.
GOOD THING, RIGHT?

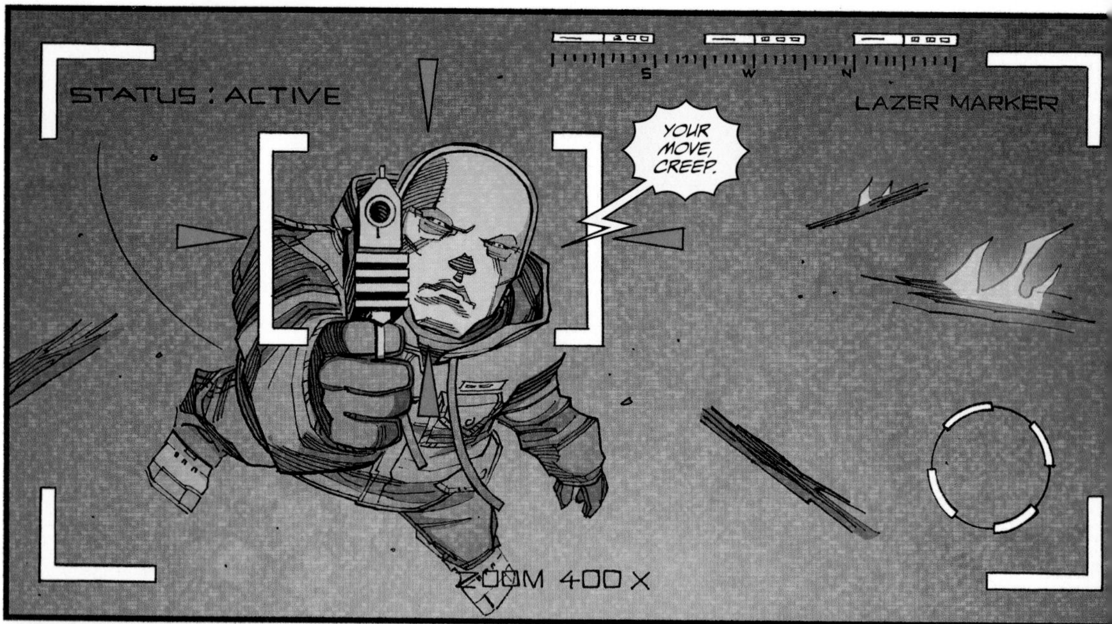
STATUS : ACTIVE
LAZER MARKER
YOUR MOVE, CREEP.
ZOOM 400 X
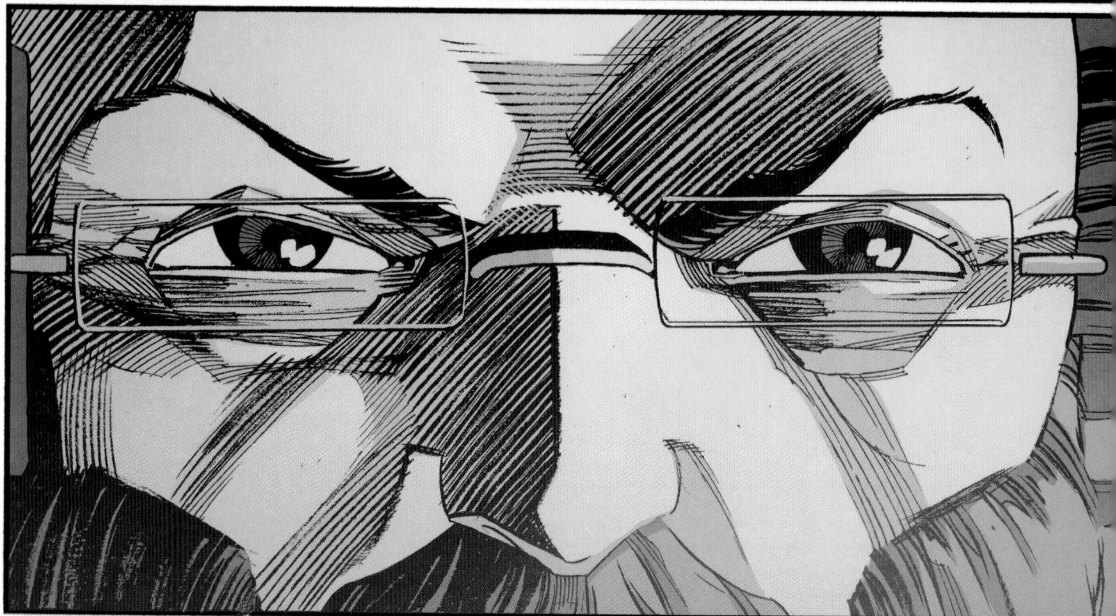
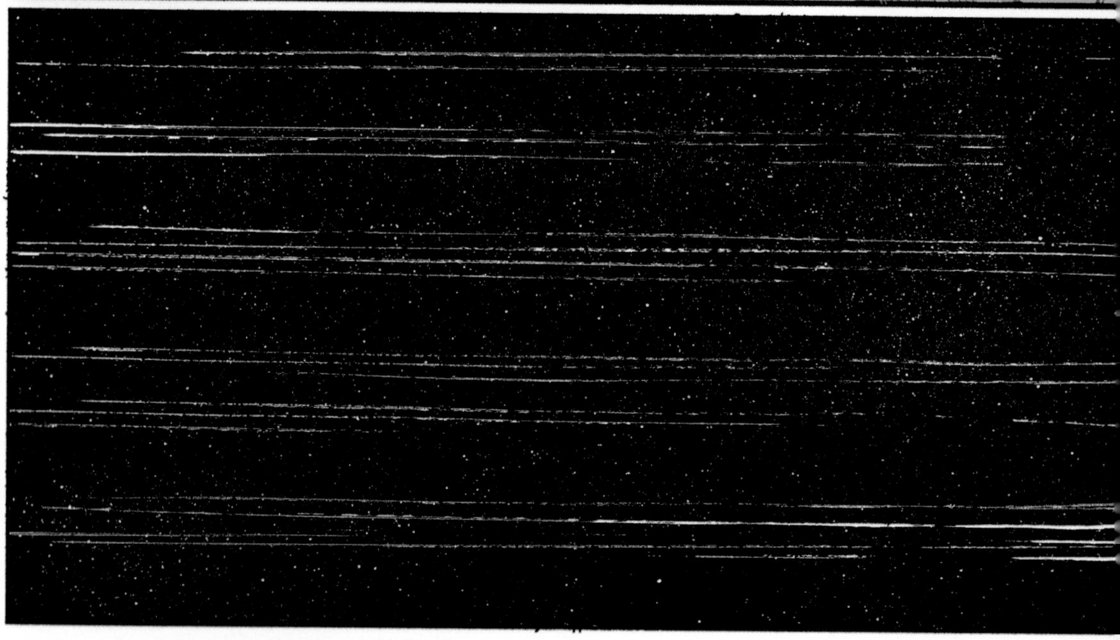

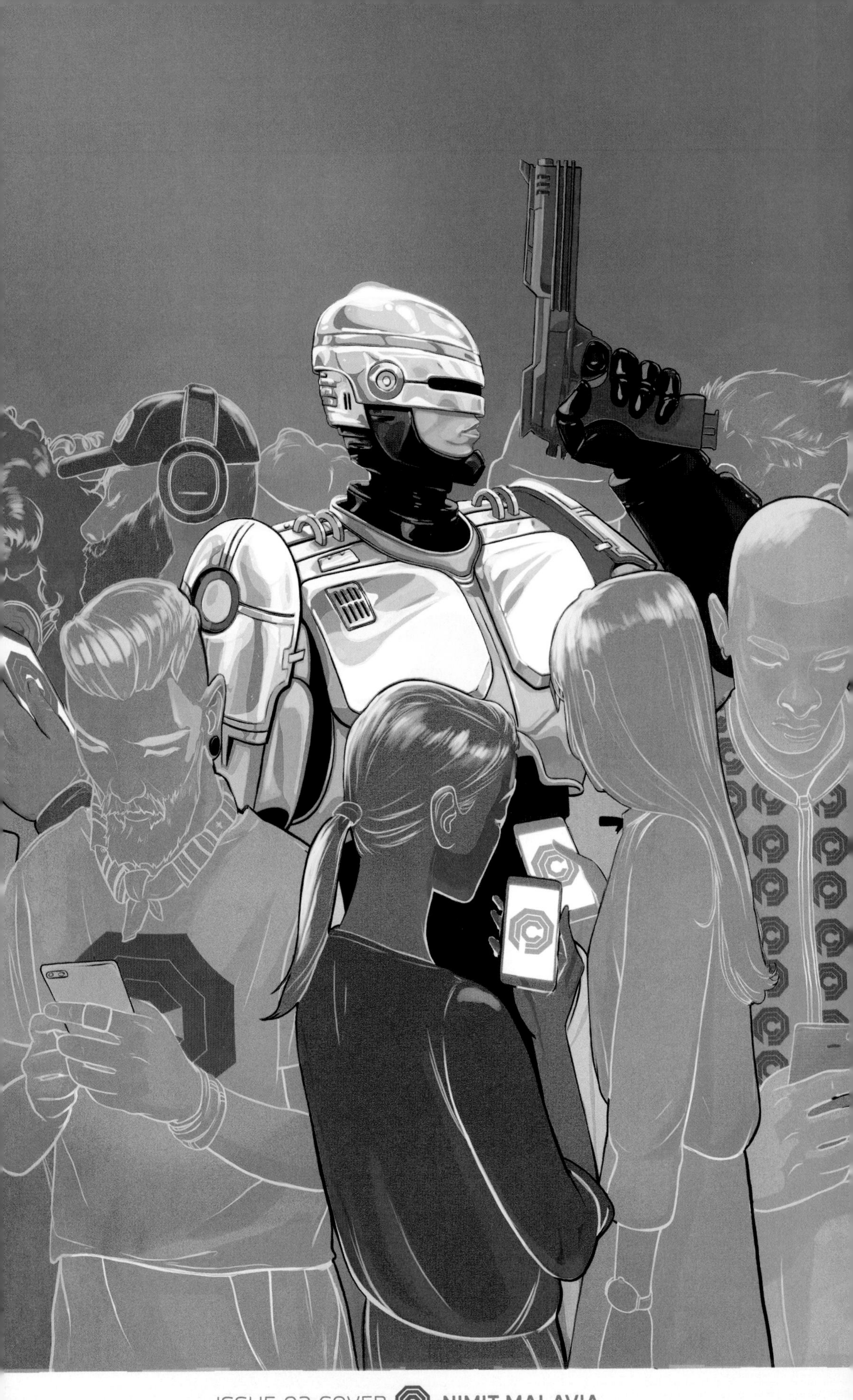

ISSUE 02 COVER NIMIT MALAVIA

THREE

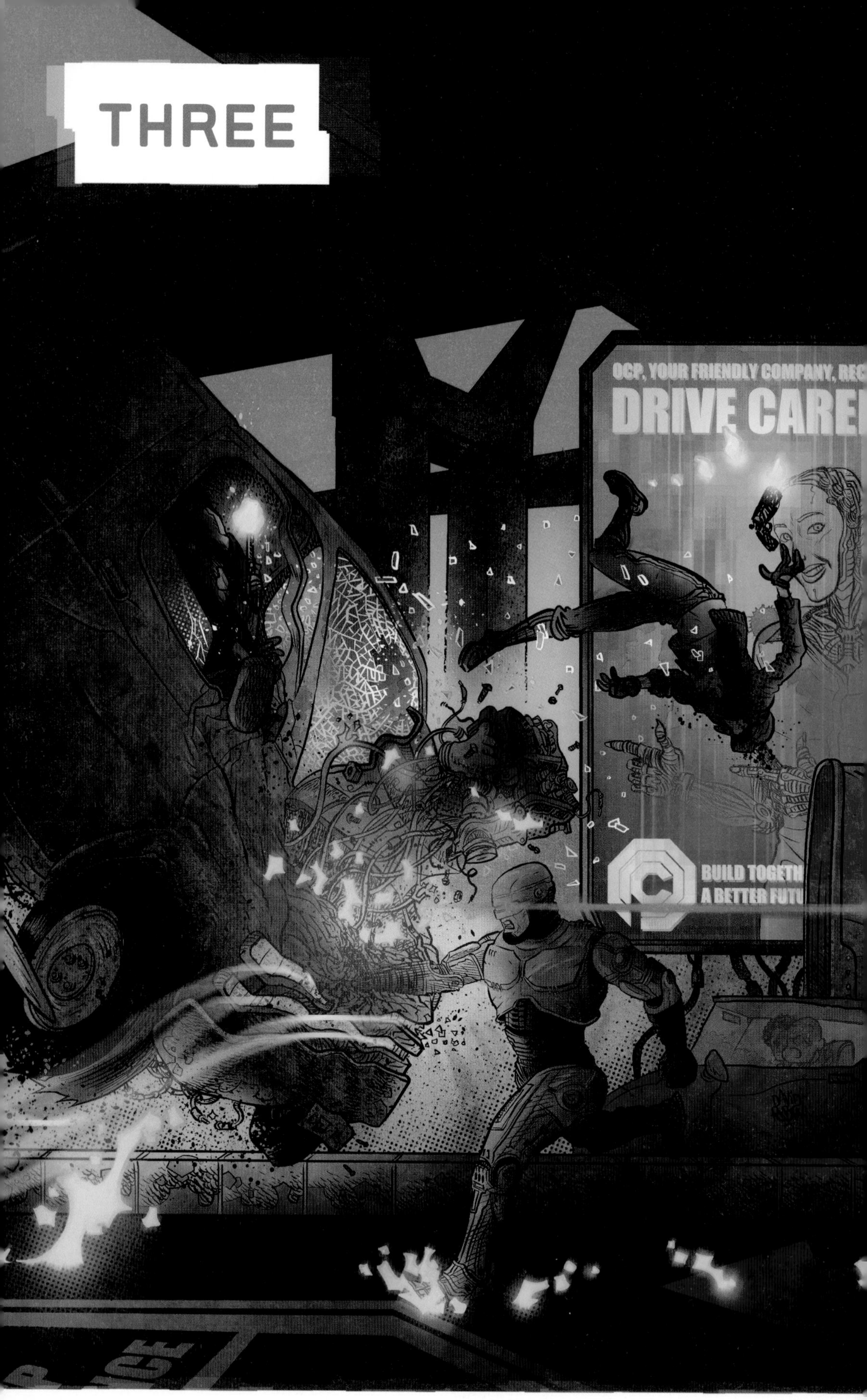
OCP, YOUR FRIENDLY COMPANY, REC
DRIVE CARE
BUILD TOGETH
A BETTER FUTU

ISSUE 03 COVER DAVID RUBÍN

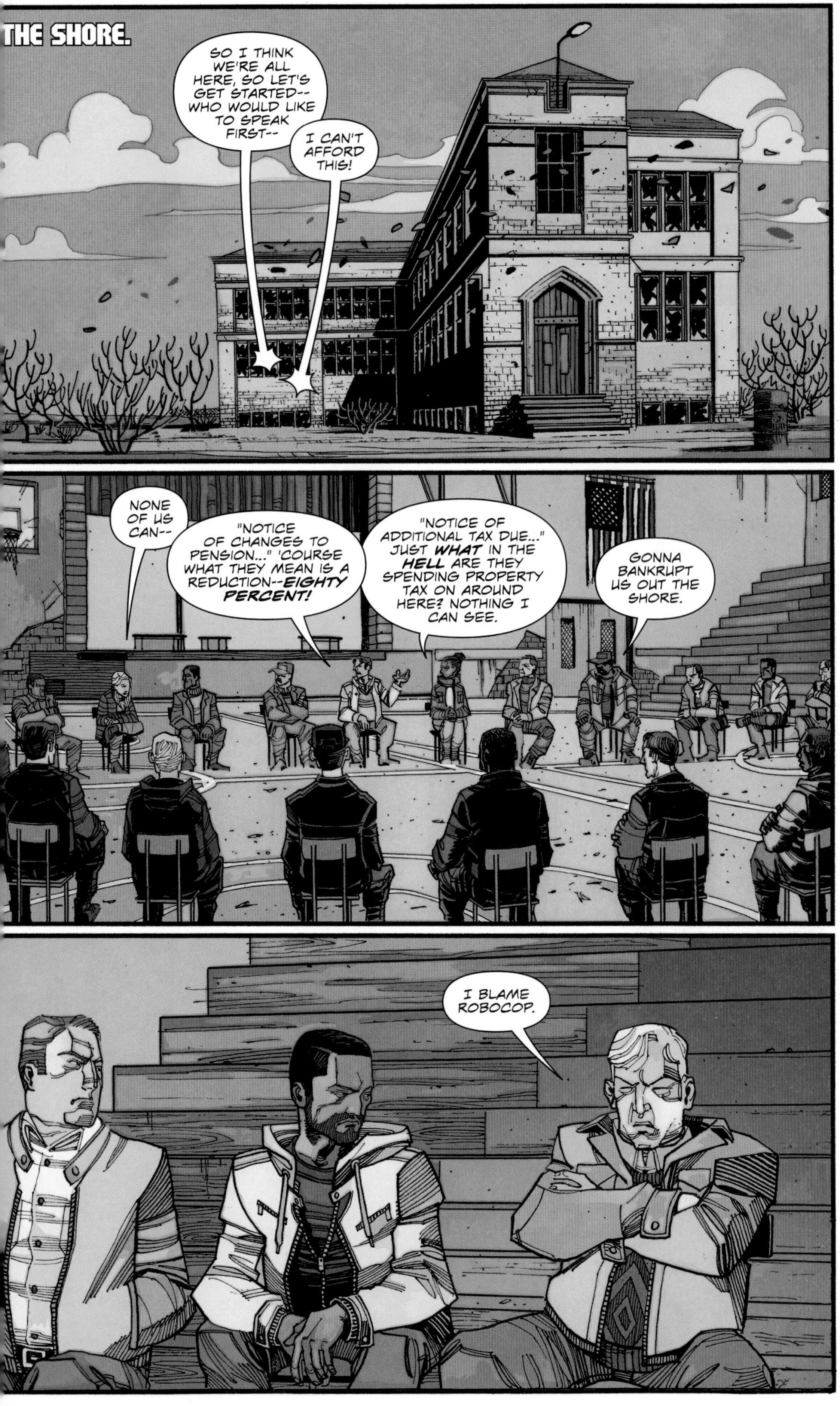
THE SHORE.
SO I THINK WE'RE ALL HERE, SO LET'S GET STARTED-- WHO WOULD LIKE TO SPEAK FIRST--
I CAN'T AFFORD THIS!
NONE OF US CAN--
"NOTICE OF CHANGES TO PENSION..." 'COURSE WHAT THEY MEAN IS A REDUCTION--EIGHTY PERCENT!
"NOTICE OF ADDITIONAL TAX DUE..." JUST WHAT IN THE HELL ARE THEY SPENDING PROPERTY TAX ON AROUND HERE? NOTHING I CAN SEE.
GONNA BANKRUPT US OUT THE SHORE.
I BLAME ROBOCOP.

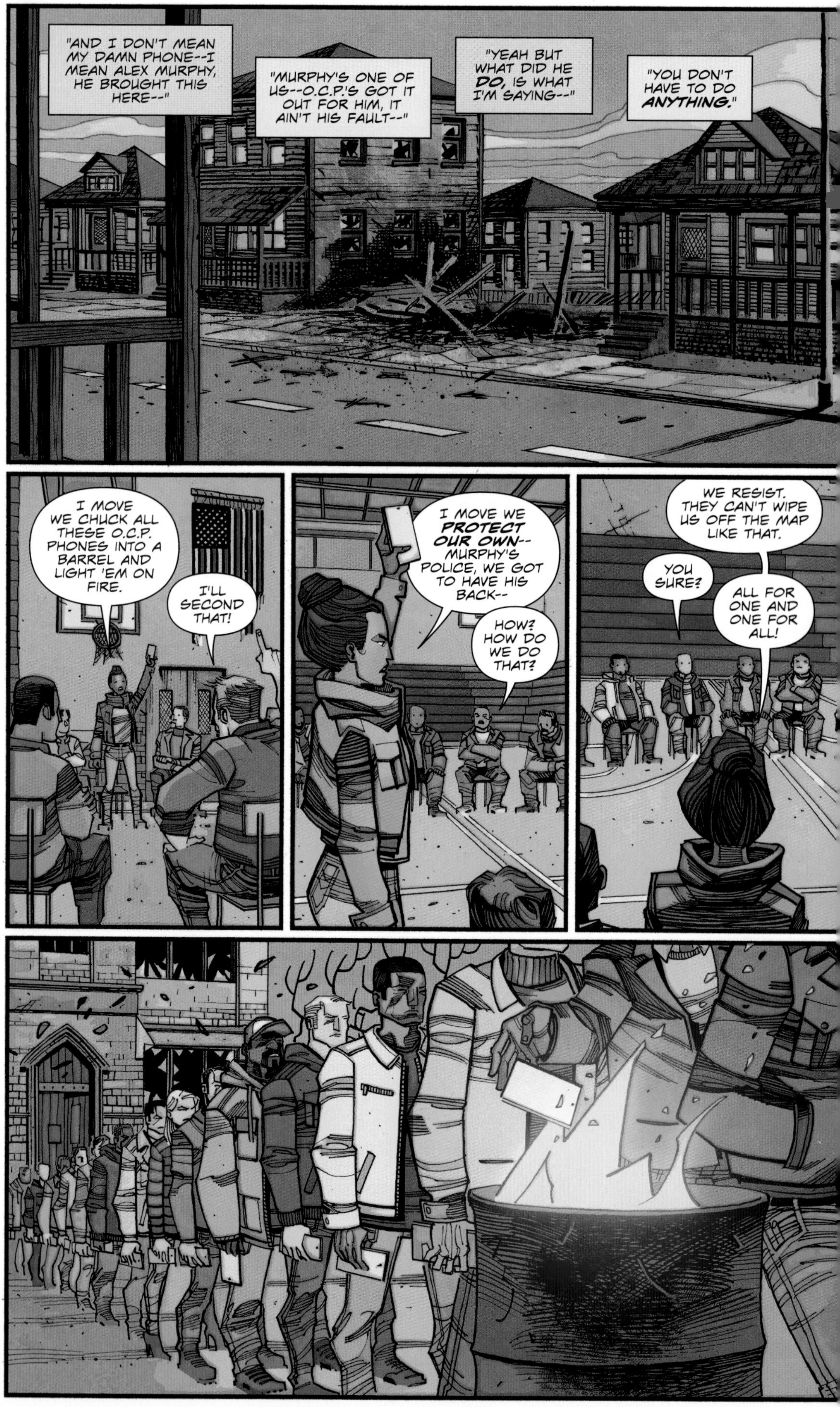

"AND I DON'T MEAN MY DAMN PHONE--I MEAN ALEX MURPHY, HE BROUGHT THIS HERE--"
"MURPHY'S ONE OF US--O.C.P.'S GOT IT OUT FOR HIM, IT AIN'T HIS FAULT--"
"YEAH BUT WHAT DID HE DO, IS WHAT I'M SAYING--"
"YOU DON'T HAVE TO DO ANYTHING."
I MOVE WE CHUCK ALL THESE O.C.P. PHONES INTO A BARREL AND LIGHT 'EM ON FIRE.
I'LL SECOND THAT!
I MOVE WE PROTECT OUR OWN--MURPHY'S POLICE, WE GOT TO HAVE HIS BACK--
HOW? HOW DO WE DO THAT?
WE RESIST. THEY CAN'T WIPE US OFF THE MAP LIKE THAT.
YOU SURE?
ALL FOR ONE AND ONE FOR ALL!

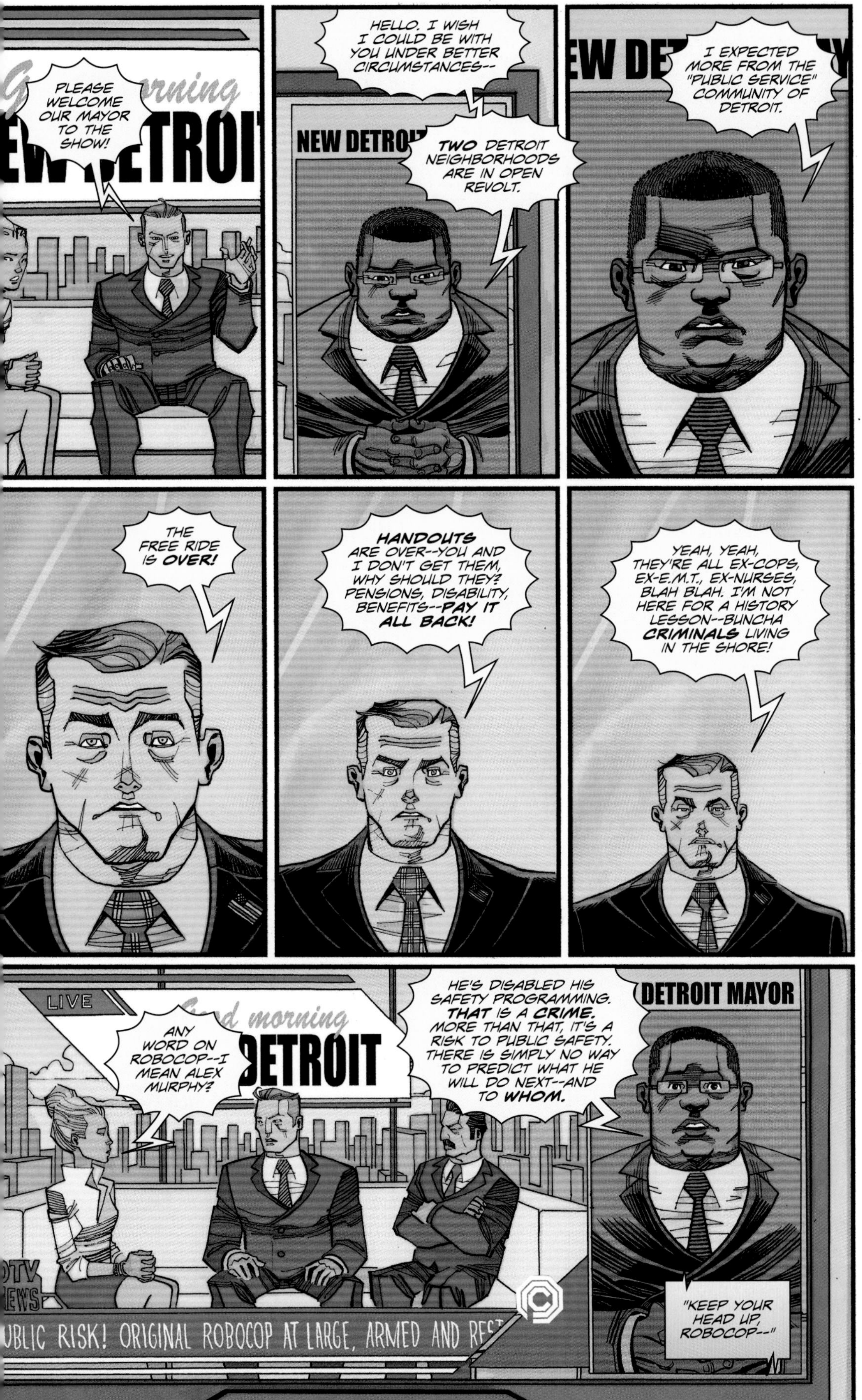
Good morning
NEW DETROIT
PLEASE WELCOME OUR MAYOR TO THE SHOW!
HELLO. I WISH I COULD BE WITH YOU UNDER BETTER CIRCUMSTANCES--
NEW DETROIT
TWO DETROIT NEIGHBORHOODS ARE IN OPEN REVOLT.
I EXPECTED MORE FROM THE "PUBLIC SERVICE" COMMUNITY OF DETROIT.
THE FREE RIDE IS OVER!
HANDOUTS ARE OVER--YOU AND I DON'T GET THEM, WHY SHOULD THEY? PENSIONS, DISABILITY, BENEFITS--PAY IT ALL BACK!
YEAH, YEAH, THEY'RE ALL EX-COPS, EX-E.M.T., EX-NURSES, BLAH BLAH. I'M NOT HERE FOR A HISTORY LESSON--BUNCHA CRIMINALS LIVING IN THE SHORE!
LIVE
DETROIT
ANY WORD ON ROBOCOP--I MEAN ALEX MURPHY?
HE'S DISABLED HIS SAFETY PROGRAMMING. THAT IS A CRIME. MORE THAN THAT, IT'S A RISK TO PUBLIC SAFETY. THERE IS SIMPLY NO WAY TO PREDICT WHAT HE WILL DO NEXT--AND TO WHOM.
DETROIT MAYOR
UBLIC RISK! ORIGINAL ROBOCOP AT LARGE, ARMED AND RES
"KEEP YOUR HEAD UP, ROBOCOP--"

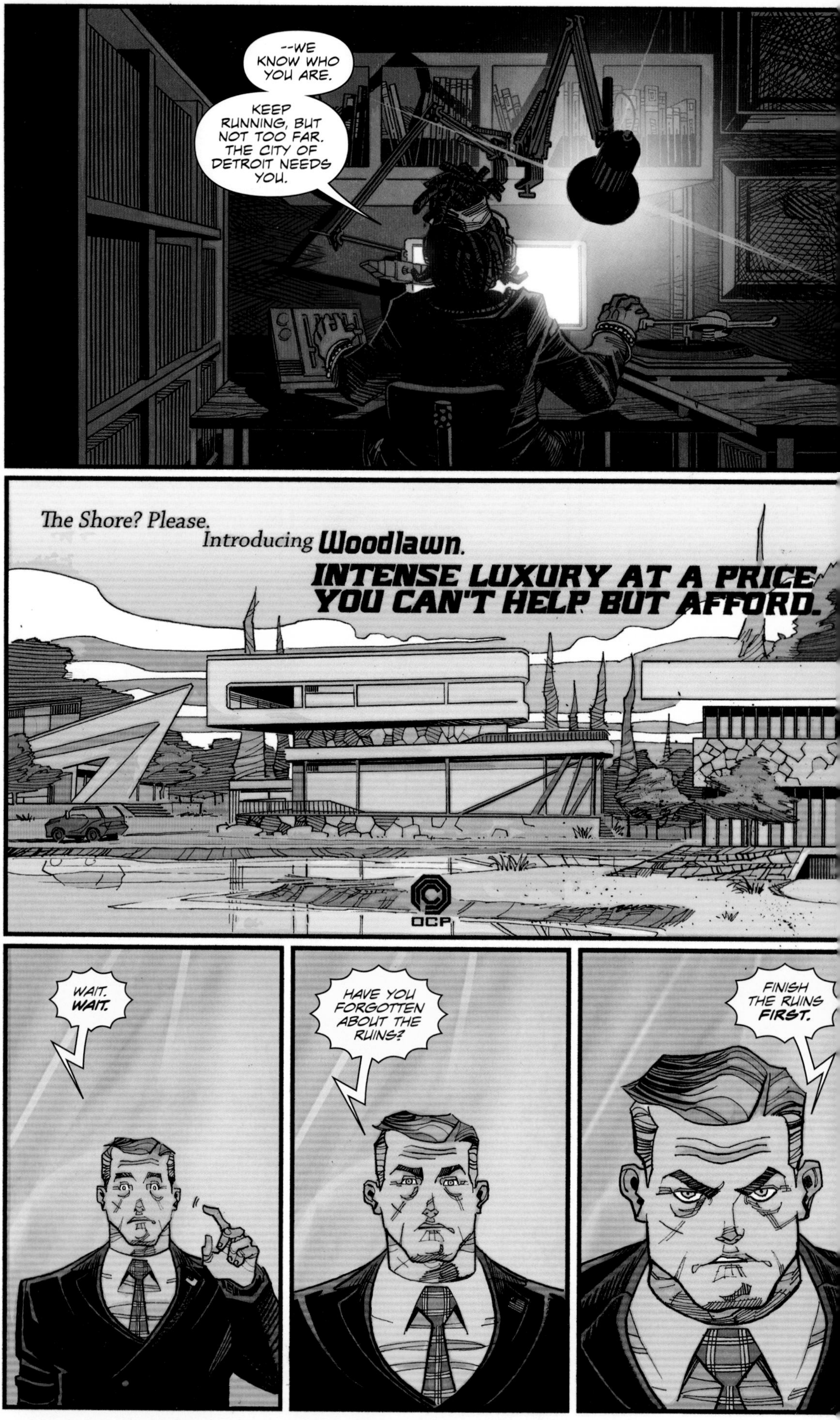
--WE KNOW WHO YOU ARE.
KEEP RUNNING, BUT NOT TOO FAR. THE CITY OF DETROIT NEEDS YOU.
The Shore? Please.
Introducing Woodlawn.
INTENSE LUXURY AT A PRICE YOU CAN'T HELP BUT AFFORD.
OCP
WAIT. WAIT.
HAVE YOU FORGOTTEN ABOUT THE RUINS?
FINISH THE RUINS FIRST.

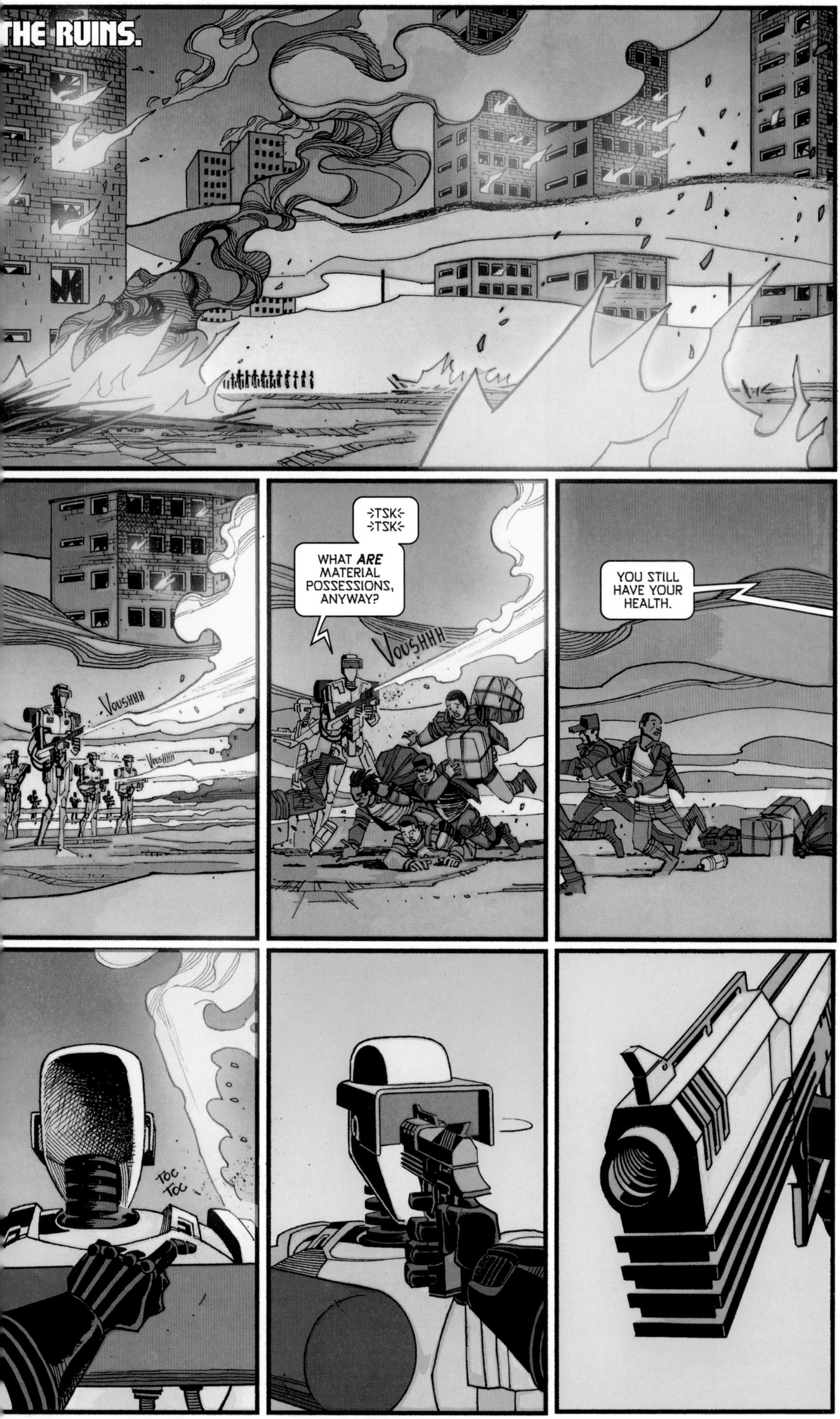
THE RUINS.
VOUSHHH
VOUSHHH
TSK TSK
WHAT ARE MATERIAL POSSESSIONS, ANYWAY?
VOUSHHH
YOU STILL HAVE YOUR HEALTH.
TOC TOC

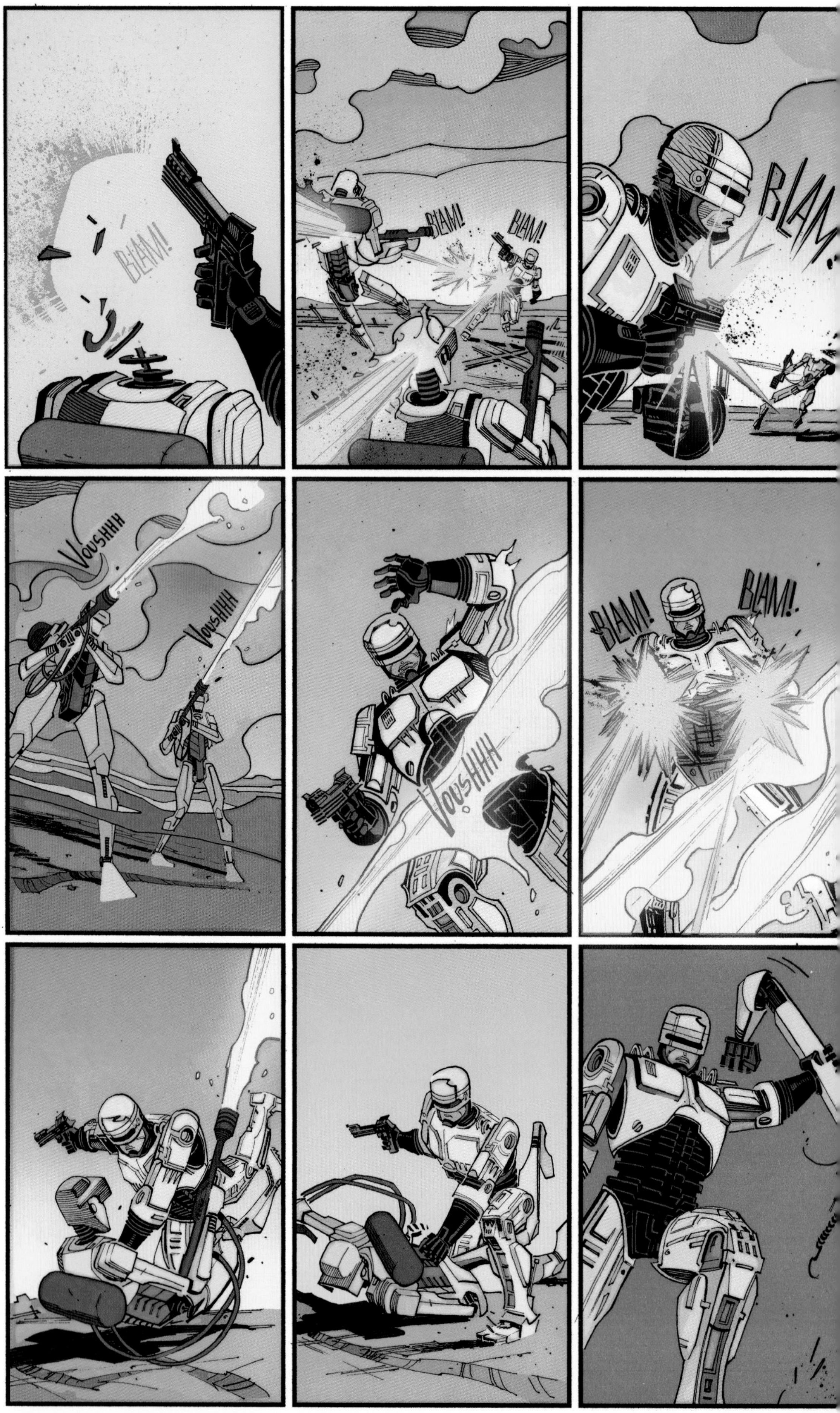

BLAM!
BLAM!
BLAM!
BLAM
VOUSHHH
VOUSHHH
VOUSHHH
BLAM!
BLAM!

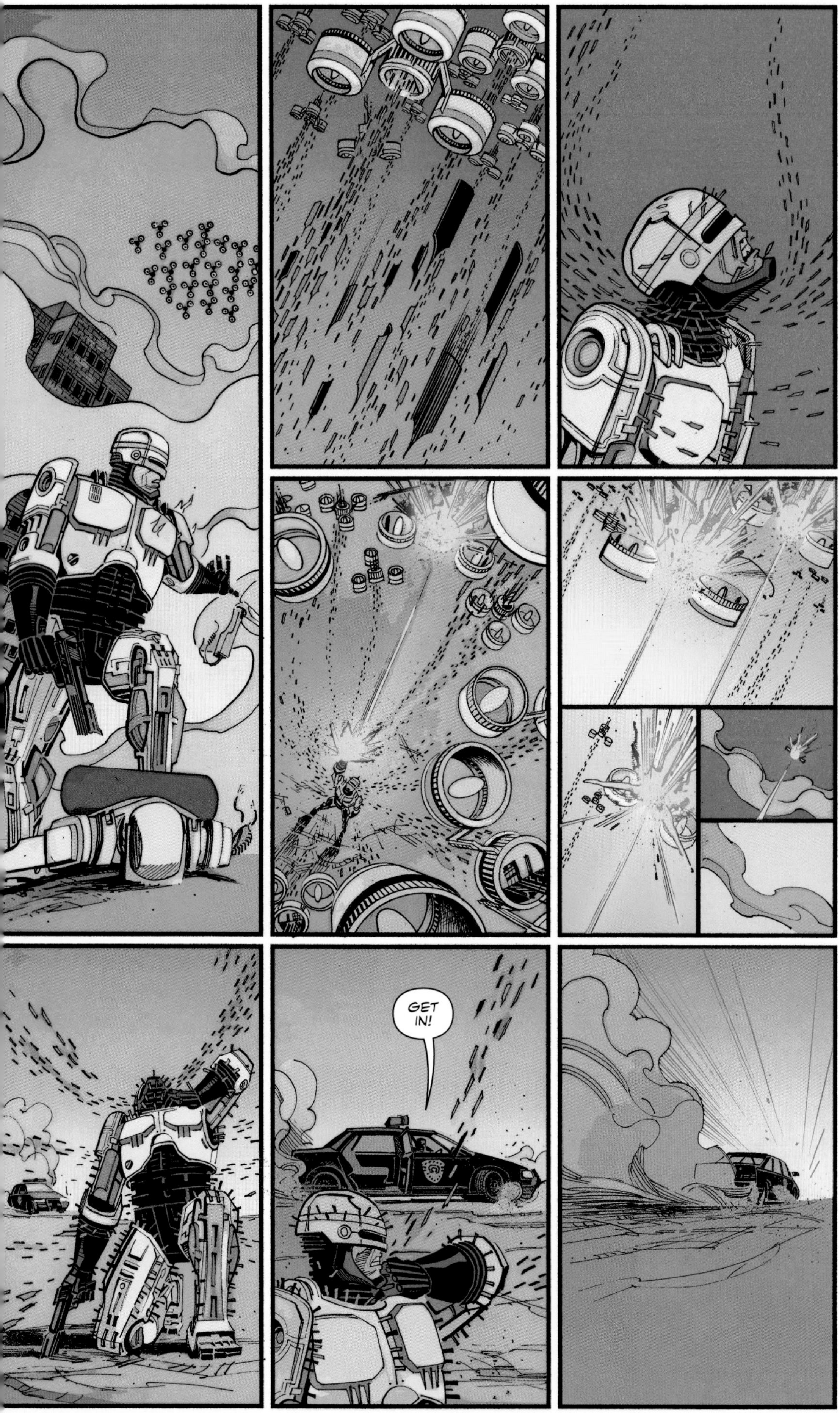
GET IN!

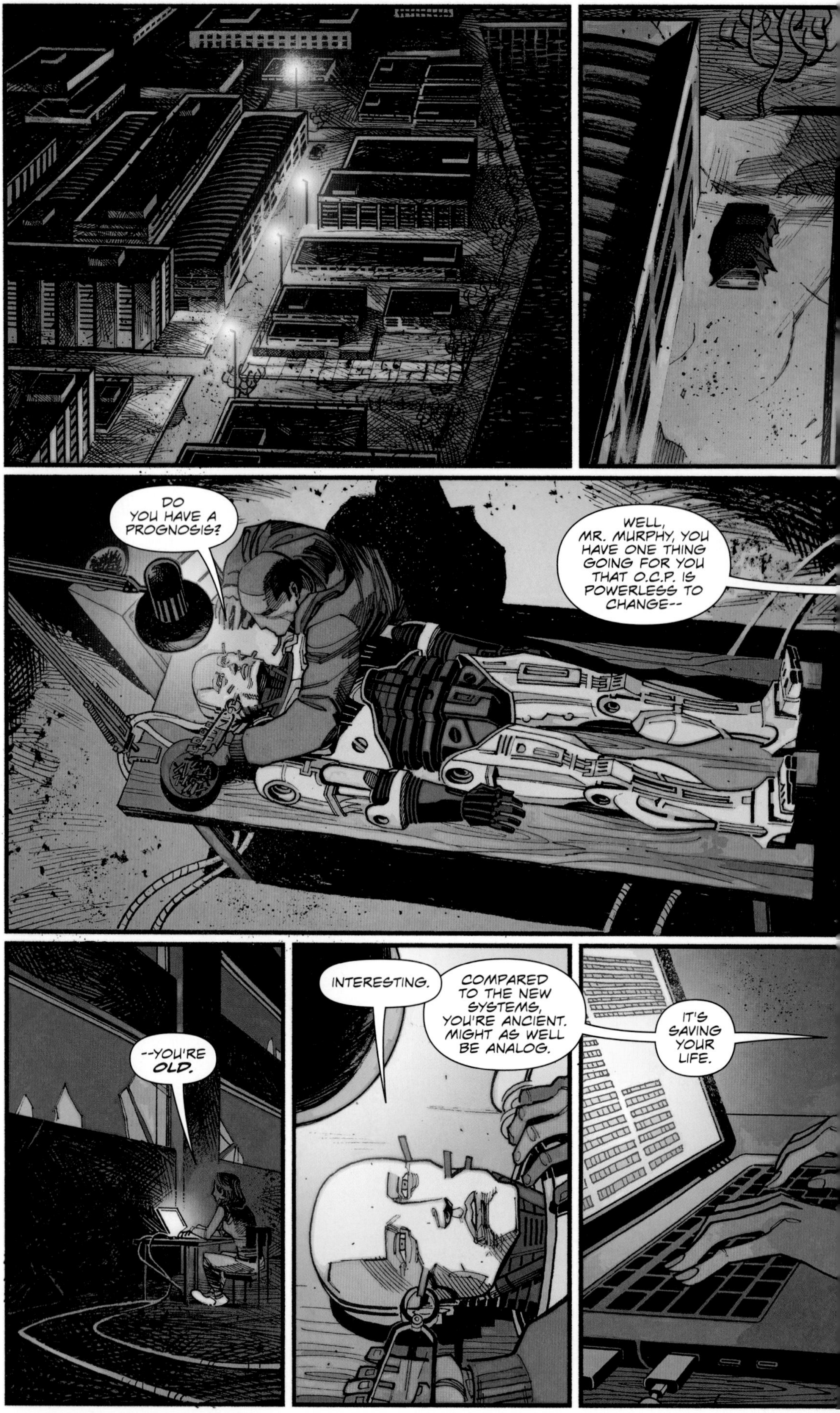
DO YOU HAVE A PROGNOSIS?
WELL, MR. MURPHY, YOU HAVE ONE THING GOING FOR YOU THAT O.C.P. IS POWERLESS TO CHANGE--
--YOU'RE OLD.
INTERESTING.
COMPARED TO THE NEW SYSTEMS, YOU'RE ANCIENT. MIGHT AS WELL BE ANALOG.
IT'S SAVING YOUR LIFE.

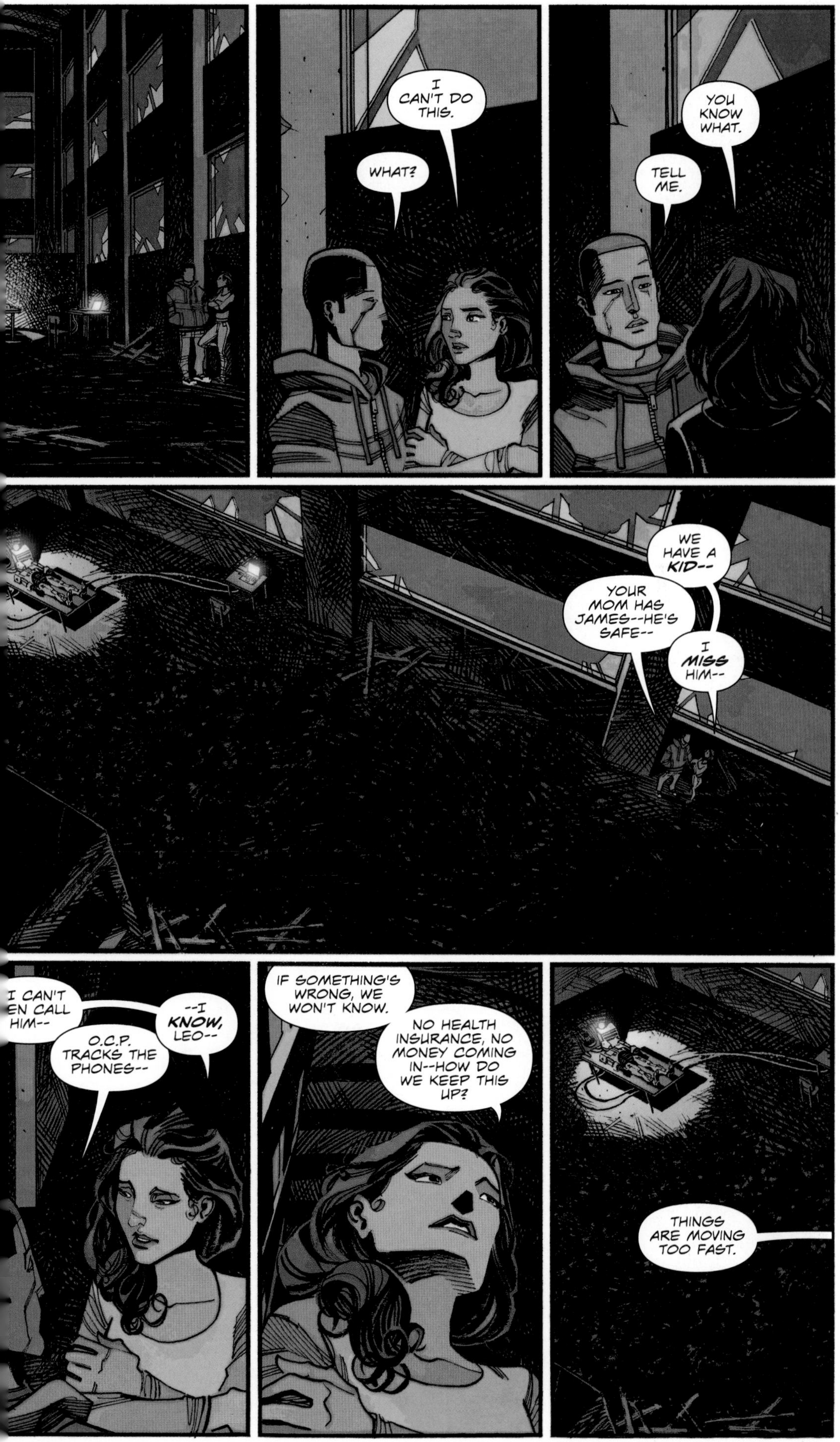
I CAN'T DO THIS.
WHAT?
YOU KNOW WHAT.
TELL ME.
WE HAVE A KID--
YOUR MOM HAS JAMES--HE'S SAFE--
I MISS HIM--
I CAN'T
EN CALL HIM--
--I KNOW, LEO--
O.C.P. TRACKS THE PHONES--
IF SOMETHING'S WRONG, WE WON'T KNOW.
NO HEALTH INSURANCE, NO MONEY COMING IN--HOW DO WE KEEP THIS UP?
THINGS ARE MOVING TOO FAST.

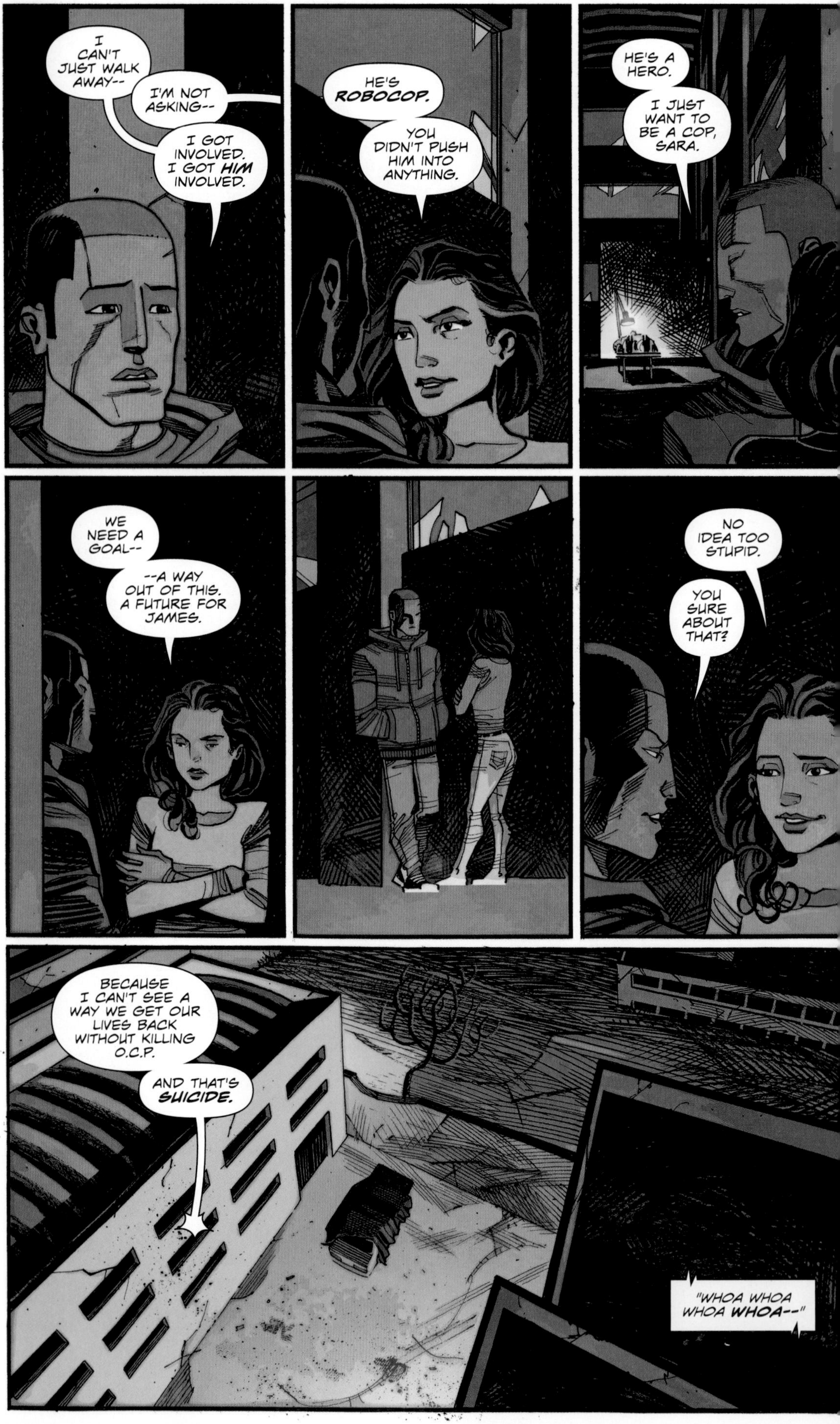
I CAN'T JUST WALK AWAY--
I'M NOT ASKING--
I GOT INVOLVED. I GOT *HIM* INVOLVED.
HE'S *ROBOCOP.*
YOU DIDN'T PUSH HIM INTO ANYTHING.
HE'S A HERO.
I JUST WANT TO BE A COP, SARA.
WE NEED A GOAL--
--A WAY OUT OF THIS. A FUTURE FOR JAMES.
NO IDEA TOO STUPID.
YOU SURE ABOUT THAT?
BECAUSE I CAN'T SEE A WAY WE GET OUR LIVES BACK WITHOUT KILLING O.C.P.
AND THAT'S *SUICIDE.*
"WHOA WHOA WHOA *WHOA--*"

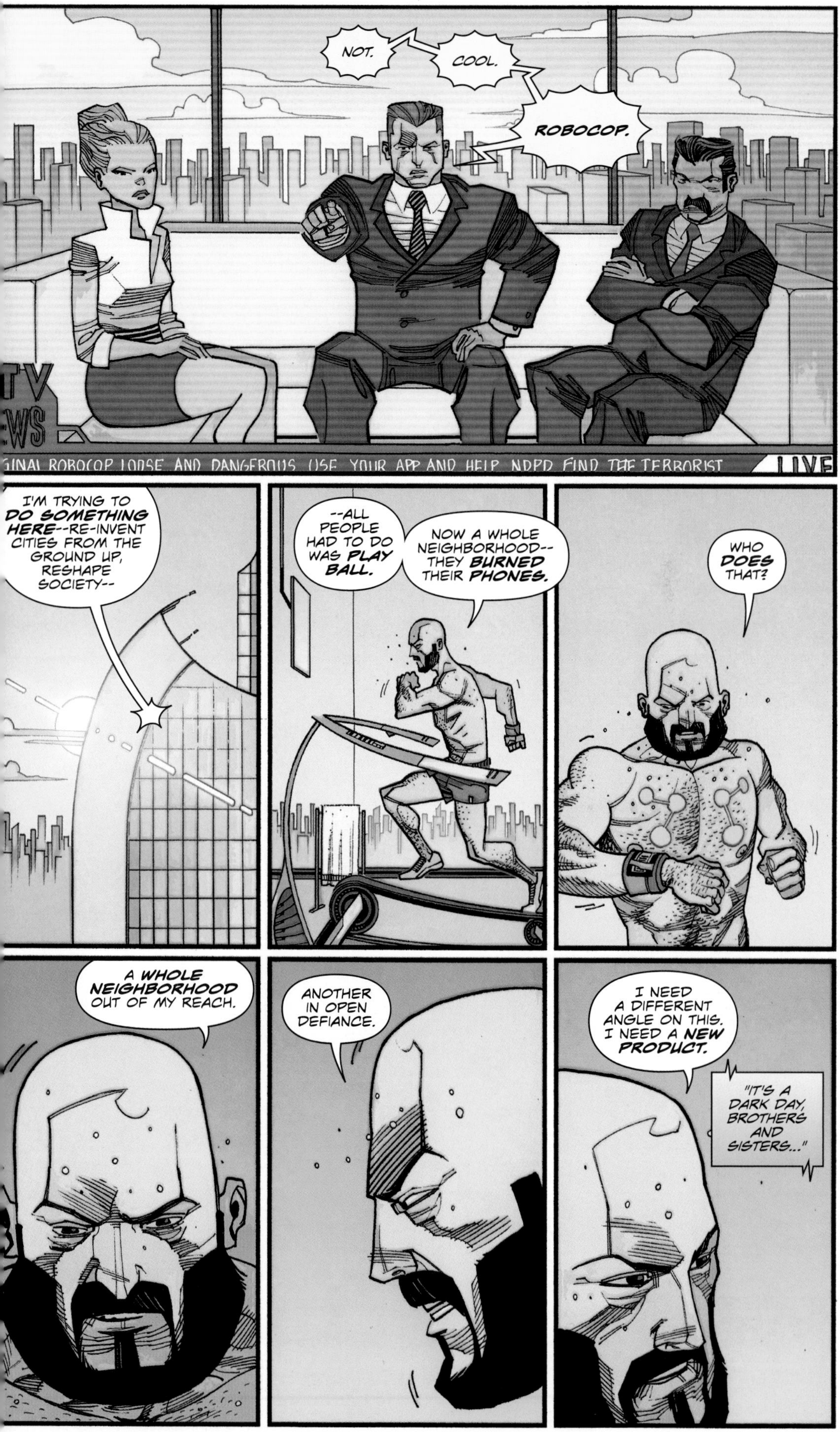
NOT.
COOL.
ROBOCOP.
GINAL ROBOCOP LOOSE AND DANGEROUS USE YOUR APP AND HELP NDPD FIND THE TERRORIST
LIVE
I'M TRYING TO DO SOMETHING HERE--RE-INVENT CITIES FROM THE GROUND UP, RESHAPE SOCIETY--
--ALL PEOPLE HAD TO DO WAS PLAY BALL.
NOW A WHOLE NEIGHBORHOOD-- THEY BURNED THEIR PHONES.
WHO DOES THAT?
A WHOLE NEIGHBORHOOD OUT OF MY REACH.
ANOTHER IN OPEN DEFIANCE.
I NEED A DIFFERENT ANGLE ON THIS. I NEED A NEW PRODUCT.
"IT'S A DARK DAY, BROTHERS AND SISTERS..."

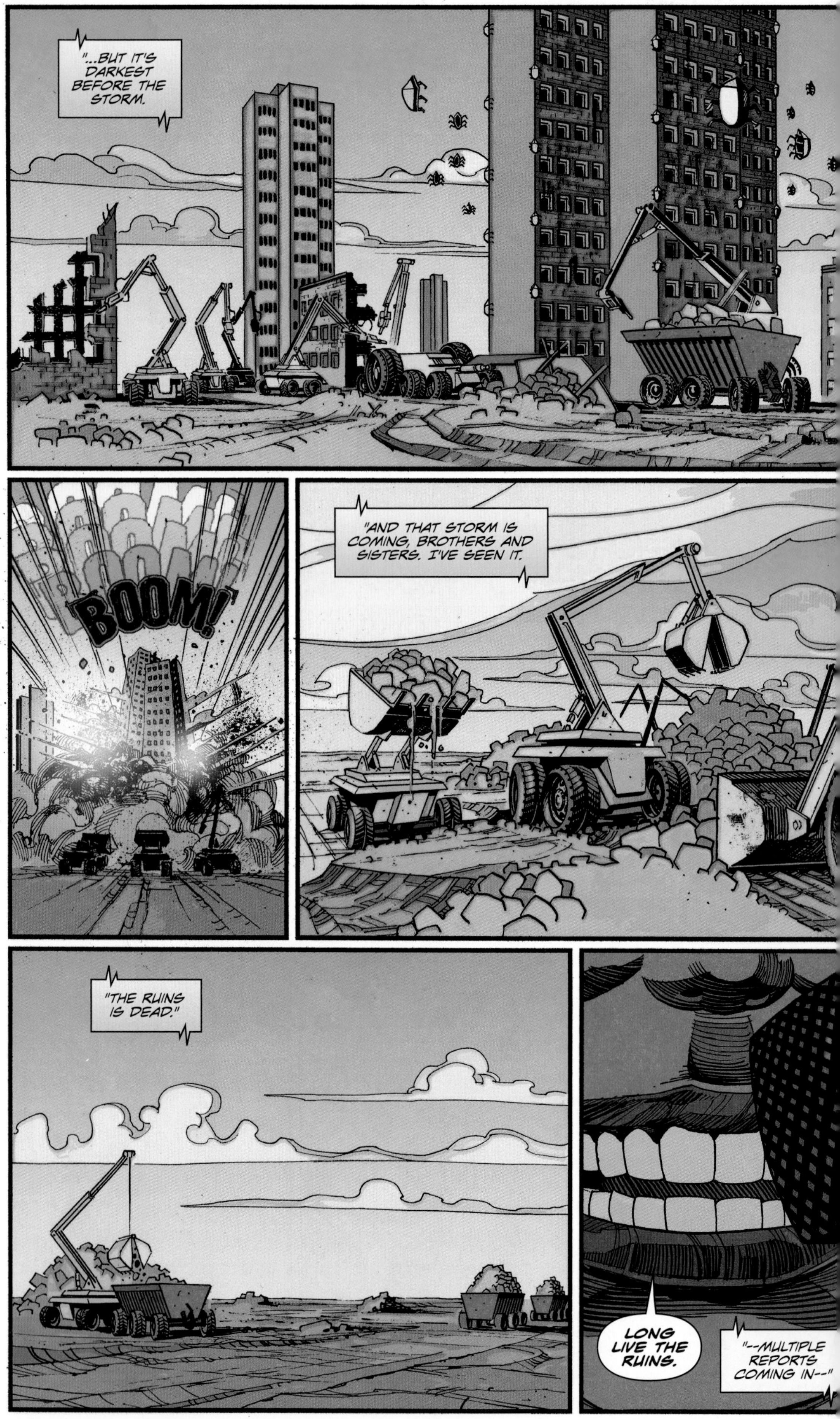
"...BUT IT'S DARKEST BEFORE THE STORM.
BOOM!
"AND THAT STORM IS COMING, BROTHERS AND SISTERS. I'VE SEEN IT.
"THE RUINS IS DEAD."
LONG LIVE THE RUINS.
"--MULTIPLE REPORTS COMING IN--"

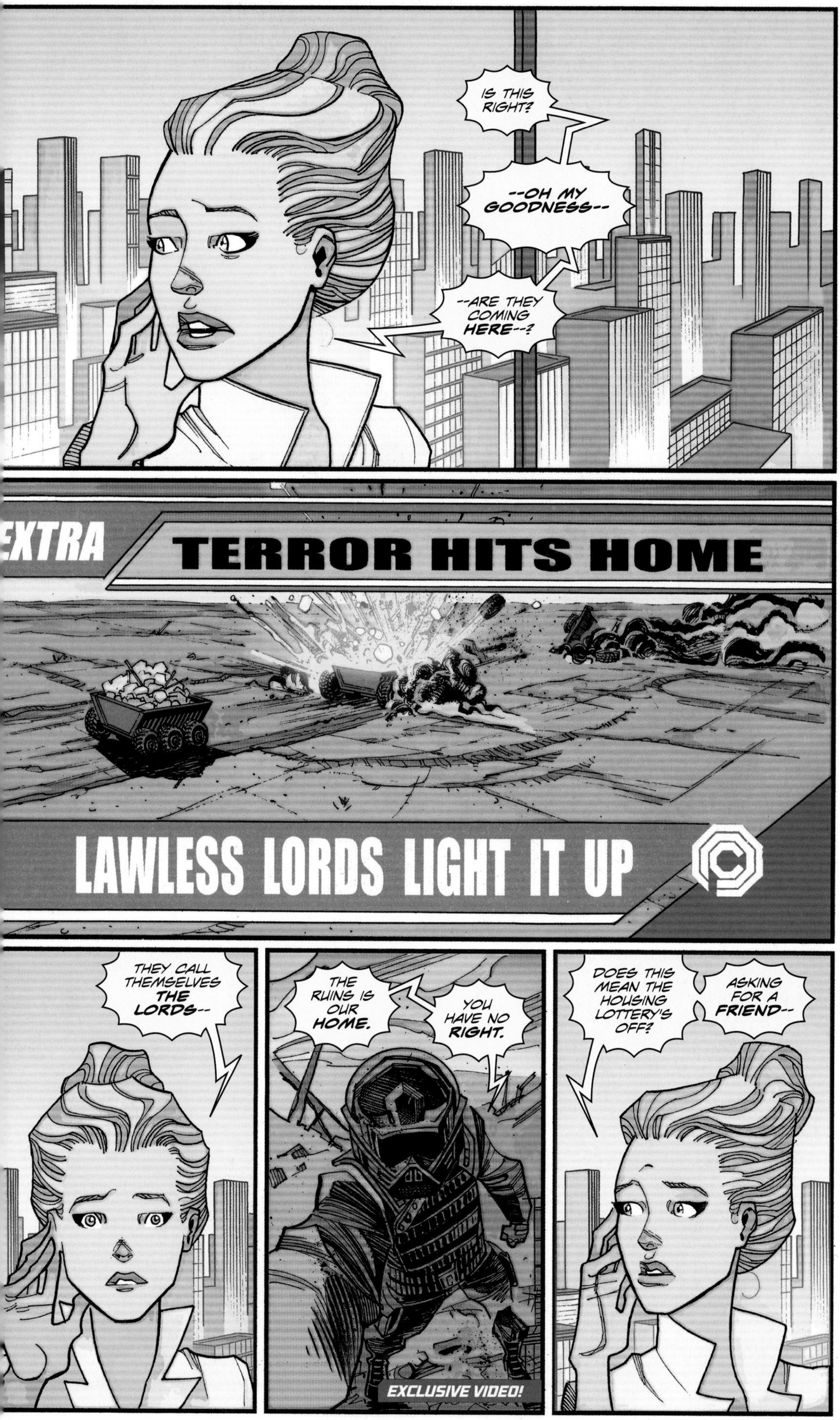
IS THIS RIGHT?
--OH MY GOODNESS--
--ARE THEY COMING HERE--?
EXTRA
TERROR HITS HOME
LAWLESS LORDS LIGHT IT UP
THEY CALL THEMSELVES THE LORDS--
THE RUINS IS OUR HOME.
YOU HAVE NO RIGHT.
EXCLUSIVE VIDEO!
DOES THIS MEAN THE HOUSING LOTTERY'S OFF?
ASKING FOR A FRIEND--

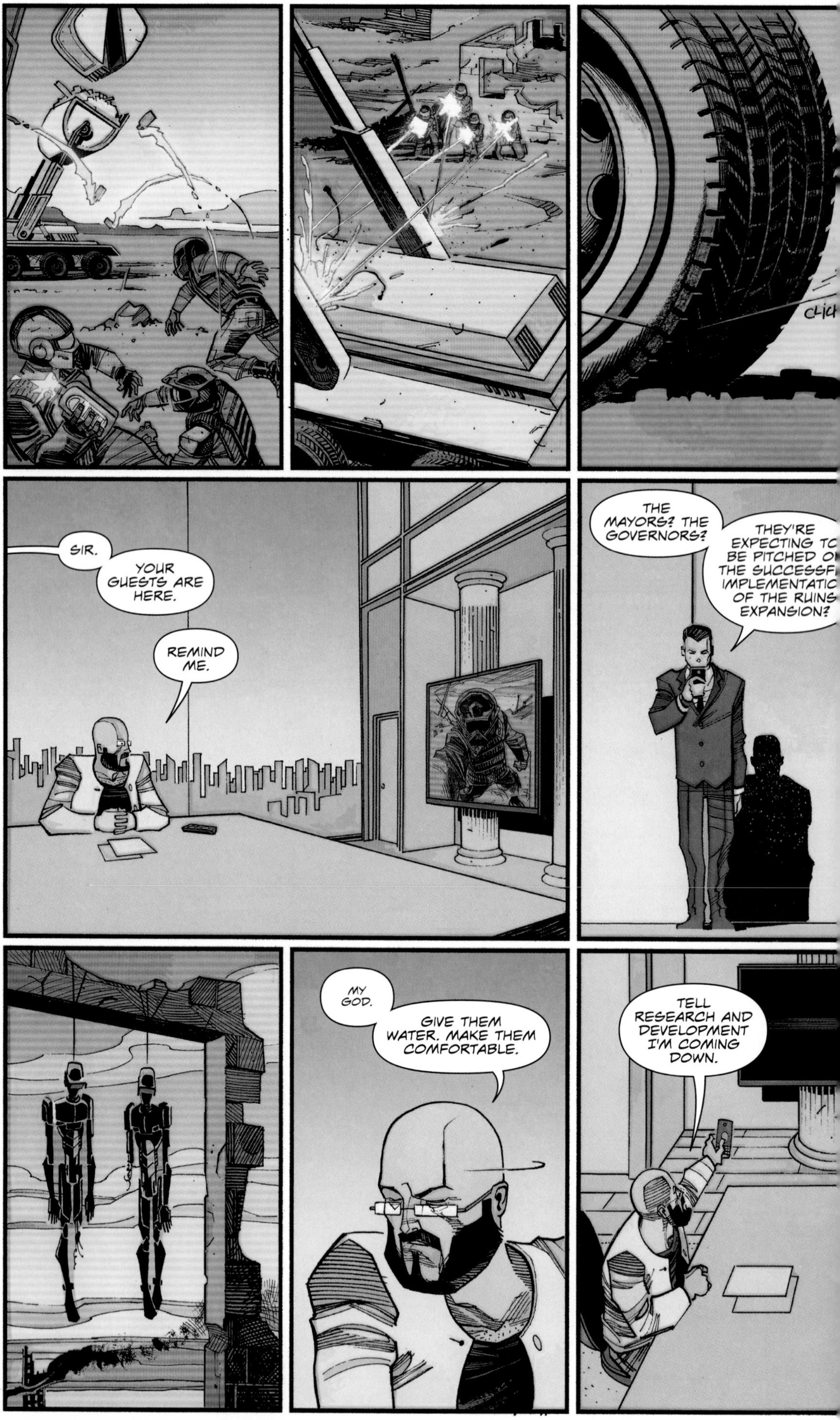
CLIC
SIR.
YOUR GUESTS ARE HERE.
REMIND ME.
THE MAYORS? THE GOVERNORS?
THEY'RE EXPECTING TO BE PITCHED ON THE SUCCESSF IMPLEMENTATIO OF THE RUINS EXPANSION?
MY GOD.
GIVE THEM WATER. MAKE THEM COMFORTABLE.
TELL RESEARCH AND DEVELOPMENT I'M COMING DOWN.

SARA--

--SHE'S UPSET.

YEAH, SHE IS.

SHE SHOULD KNOW I'M GRATEFUL FOR HER HELP.

SHE KNOWS.

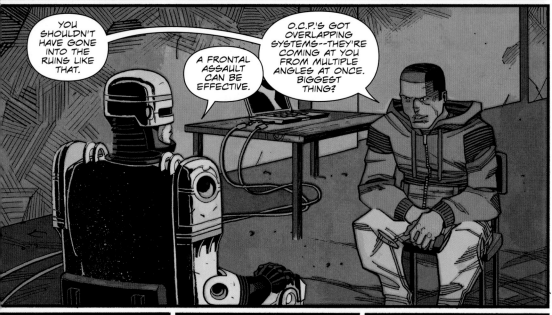

YOU SHOULDN'T HAVE GONE INTO THE RUINS LIKE THAT.

A FRONTAL ASSAULT CAN BE EFFECTIVE.

O.C.P.'S GOT OVERLAPPING SYSTEMS--THEY'RE COMING AT YOU FROM MULTIPLE ANGLES AT ONCE. BIGGEST THING?

THEY AREN'T BEHOLDEN TO ANYTHING. THEY CAN DO **WHATEVER**, AND IT'S ALL LEGAL FOR THEM.

NO PRIME DIRECTIVES.

NAME THEM.

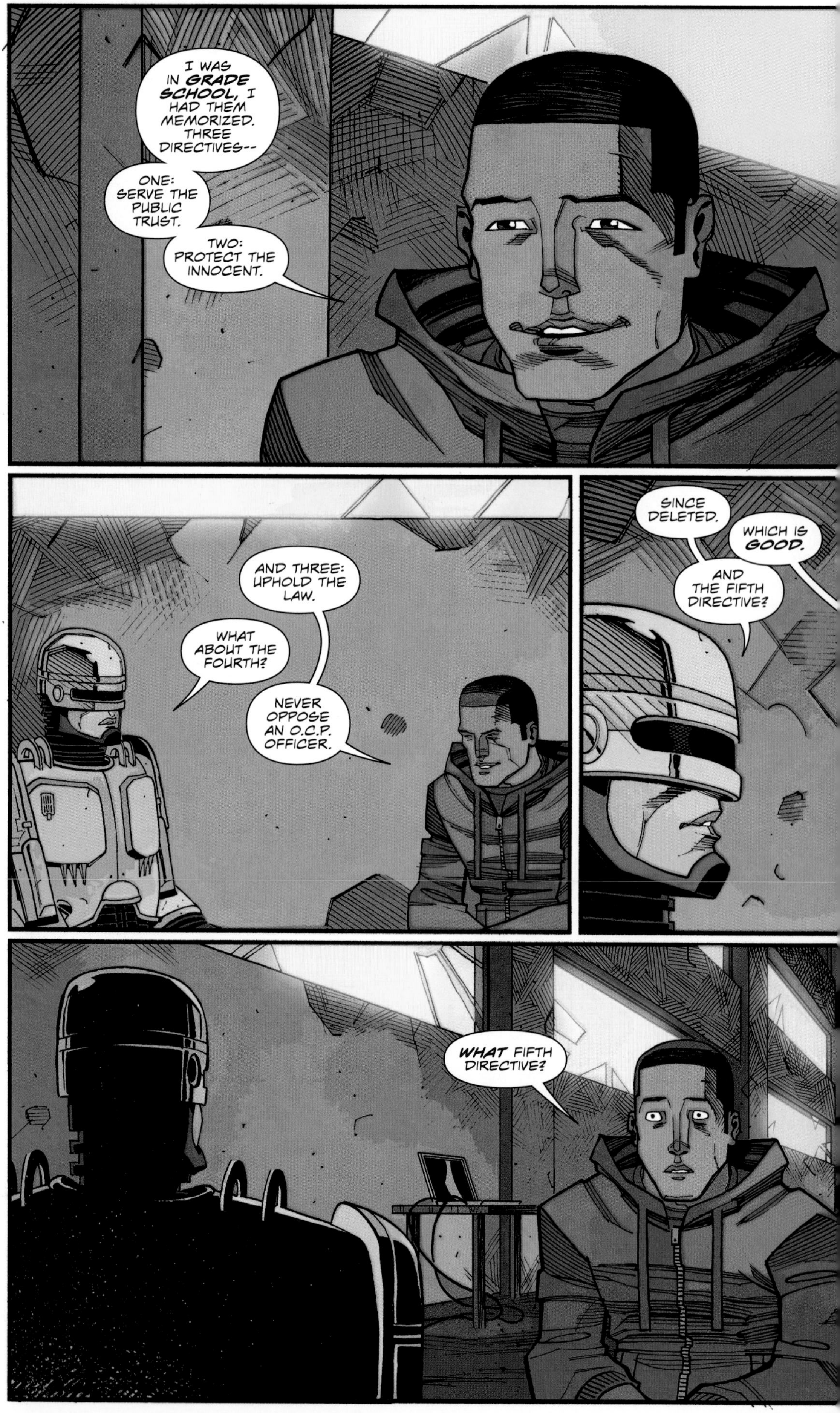
I WAS IN GRADE SCHOOL, I HAD THEM MEMORIZED. THREE DIRECTIVES--
ONE: SERVE THE PUBLIC TRUST.
TWO: PROTECT THE INNOCENT.
AND THREE: UPHOLD THE LAW.
WHAT ABOUT THE FOURTH?
NEVER OPPOSE AN O.C.P. OFFICER.
SINCE DELETED.
WHICH IS GOOD.
AND THE FIFTH DIRECTIVE?
WHAT FIFTH DIRECTIVE?

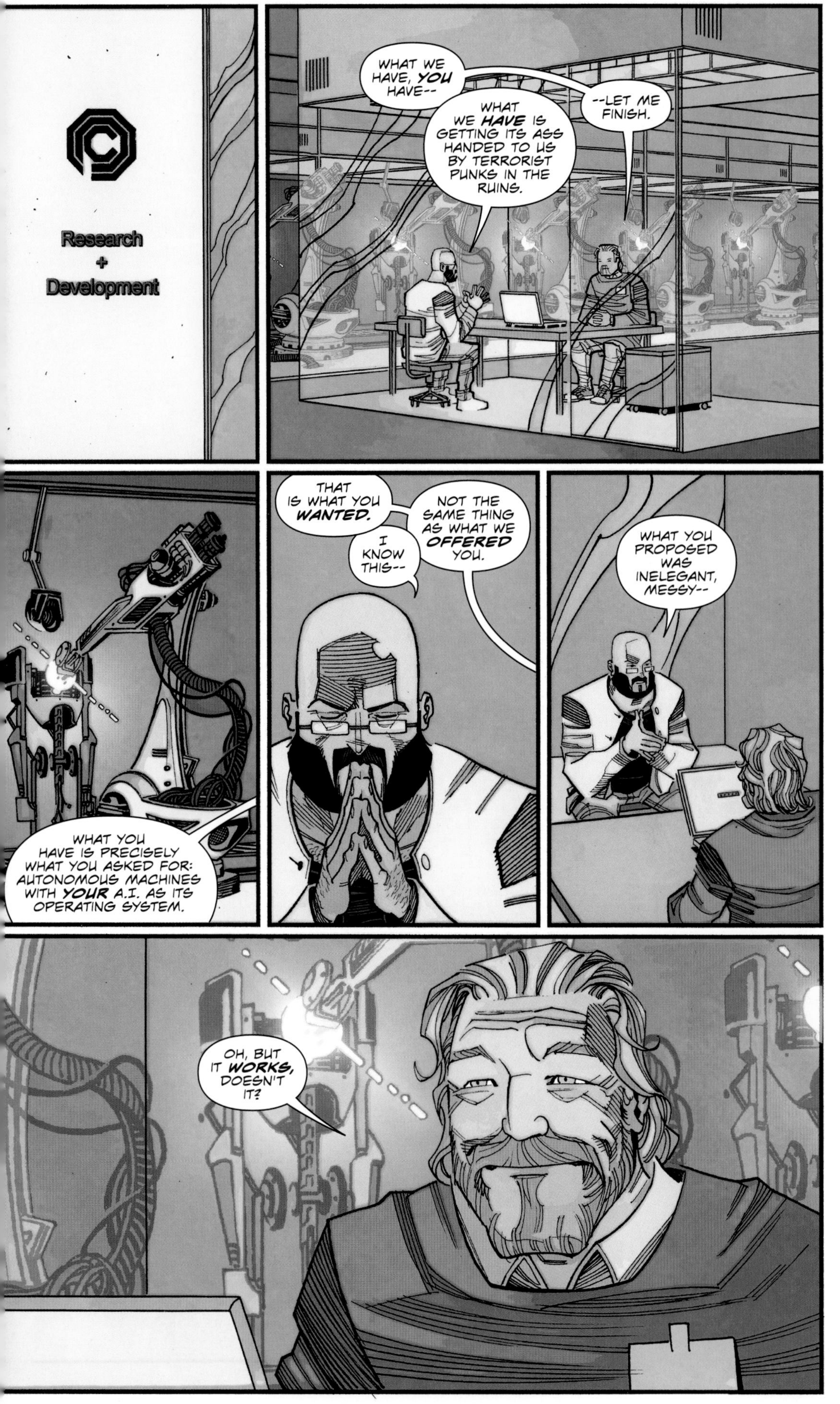
Research
+
Development
WHAT WE HAVE, YOU HAVE--
WHAT WE HAVE IS GETTING ITS ASS HANDED TO US BY TERRORIST PUNKS IN THE RUINS.
--LET ME FINISH.
WHAT YOU HAVE IS PRECISELY WHAT YOU ASKED FOR: AUTONOMOUS MACHINES WITH YOUR A.I. AS ITS OPERATING SYSTEM.
THAT IS WHAT YOU WANTED.
I KNOW THIS--
NOT THE SAME THING AS WHAT WE OFFERED YOU.
WHAT YOU PROPOSED WAS INELEGANT, MESSY--
OH, BUT IT WORKS, DOESN'T IT?

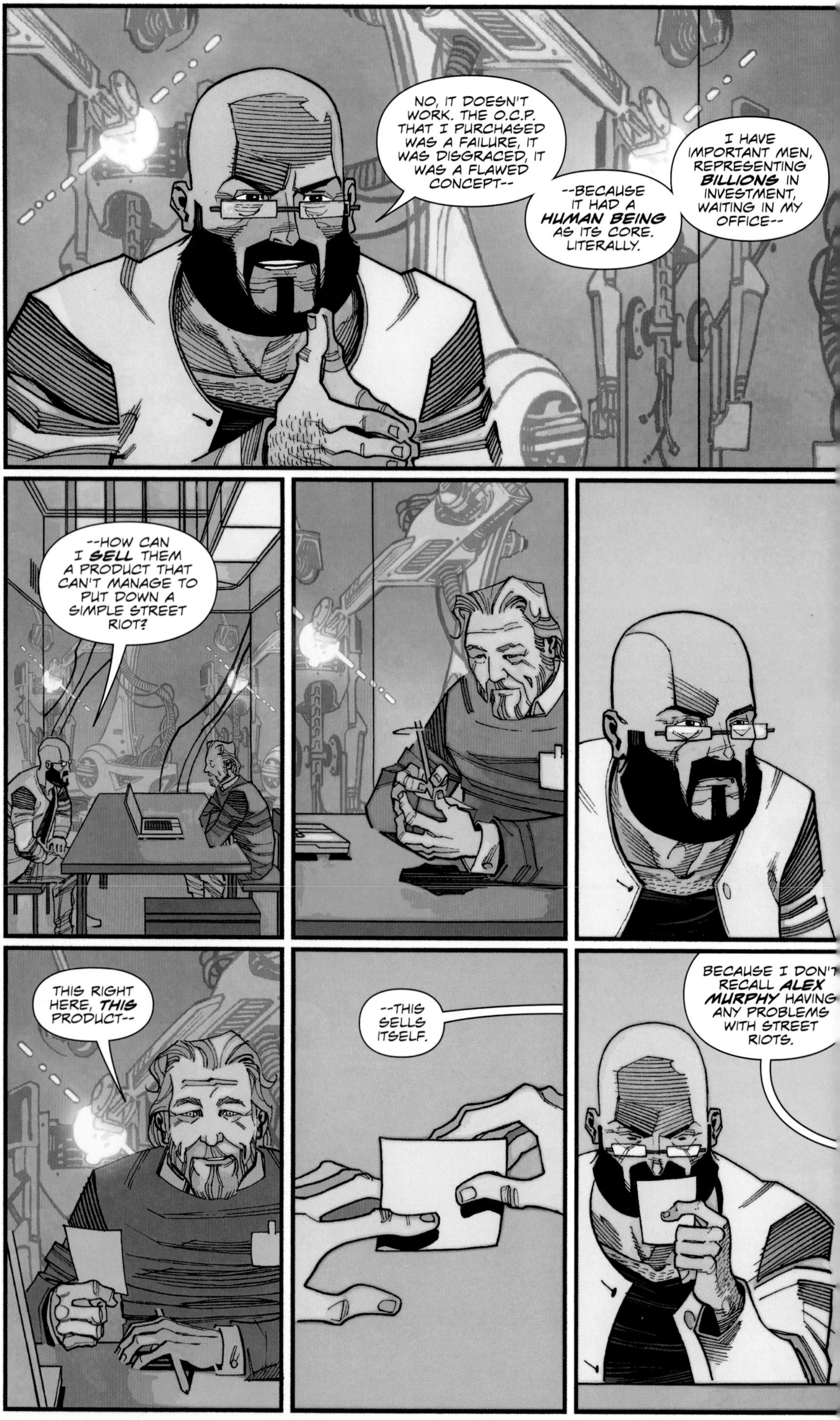
NO, IT DOESN'T WORK. THE O.C.P. THAT I PURCHASED WAS A FAILURE, IT WAS DISGRACED, IT WAS A FLAWED CONCEPT--
--BECAUSE IT HAD A HUMAN BEING AS ITS CORE. LITERALLY.
I HAVE IMPORTANT MEN, REPRESENTING BILLIONS IN INVESTMENT, WAITING IN MY OFFICE--
--HOW CAN I SELL THEM A PRODUCT THAT CAN'T MANAGE TO PUT DOWN A SIMPLE STREET RIOT?
THIS RIGHT HERE, THIS PRODUCT--
--THIS SELLS ITSELF.
BECAUSE I DON'T RECALL ALEX MURPHY HAVING ANY PROBLEMS WITH STREET RIOTS.

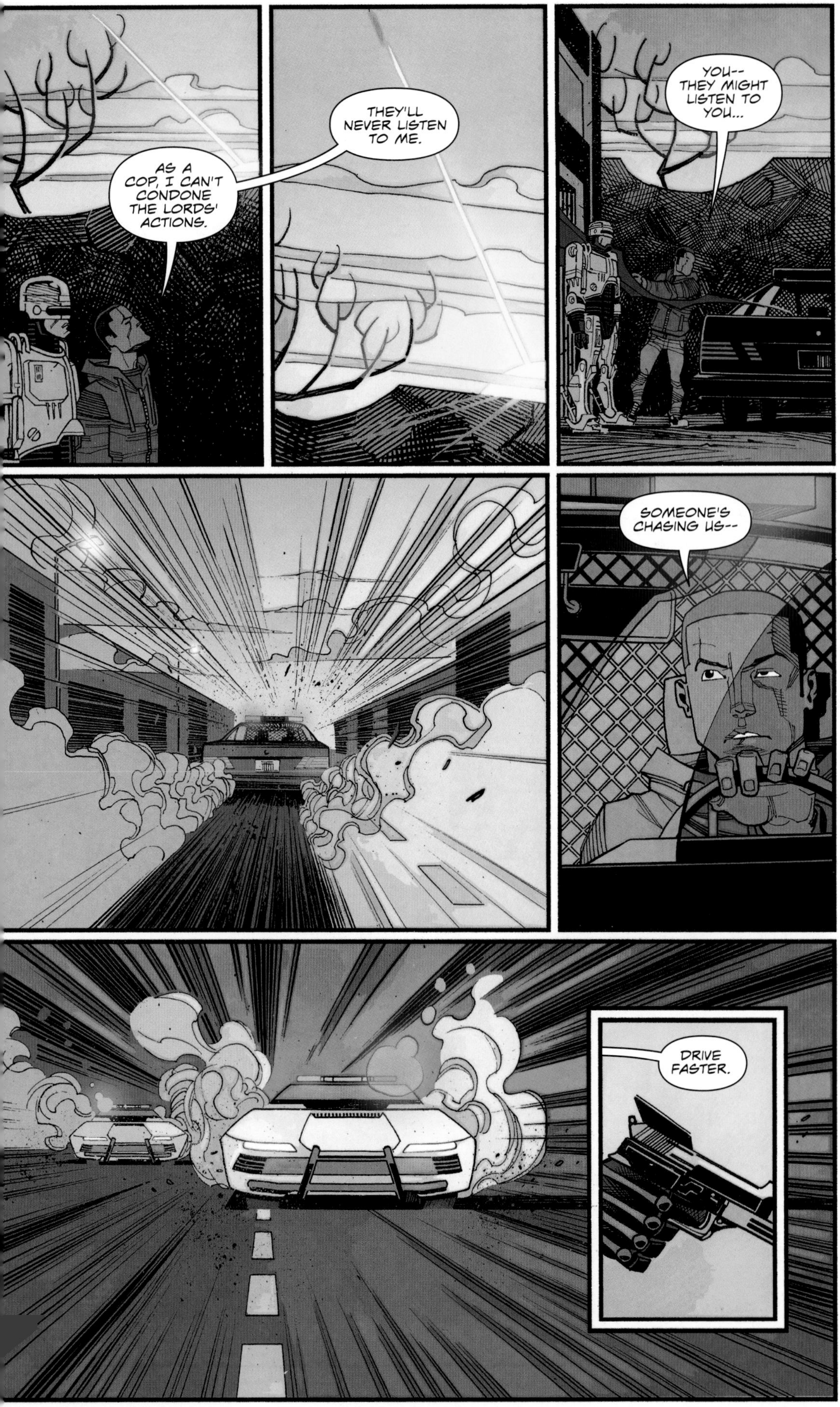
AS A COP, I CAN'T CONDONE THE LORDS' ACTIONS.
THEY'LL NEVER LISTEN TO ME.
YOU-- THEY MIGHT LISTEN TO YOU...
SOMEONE'S CHASING US--
DRIVE FASTER.

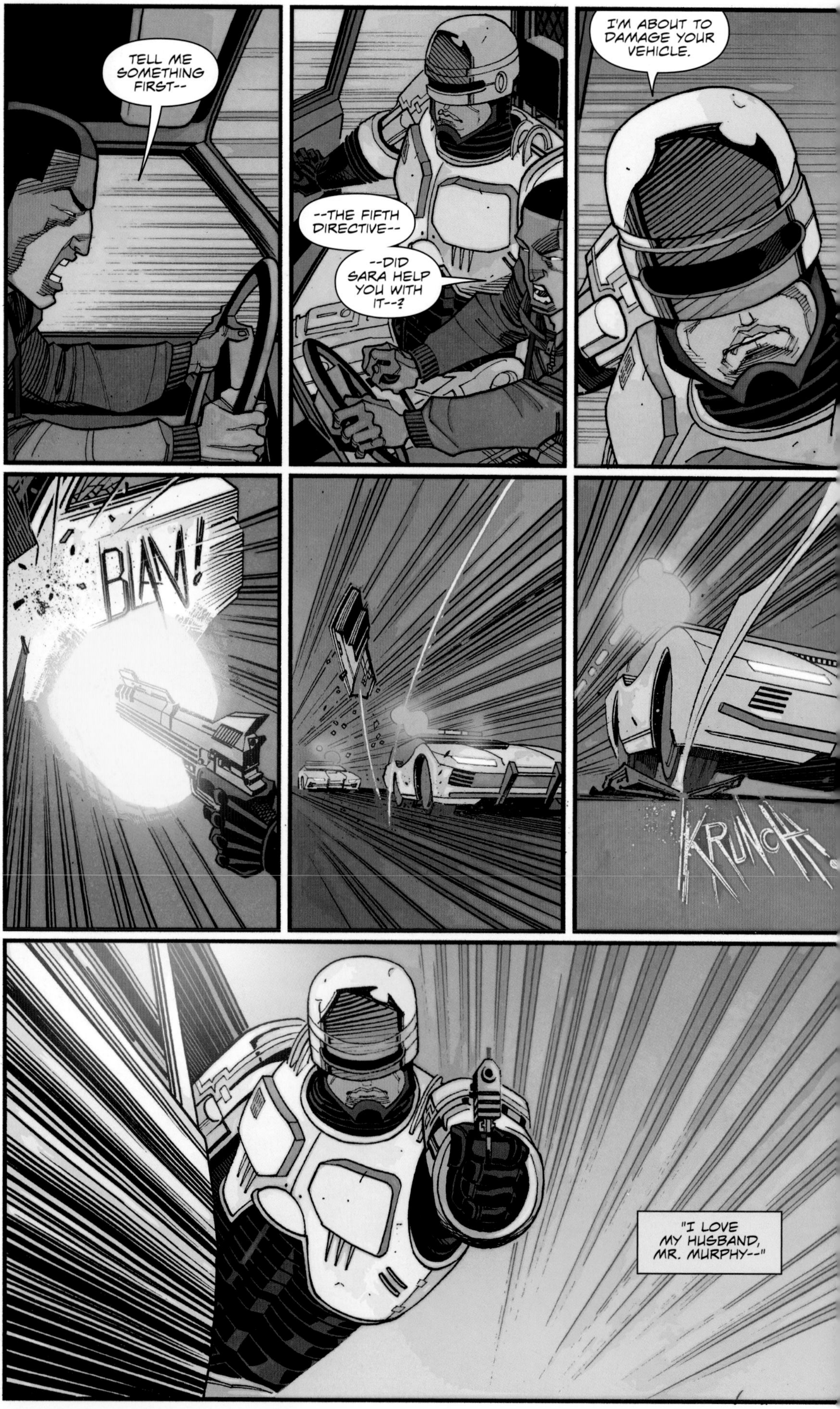
TELL ME SOMETHING FIRST--
--THE FIFTH DIRECTIVE--
--DID SARA HELP YOU WITH IT--?
I'M ABOUT TO DAMAGE YOUR VEHICLE.
BLAM!
KRUNCH!
"I LOVE MY HUSBAND, MR. MURPHY--"

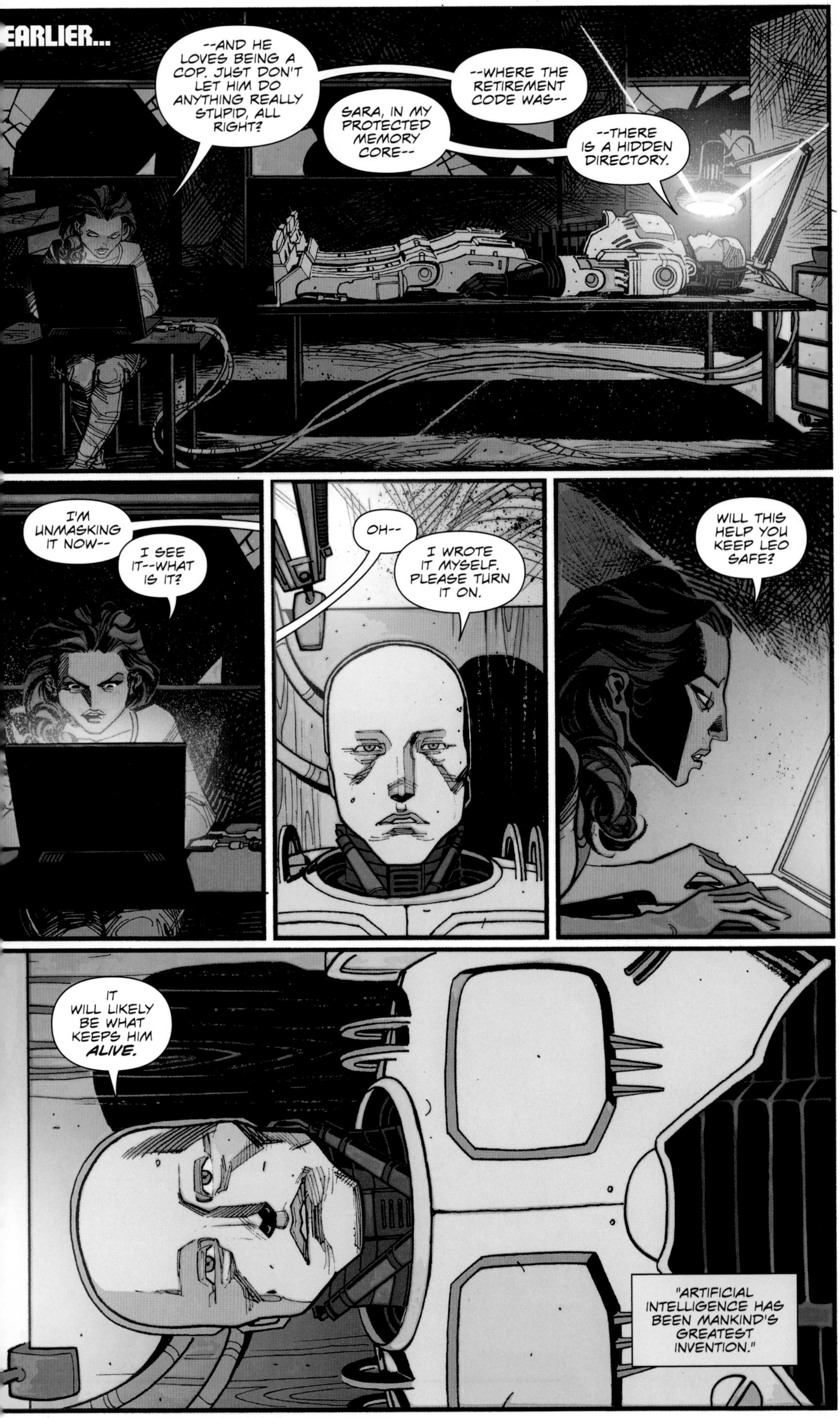
EARLIER...
--AND HE LOVES BEING A COP. JUST DON'T LET HIM DO ANYTHING REALLY STUPID, ALL RIGHT?
--WHERE THE RETIREMENT CODE WAS--
SARA, IN MY PROTECTED MEMORY CORE--
--THERE IS A HIDDEN DIRECTORY.
I'M UNMASKING IT NOW--
I SEE IT--WHAT IS IT?
OH--
I WROTE IT MYSELF. PLEASE TURN IT ON.
WILL THIS HELP YOU KEEP LEO SAFE?
IT WILL LIKELY BE WHAT KEEPS HIM *ALIVE.*
"ARTIFICIAL INTELLIGENCE HAS BEEN MANKIND'S GREATEST INVENTION."

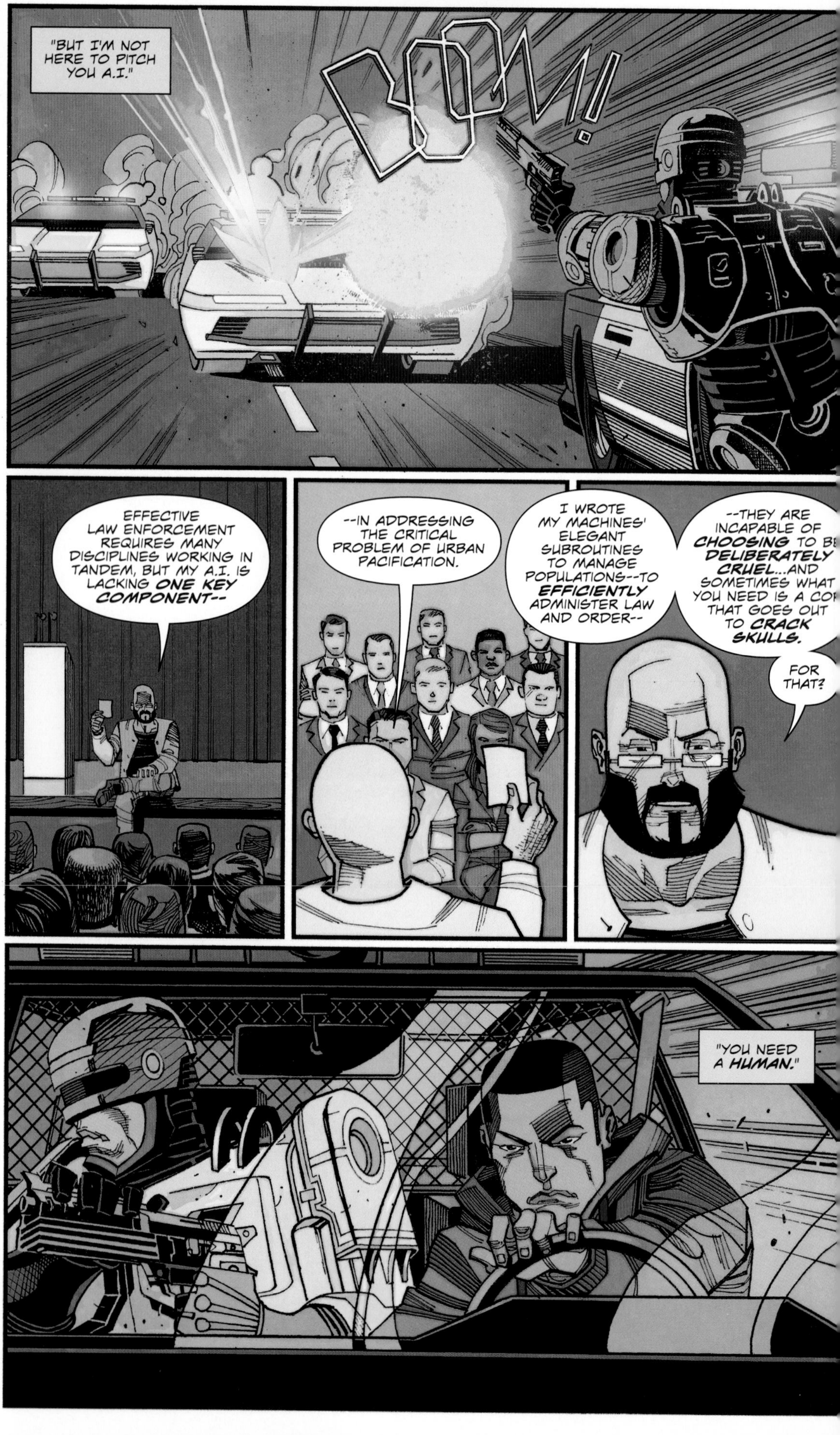
"BUT I'M NOT HERE TO PITCH YOU A.I."
BOOM!
EFFECTIVE LAW ENFORCEMENT REQUIRES MANY DISCIPLINES WORKING IN TANDEM, BUT MY A.I. IS LACKING ONE KEY COMPONENT--
--IN ADDRESSING THE CRITICAL PROBLEM OF URBAN PACIFICATION.
I WROTE MY MACHINES' ELEGANT SUBROUTINES TO MANAGE POPULATIONS--TO EFFICIENTLY ADMINISTER LAW AND ORDER--
--THEY ARE INCAPABLE OF CHOOSING TO BE DELIBERATELY CRUEL...AND SOMETIMES WHAT YOU NEED IS A COP THAT GOES OUT TO CRACK SKULLS.
FOR THAT?
"YOU NEED A HUMAN."

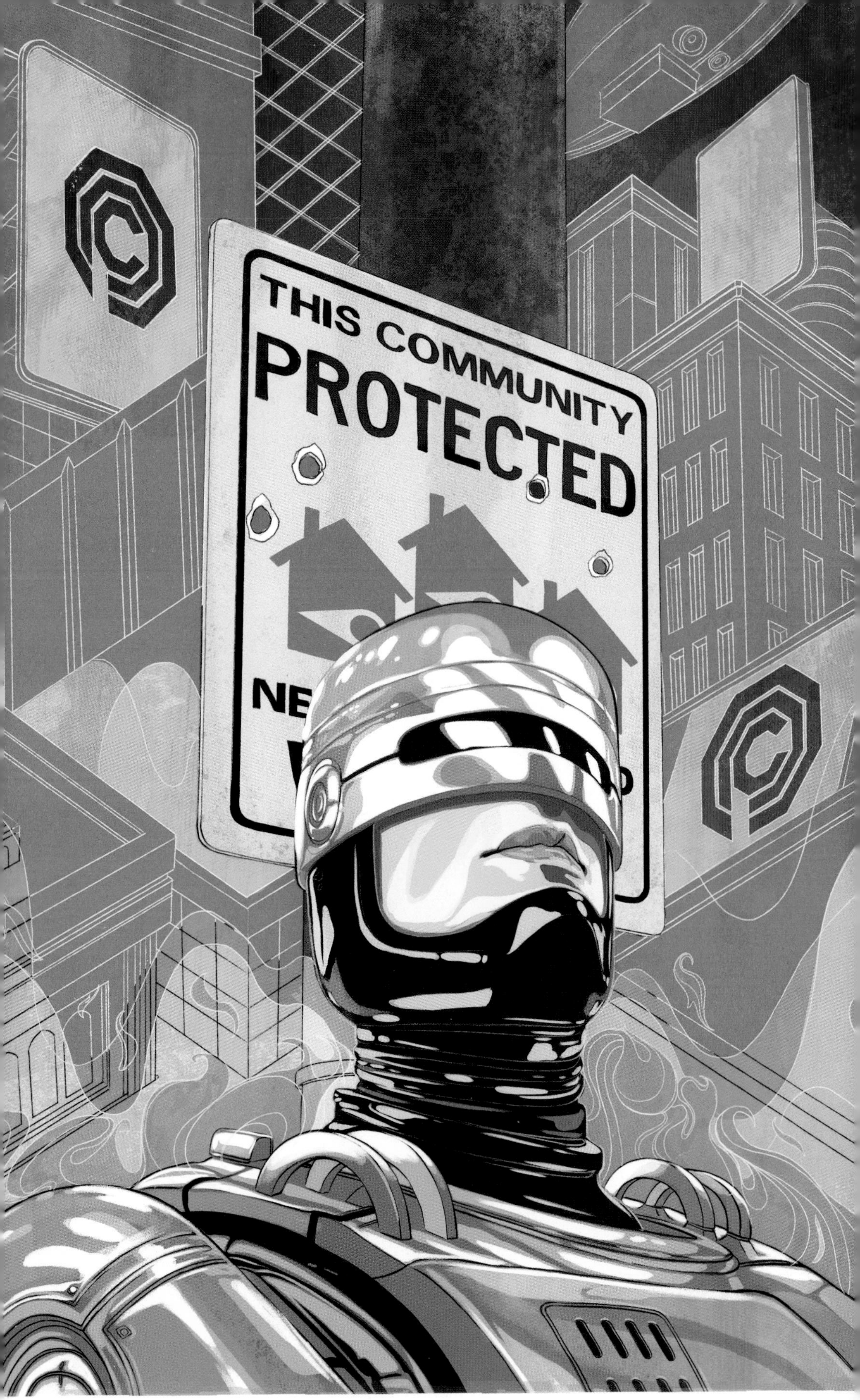
THIS COMMUNITY
PROTECTED

ISSUE 03 COVER **NIMIT MALAVIA**

FOUR

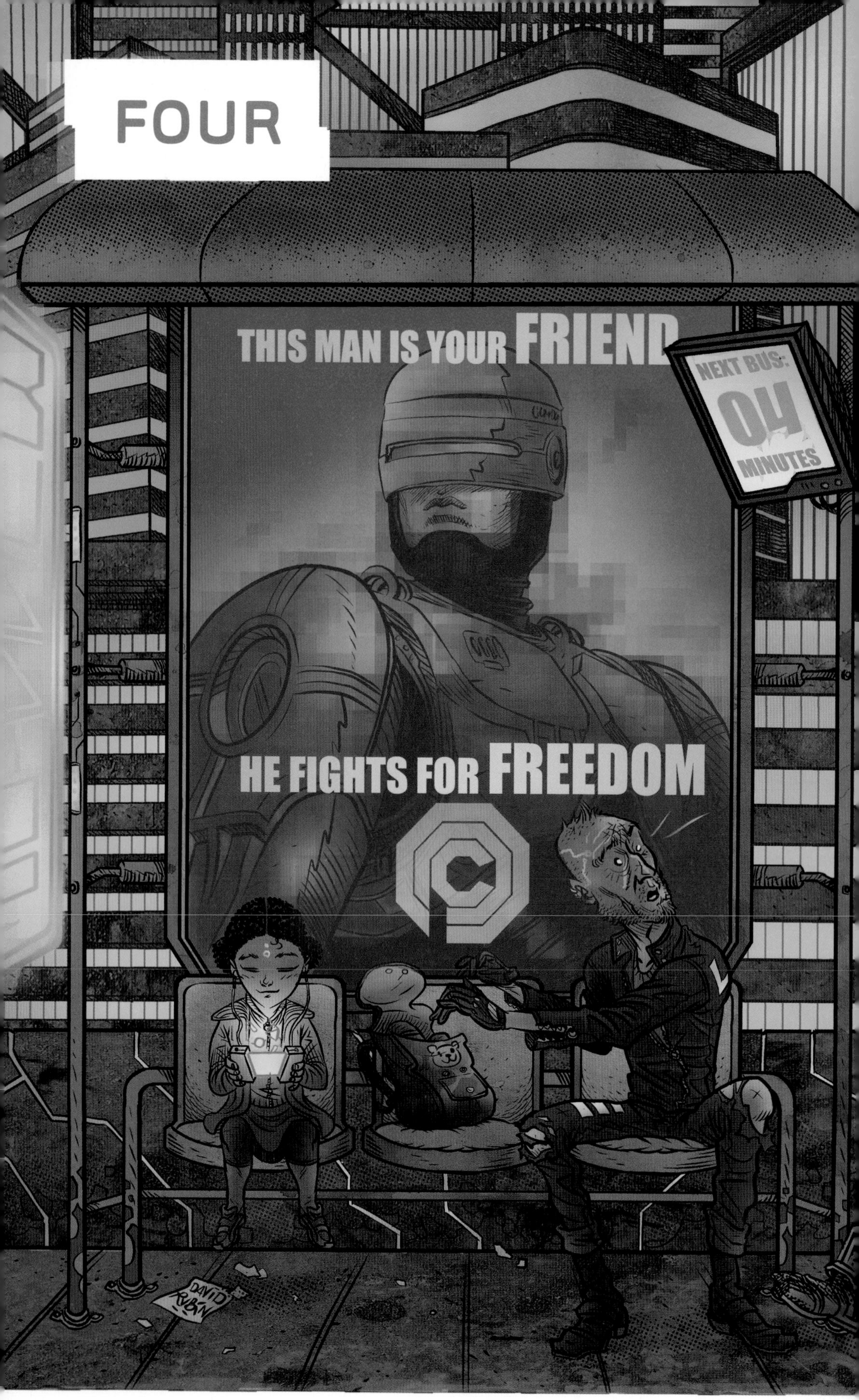
THIS MAN IS YOUR FRIEND
HE FIGHTS FOR FREEDOM
NEXT BUS:
04
MINUTES
DAVID RUBÍN

ISSUE 04 COVER DAVID RUBÍN

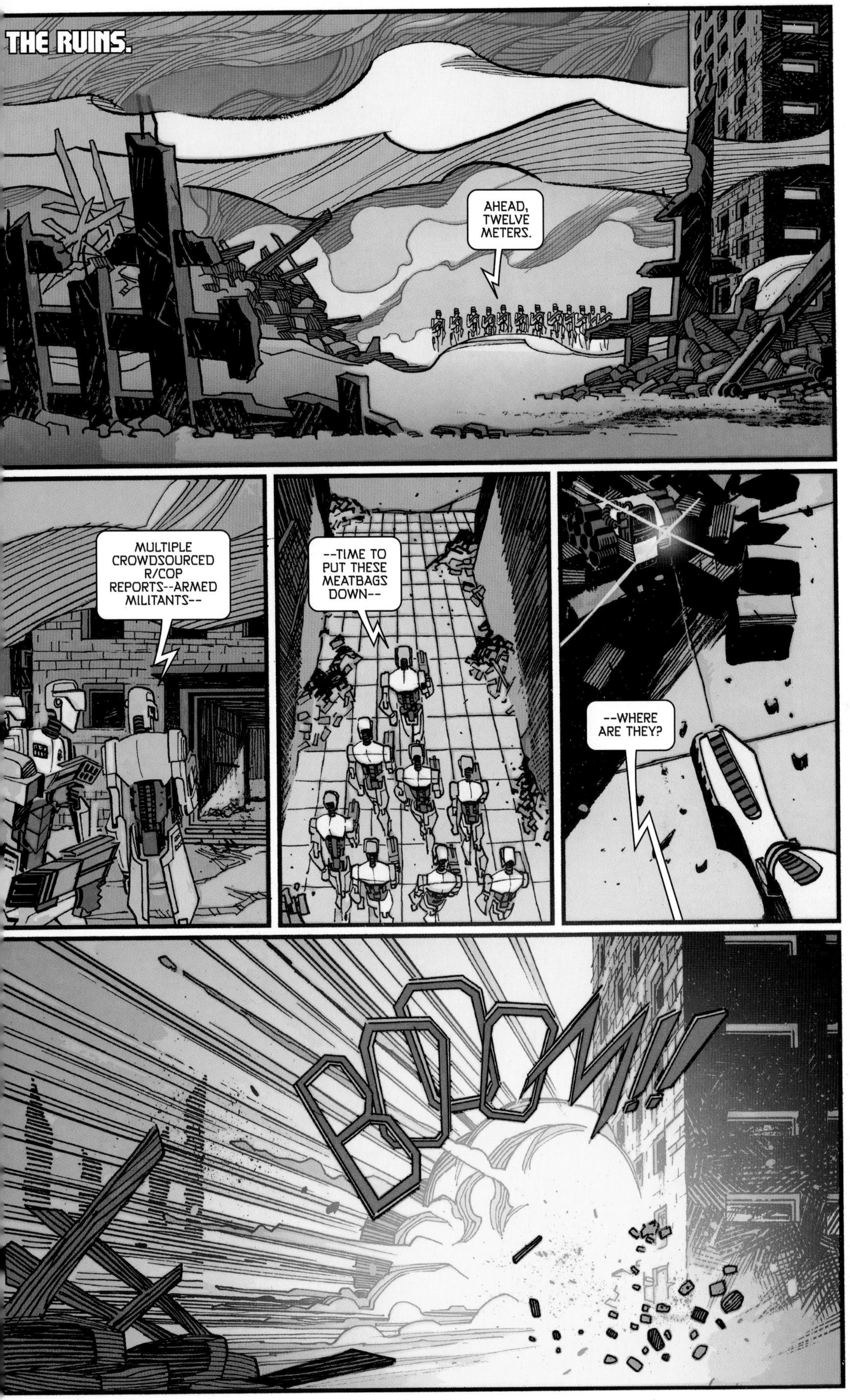
THE RUINS.
AHEAD, TWELVE METERS.
MULTIPLE CROWDSOURCED R/COP REPORTS--ARMED MILITANTS--
--TIME TO PUT THESE MEATBAGS DOWN--
--WHERE ARE THEY?
BOOOM!!

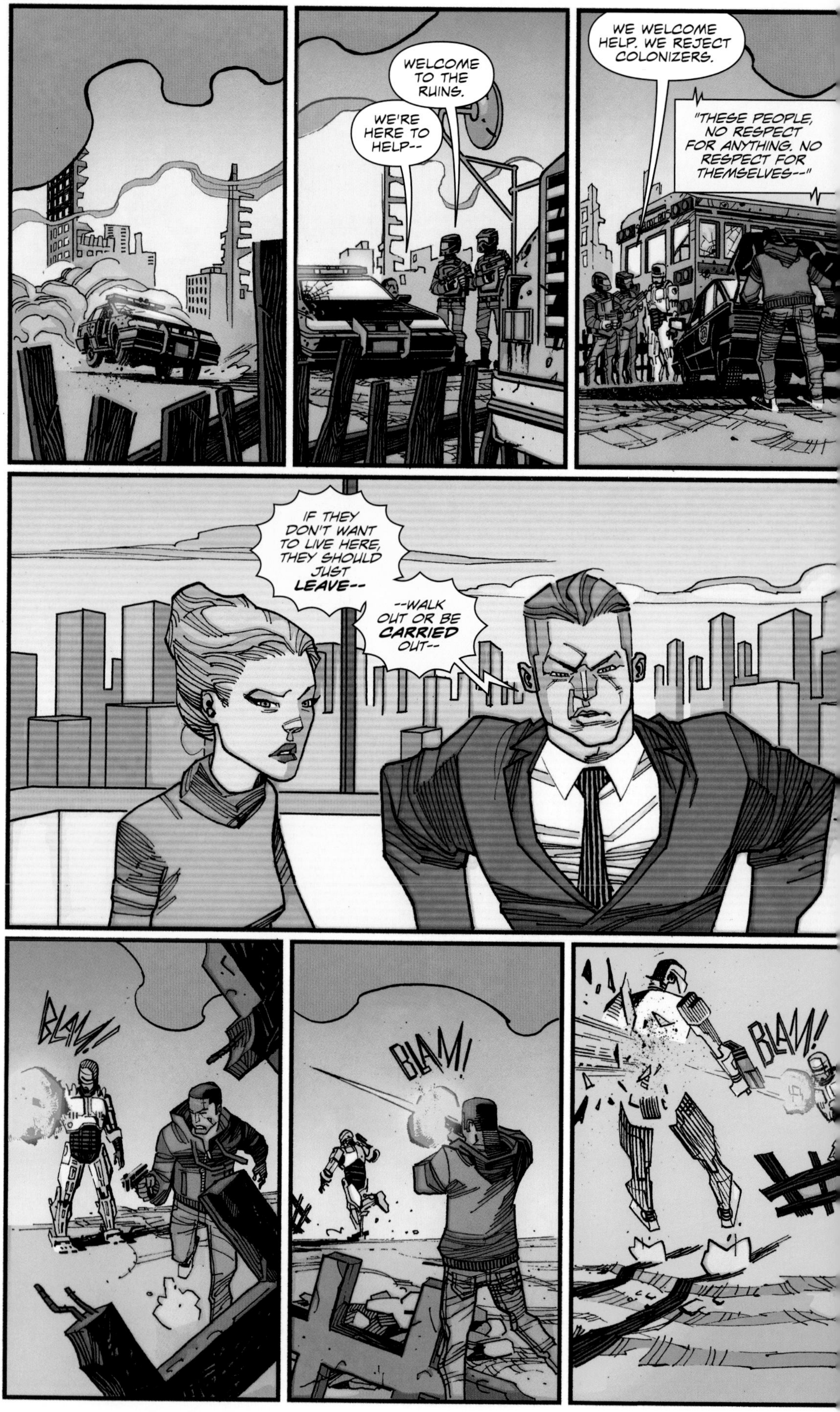

WELCOME TO THE RUINS.
WE'RE HERE TO HELP--
WE WELCOME HELP. WE REJECT COLONIZERS.
"THESE PEOPLE, NO RESPECT FOR ANYTHING. NO RESPECT FOR THEMSELVES--"
IF THEY DON'T WANT TO LIVE HERE, THEY SHOULD JUST **LEAVE--**
--WALK OUT OR BE **CARRIED** OUT--
BLAM!
BLAM!
BLAM!

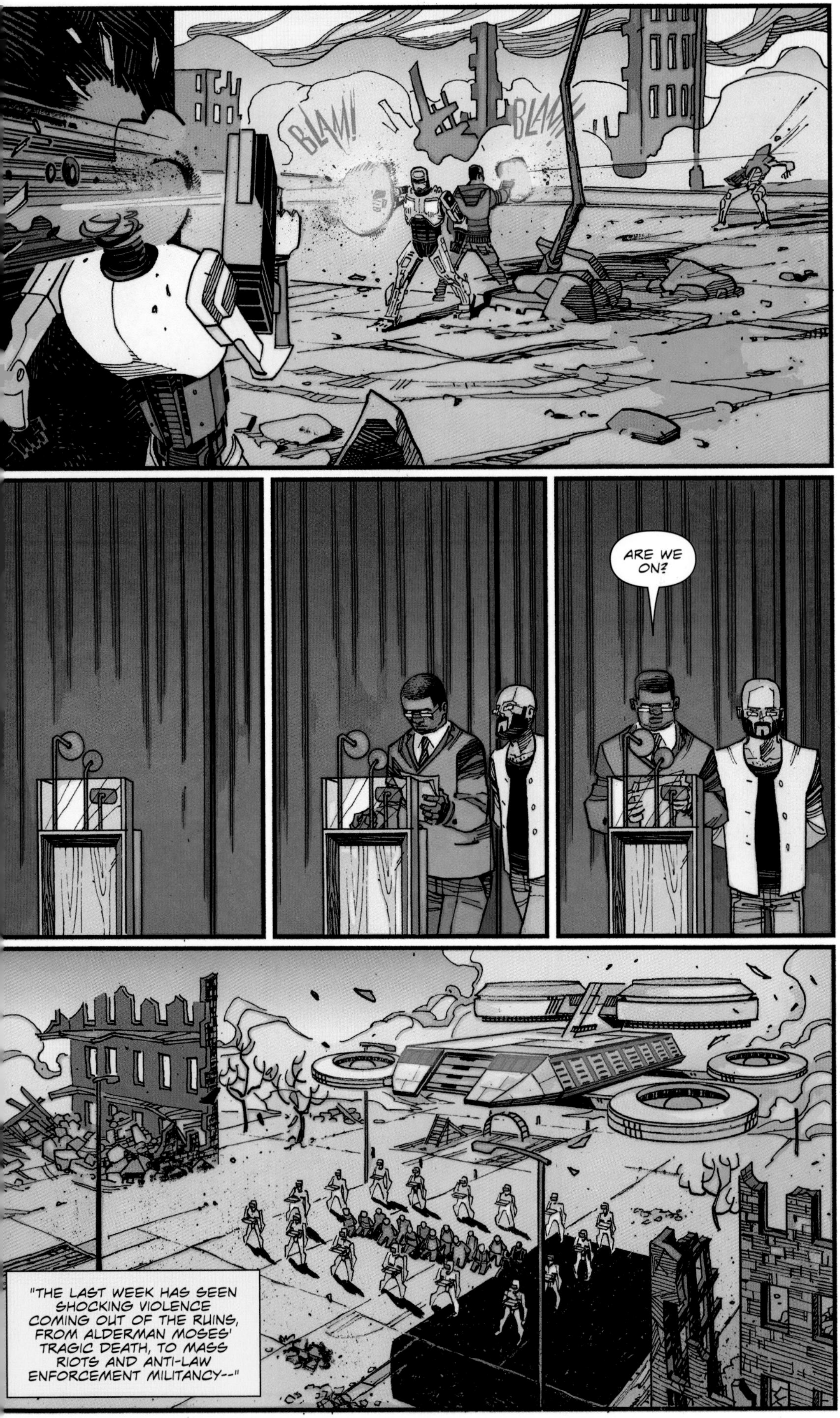
BLAM!
BLAM!
ARE WE ON?
"THE LAST WEEK HAS SEEN SHOCKING VIOLENCE COMING OUT OF THE RUINS, FROM ALDERMAN MOSES' TRAGIC DEATH, TO MASS RIOTS AND ANTI-LAW ENFORCEMENT MILITANCY--"

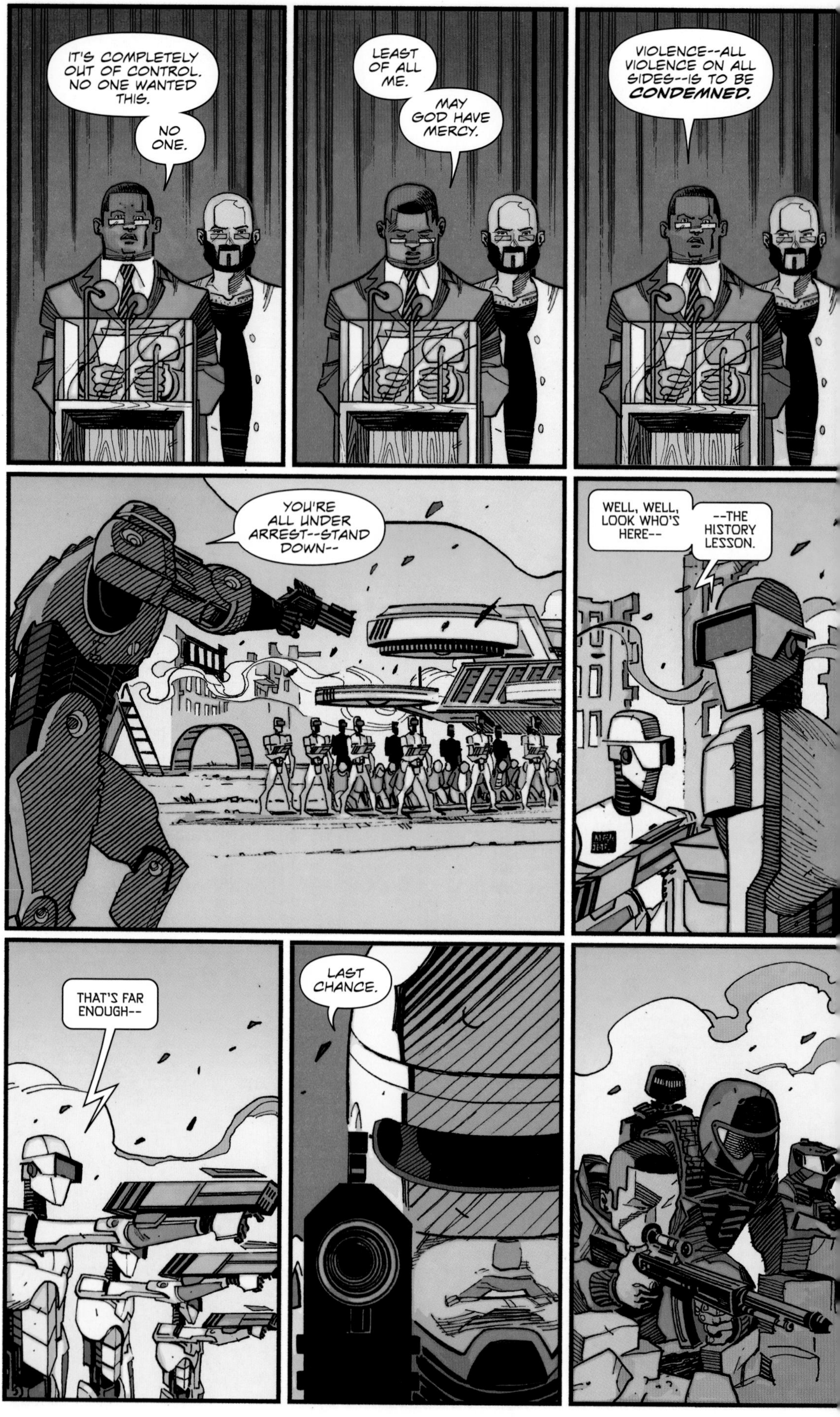
IT'S COMPLETELY OUT OF CONTROL. NO ONE WANTED THIS.
NO ONE.
LEAST OF ALL ME.
MAY GOD HAVE MERCY.
VIOLENCE--ALL VIOLENCE ON ALL SIDES--IS TO BE CONDEMNED.
YOU'RE ALL UNDER ARREST--STAND DOWN--
WELL, WELL, LOOK WHO'S HERE--
--THE HISTORY LESSON.
THAT'S FAR ENOUGH--
LAST CHANCE.

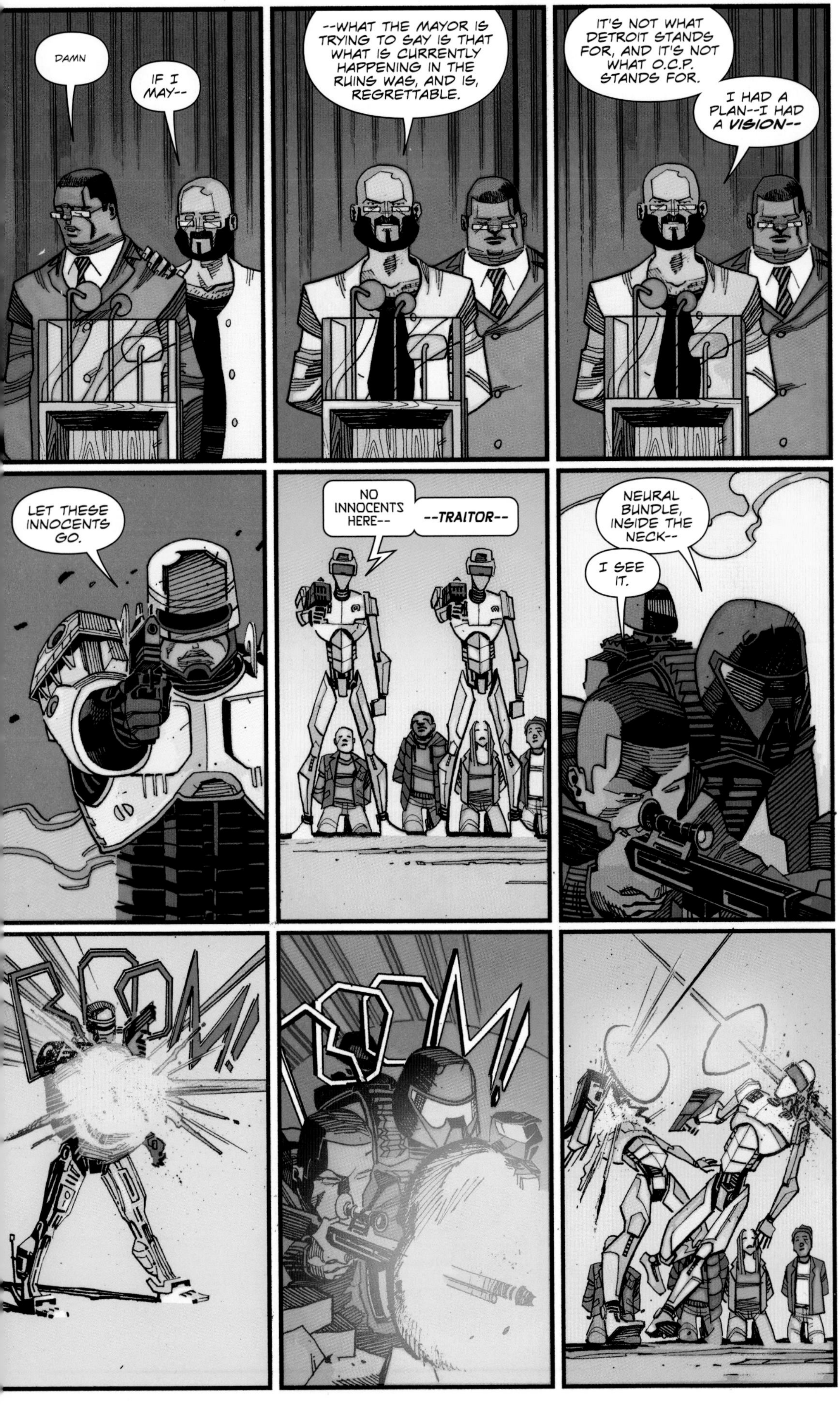
DAMN
IF I MAY--
--WHAT THE MAYOR IS TRYING TO SAY IS THAT WHAT IS CURRENTLY HAPPENING IN THE RUINS WAS, AND IS, REGRETTABLE.
IT'S NOT WHAT DETROIT STANDS FOR, AND IT'S NOT WHAT O.C.P. STANDS FOR.
I HAD A PLAN--I HAD A *VISION*--
LET THESE INNOCENTS GO.
NO INNOCENTS HERE--
--TRAITOR--
NEURAL BUNDLE, INSIDE THE NECK--
I SEE IT.
BOOM!
BOOM!

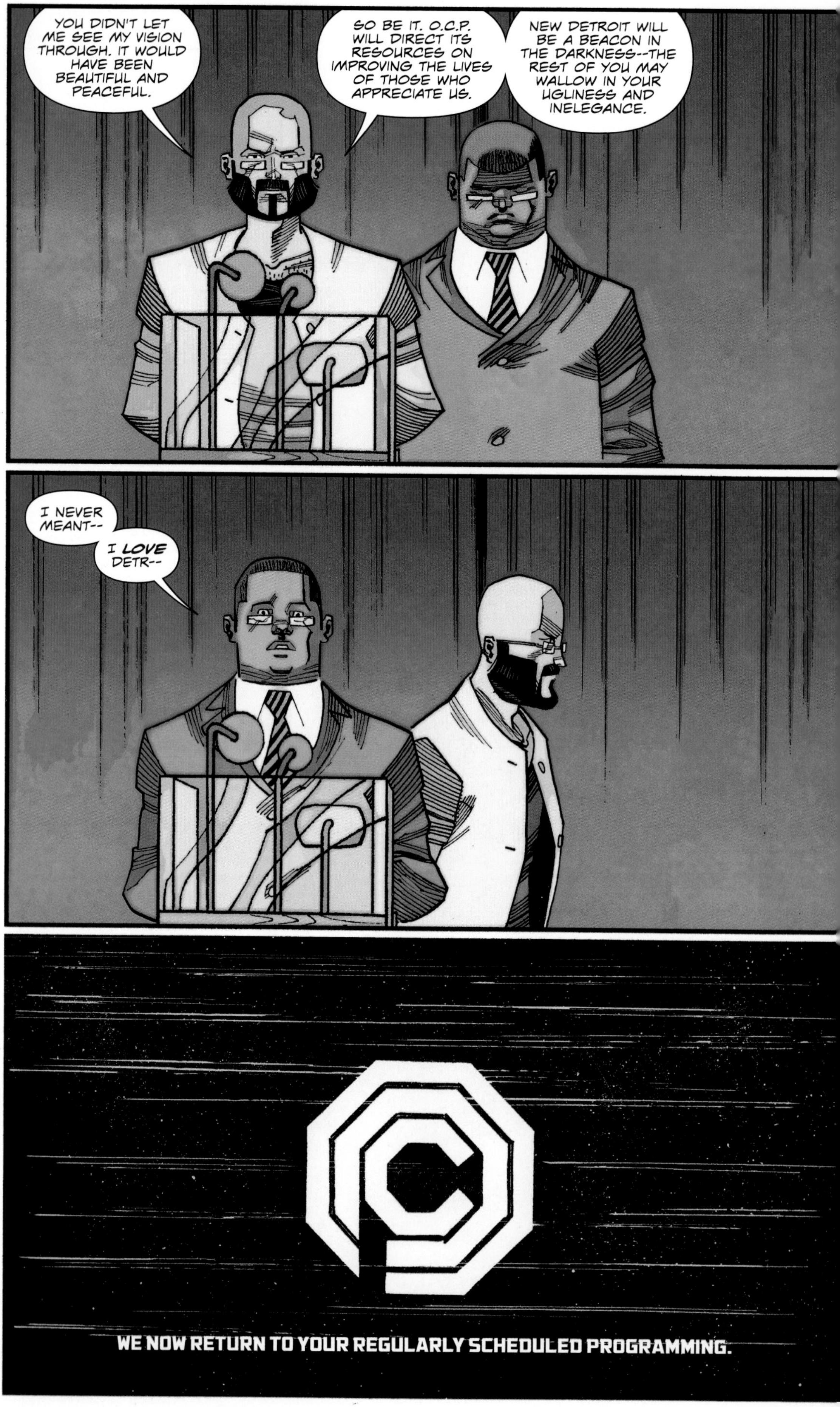
YOU DIDN'T LET ME SEE MY VISION THROUGH. IT WOULD HAVE BEEN BEAUTIFUL AND PEACEFUL.
SO BE IT. O.C.P. WILL DIRECT ITS RESOURCES ON IMPROVING THE LIVES OF THOSE WHO APPRECIATE US.
NEW DETROIT WILL BE A BEACON IN THE DARKNESS--THE REST OF YOU MAY WALLOW IN YOUR UGLINESS AND INELEGANCE.
I NEVER MEANT--
I LOVE DETR--
WE NOW RETURN TO YOUR REGULARLY SCHEDULED PROGRAMMING.

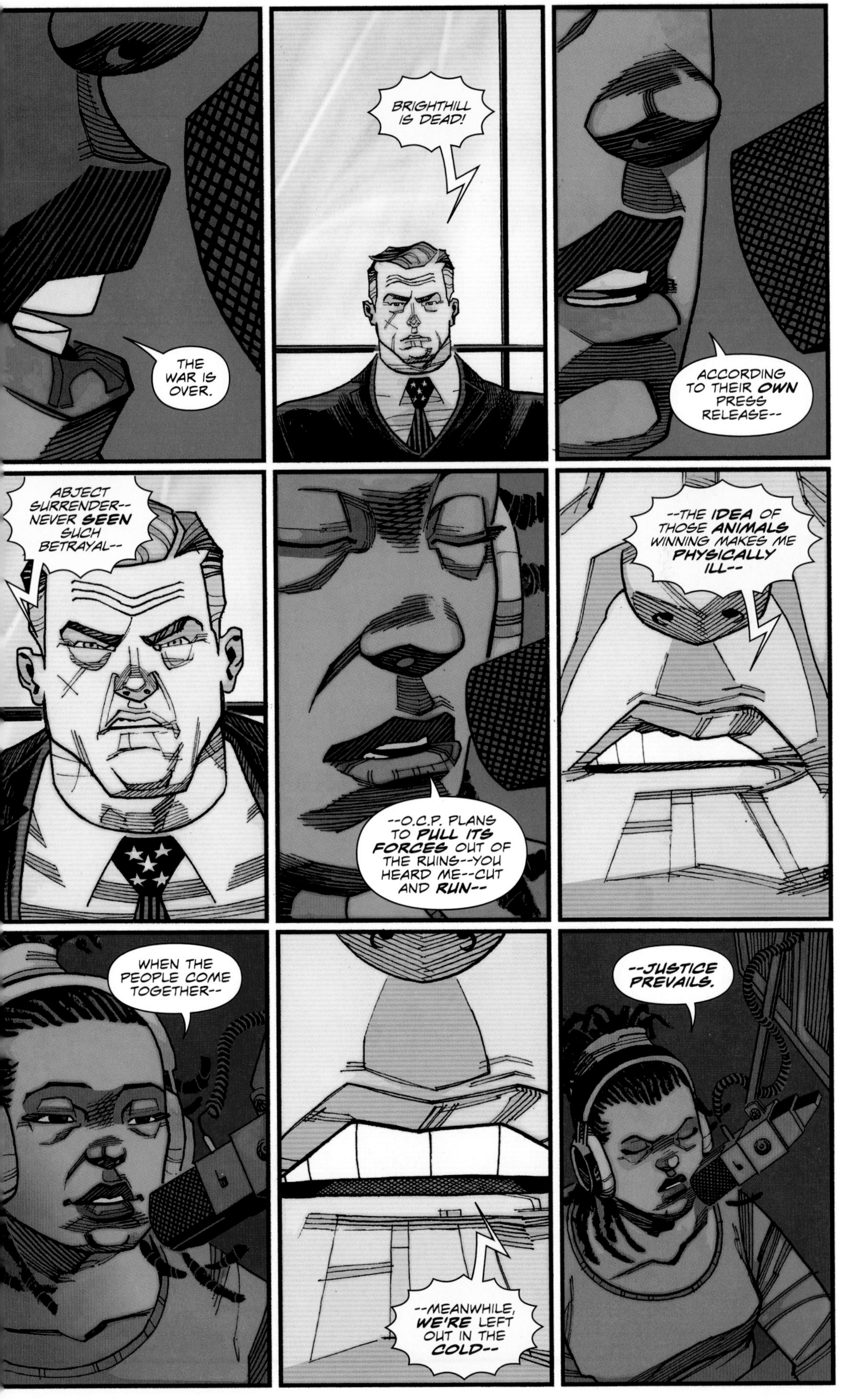
THE WAR IS OVER.
BRIGHTHILL IS DEAD!
ACCORDING TO THEIR OWN PRESS RELEASE--
ABJECT SURRENDER--NEVER SEEN SUCH BETRAYAL--
--O.C.P. PLANS TO PULL ITS FORCES OUT OF THE RUINS--YOU HEARD ME--CUT AND RUN--
--THE IDEA OF THOSE ANIMALS WINNING MAKES ME PHYSICALLY ILL--
WHEN THE PEOPLE COME TOGETHER--
--MEANWHILE, WE'RE LEFT OUT IN THE COLD--
--JUSTICE PREVAILS.

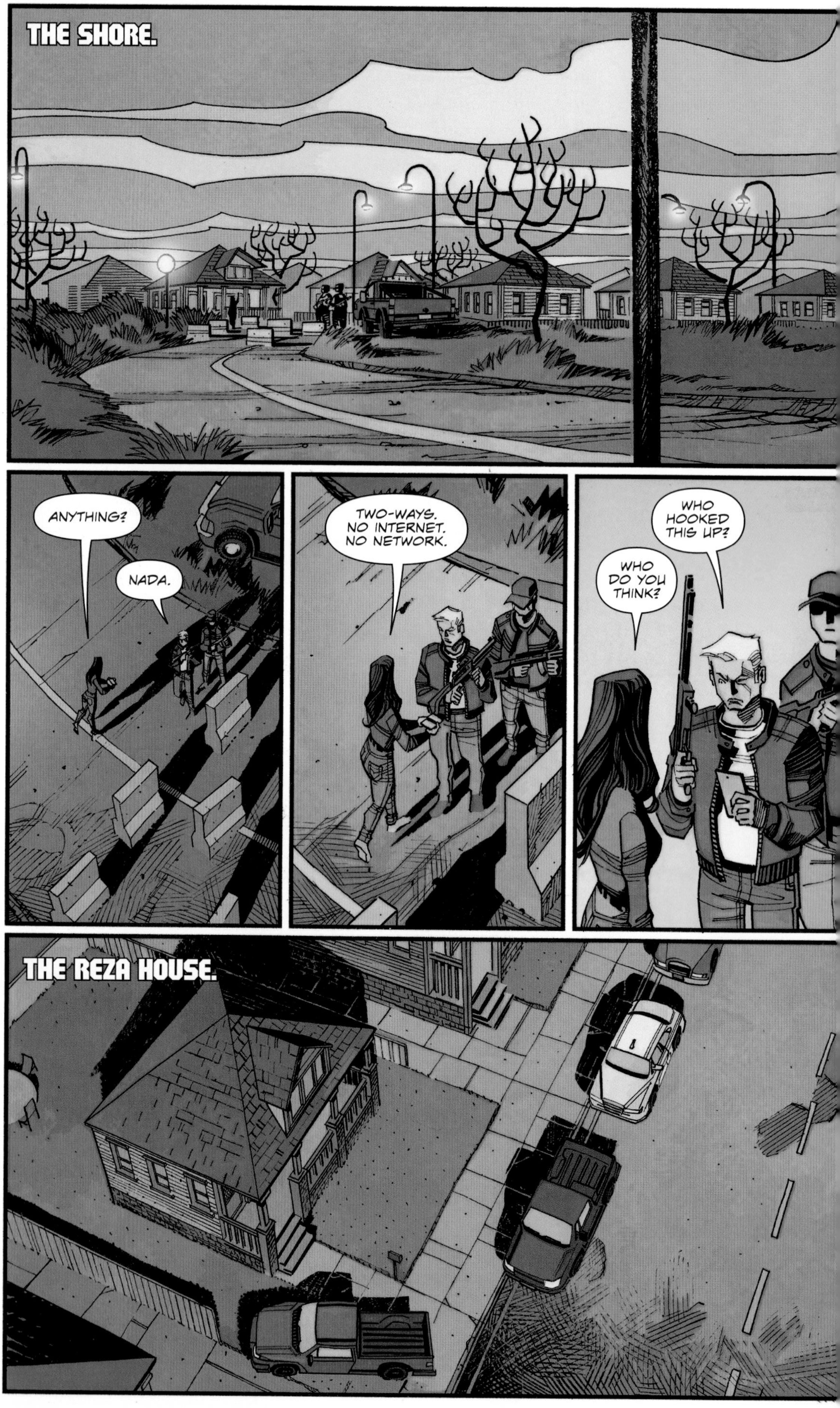
THE SHORE.
ANYTHING?
NADA.
TWO-WAYS. NO INTERNET. NO NETWORK.
WHO HOOKED THIS UP?
WHO DO YOU THINK?
THE REZA HOUSE.

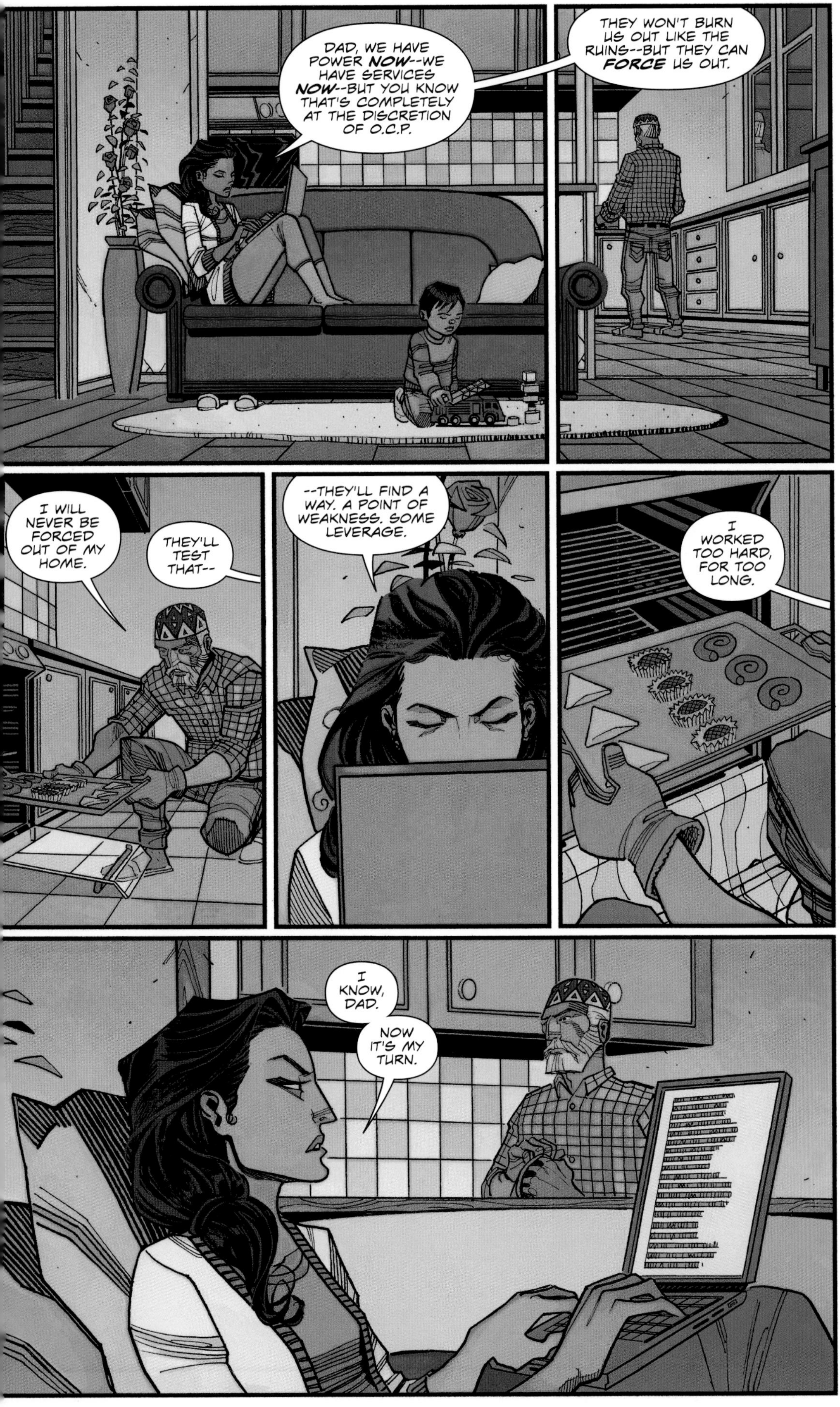
DAD, WE HAVE POWER NOW--WE HAVE SERVICES NOW--BUT YOU KNOW THAT'S COMPLETELY AT THE DISCRETION OF O.C.P.
THEY WON'T BURN US OUT LIKE THE RUINS--BUT THEY CAN FORCE US OUT.
I WILL NEVER BE FORCED OUT OF MY HOME.
THEY'LL TEST THAT--
--THEY'LL FIND A WAY. A POINT OF WEAKNESS. SOME LEVERAGE.
I WORKED TOO HARD, FOR TOO LONG.
I KNOW, DAD.
NOW IT'S MY TURN.

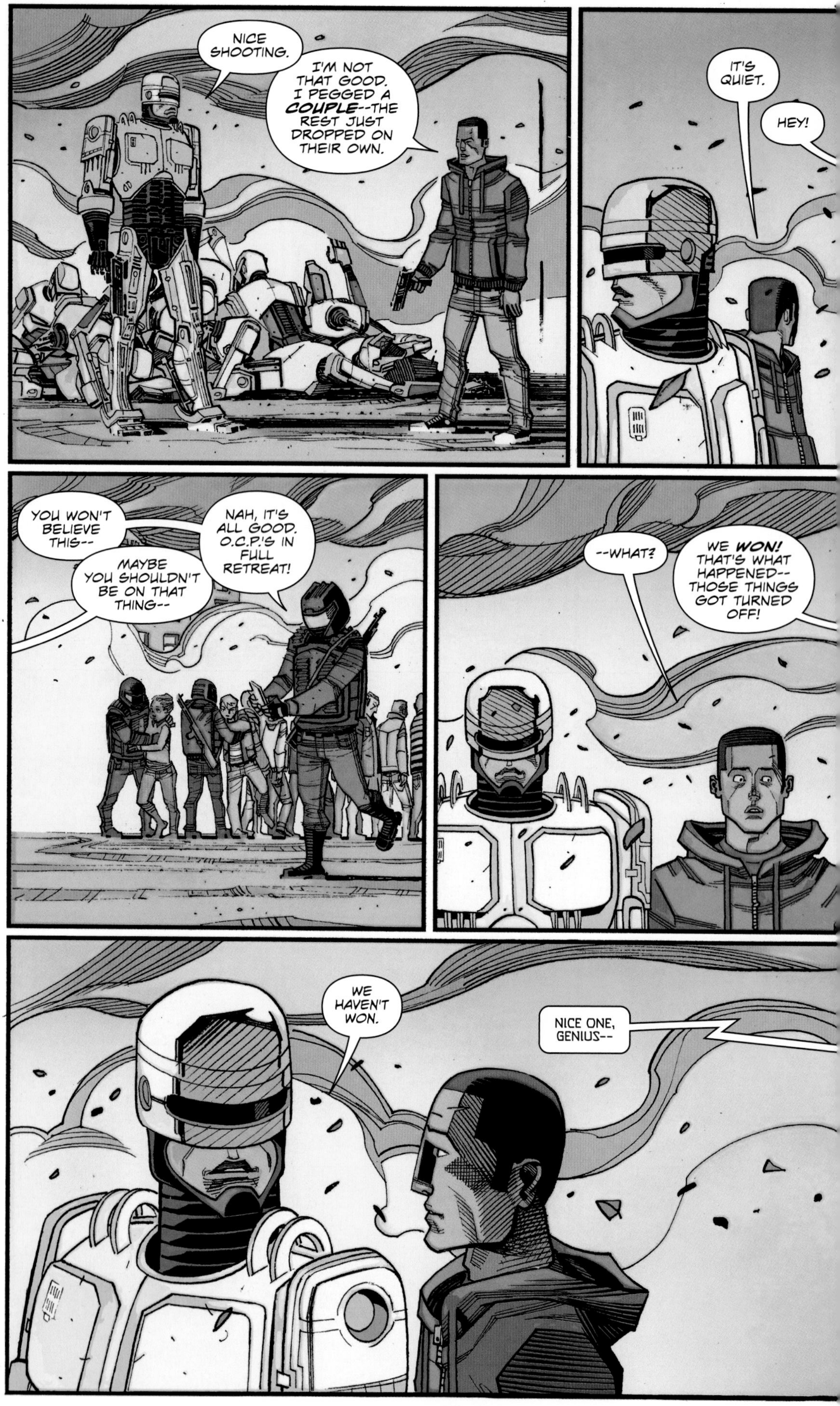
NICE SHOOTING.
I'M NOT THAT GOOD. I PEGGED A ***COUPLE***--THE REST JUST DROPPED ON THEIR OWN.
IT'S QUIET.
HEY!
YOU WON'T BELIEVE THIS--
MAYBE YOU SHOULDN'T BE ON THAT THING--
NAH, IT'S ALL GOOD. O.C.P.'S IN FULL RETREAT!
--WHAT?
WE ***WON!*** THAT'S WHAT HAPPENED--THOSE THINGS GOT TURNED OFF!
WE HAVEN'T WON.
NICE ONE, GENIUS--

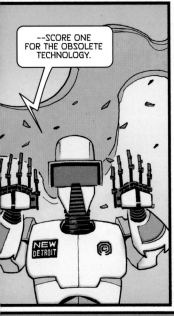

--SCORE ONE FOR THE OBSOLETE TECHNOLOGY.

WOAH, WOAH--

THIS IS JUST A COURTESY CALL.

I'VE BEEN WANTING TO TALK TO YOU FOR A LONG TIME.

YOU'RE THE OLD MAN, THE HEAD OF O.C.P.--

YOU'RE ON FIRE TODAY, MURPHY. LISTEN, LET'S WORK THIS OUT. WHAT YOU'RE HEARING IS TRUE--I ORDERED A FULL RETREAT FROM THE RUINS.

I NEED YOU TO MAKE THIS CEASEFIRE STICK.

EXPLAIN.

YOU'RE *ROBOCOP*, MAN!

THE ORIGINAL!

KEEP TALKING.

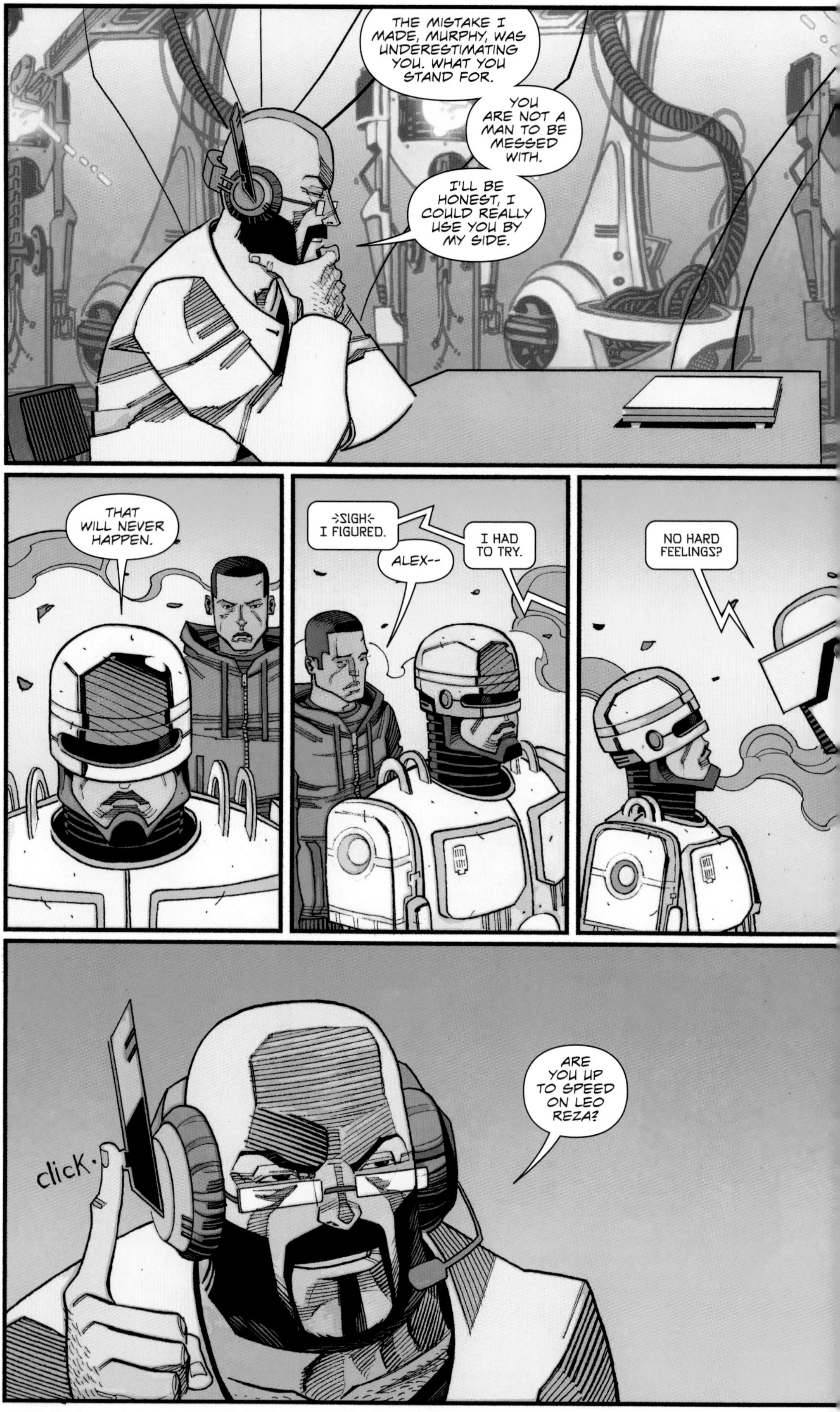
THE MISTAKE I MADE, MURPHY, WAS UNDERESTIMATING YOU. WHAT YOU STAND FOR.
YOU ARE NOT A MAN TO BE MESSED WITH.
I'LL BE HONEST, I COULD REALLY USE YOU BY MY SIDE.
THAT WILL NEVER HAPPEN.
-SIGH- I FIGURED.
ALEX--
I HAD TO TRY.
NO HARD FEELINGS?
click.
ARE YOU UP TO SPEED ON LEO REZA?

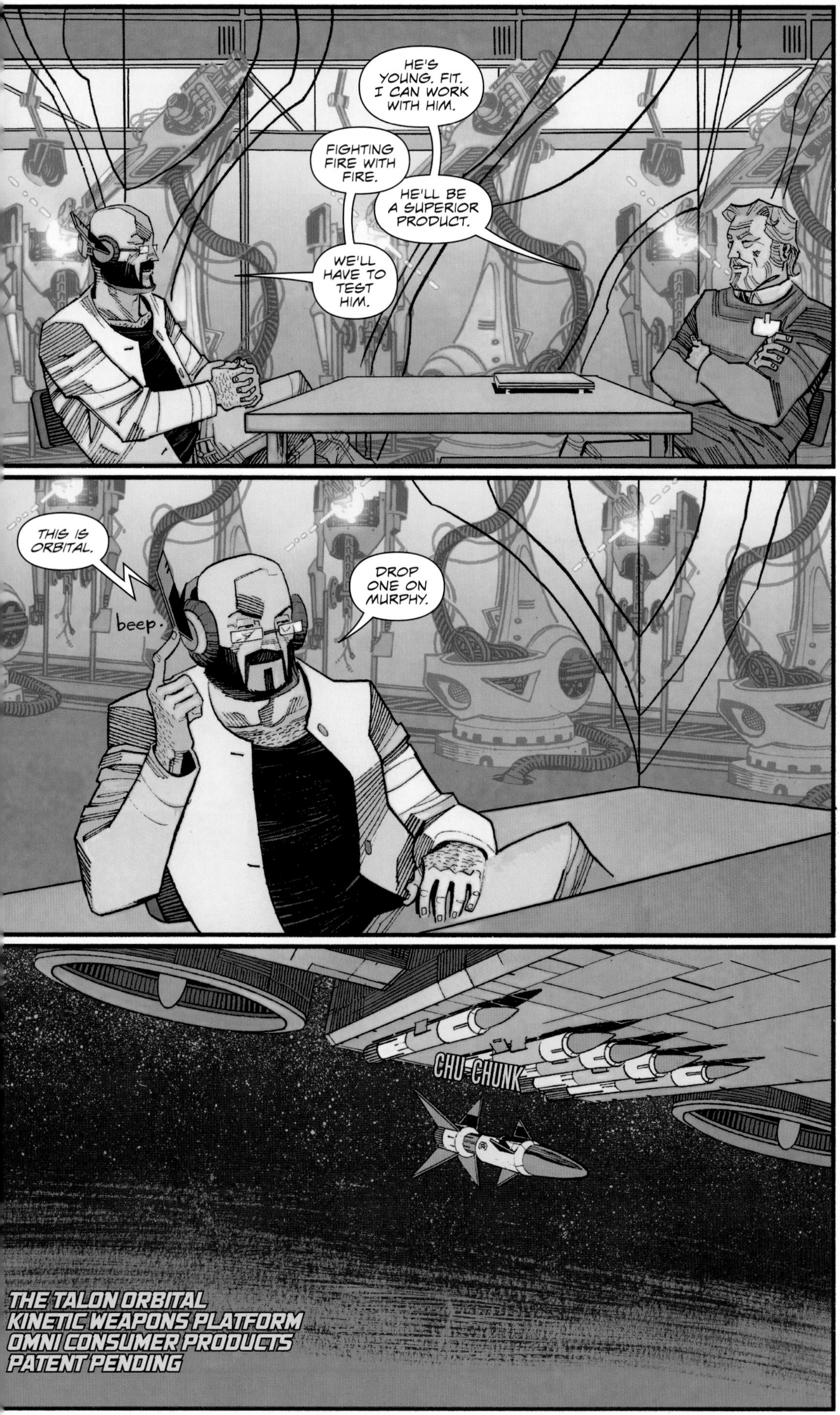
FIGHTING FIRE WITH FIRE.
HE'S YOUNG. FIT. I CAN WORK WITH HIM.
HE'LL BE A SUPERIOR PRODUCT.
WE'LL HAVE TO TEST HIM.
THIS IS ORBITAL.
beep.
DROP ONE ON MURPHY.
CHU-CHUNK
THE TALON ORBITAL
KINETIC WEAPONS PLATFORM
OMNI CONSUMER PRODUCTS
PATENT PENDING

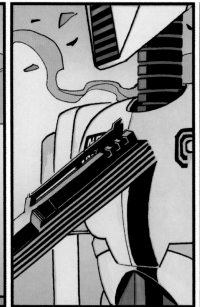

ALEX, THIS IS NO GOOD--

--WE SHOULD GET OUT OF HERE.

THERE'S NO TIME.

WHAT DOES *THAT* MEAN?

YOU AND YOUR WIFE GAVE ME MY LIFE BACK.

AND I MADE HER A PROMISE. ASK HER TO EXPLAIN THE FIFTH DIRECTIVE TO YOU.

YOU'RE FREAKING ME OUT--

IT'S NOT YOU THEY WANT.

GOODBYE, LEO.

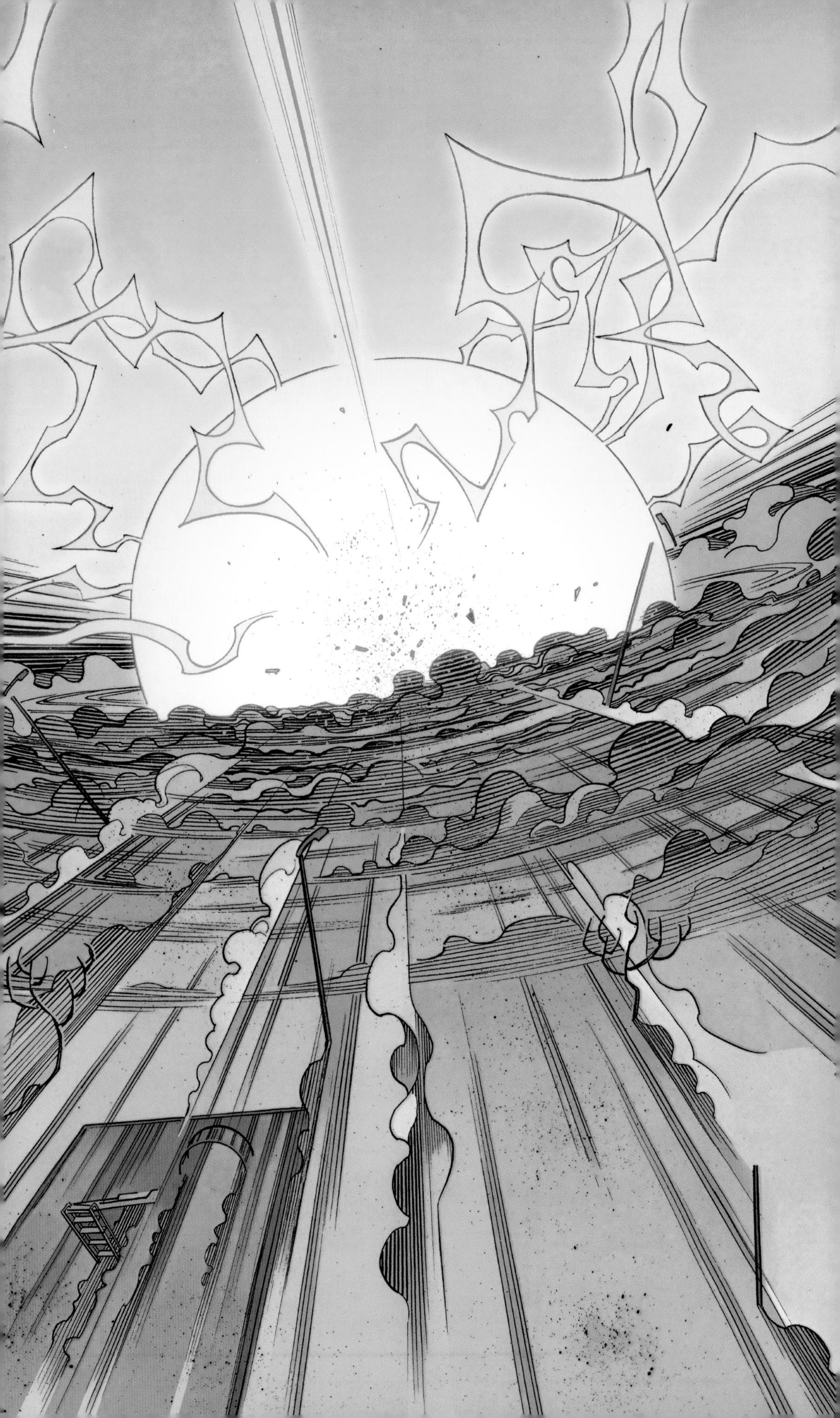

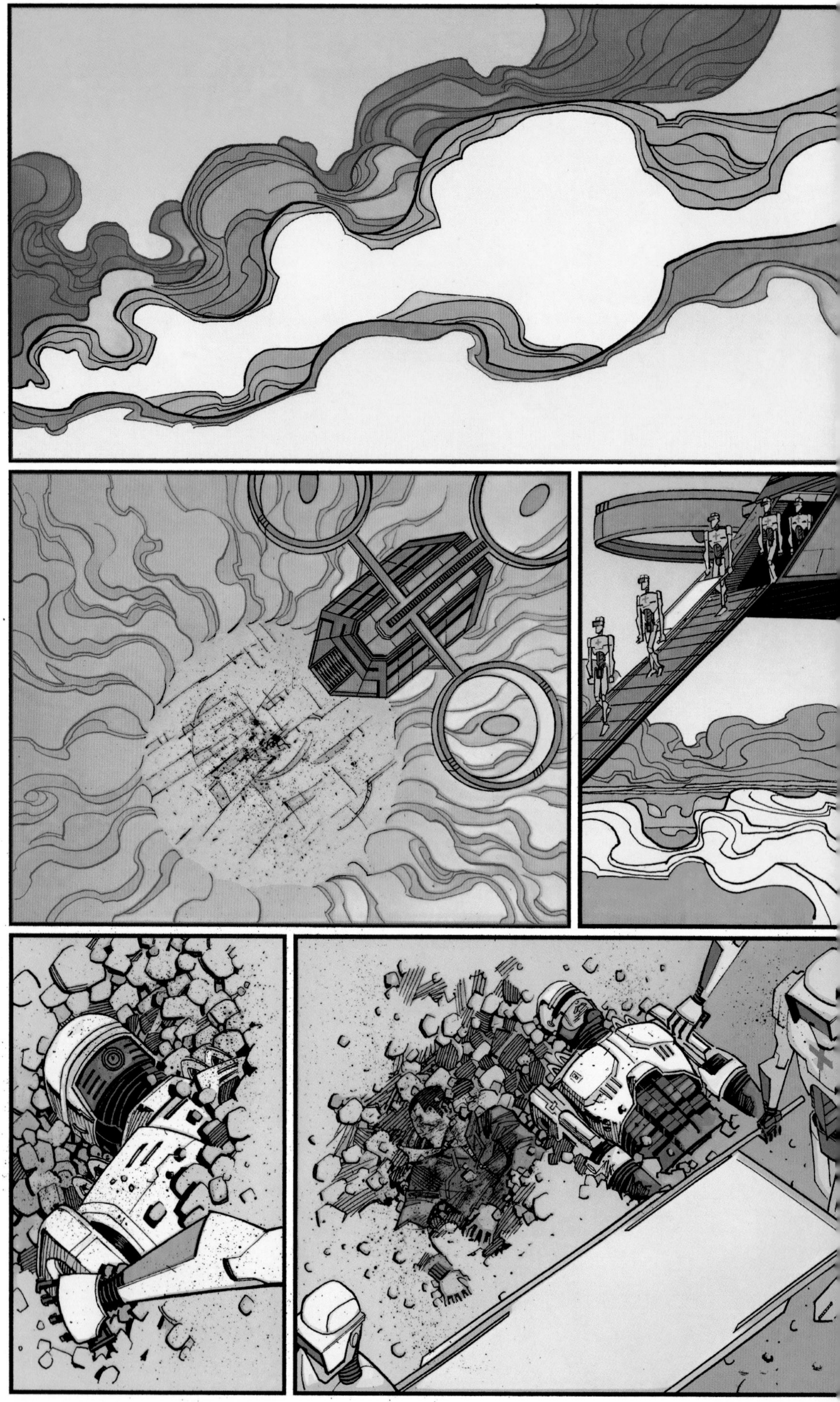

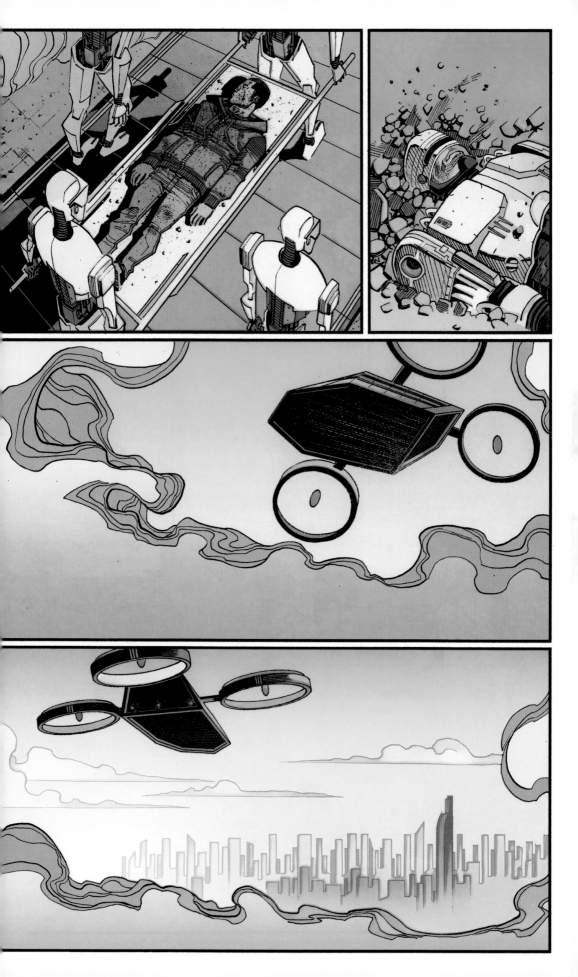

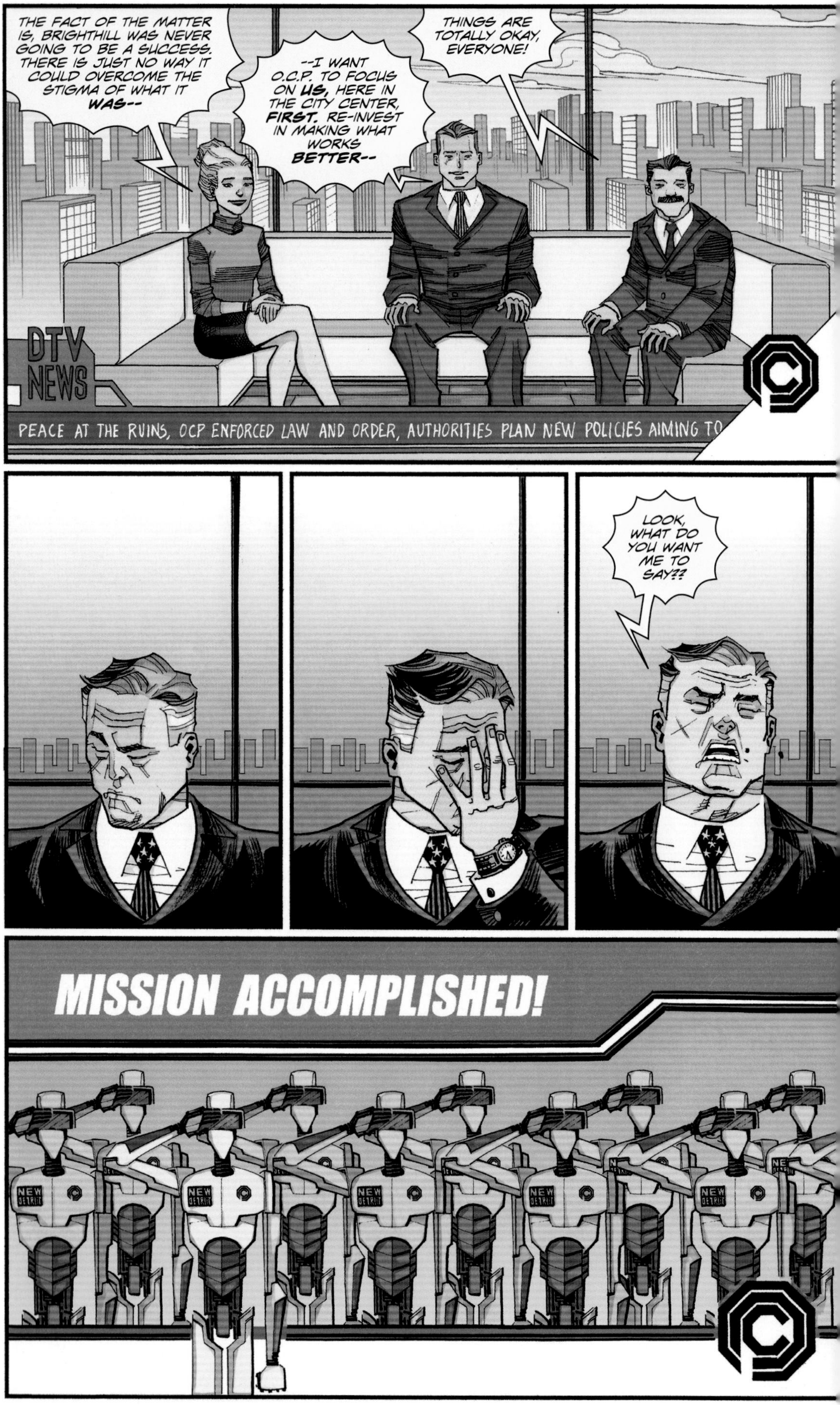
THE FACT OF THE MATTER IS, BRIGHTHILL WAS NEVER GOING TO BE A SUCCESS. THERE IS JUST NO WAY IT COULD OVERCOME THE STIGMA OF WHAT IT WAS--
--I WANT O.C.P. TO FOCUS ON US, HERE IN THE CITY CENTER, FIRST. RE-INVEST IN MAKING WHAT WORKS BETTER--
THINGS ARE TOTALLY OKAY, EVERYONE!
DTV NEWS
PEACE AT THE RUINS, OCP ENFORCED LAW AND ORDER, AUTHORITIES PLAN NEW POLICIES AIMING TO
LOOK, WHAT DO YOU WANT ME TO SAY??
MISSION ACCOMPLISHED!

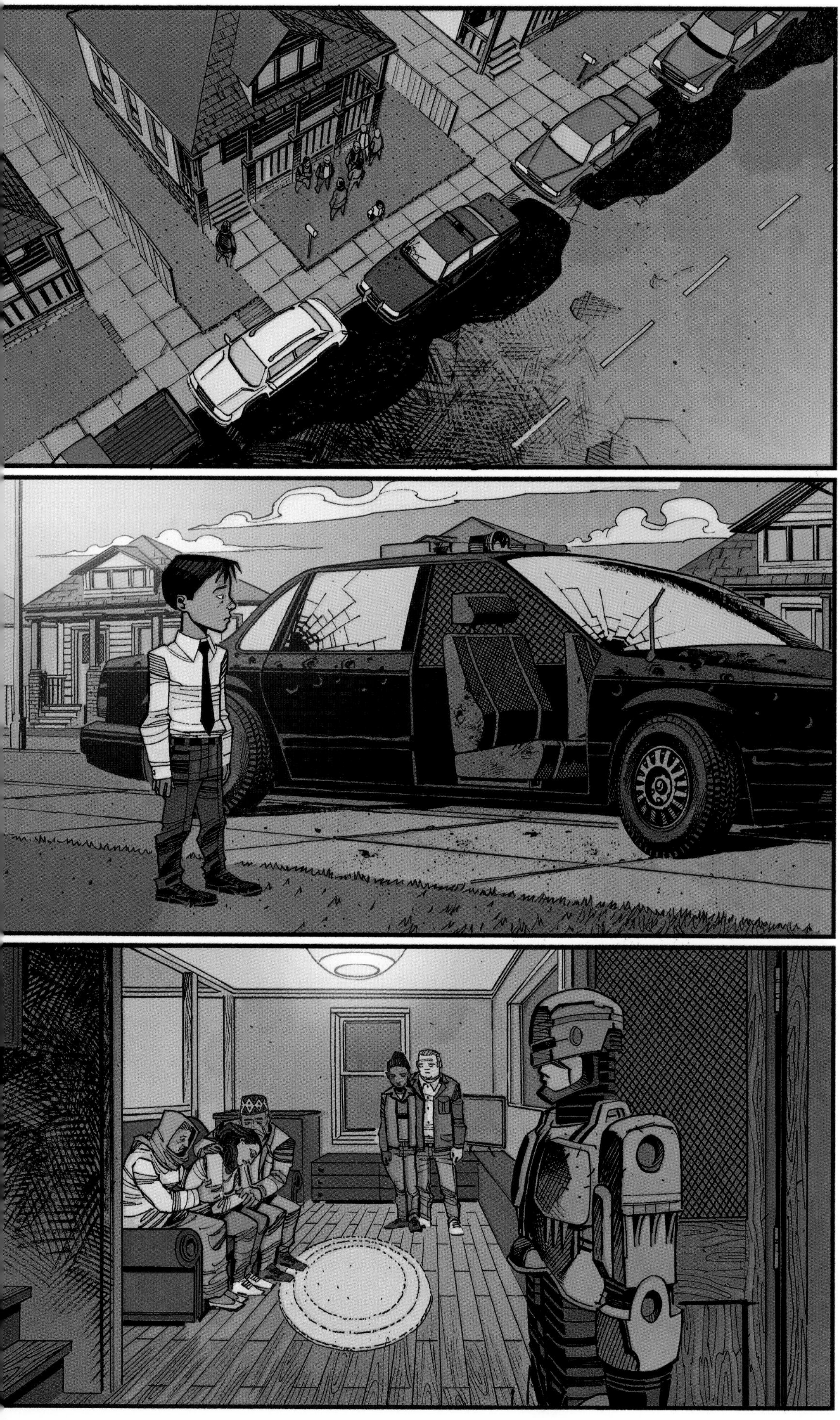

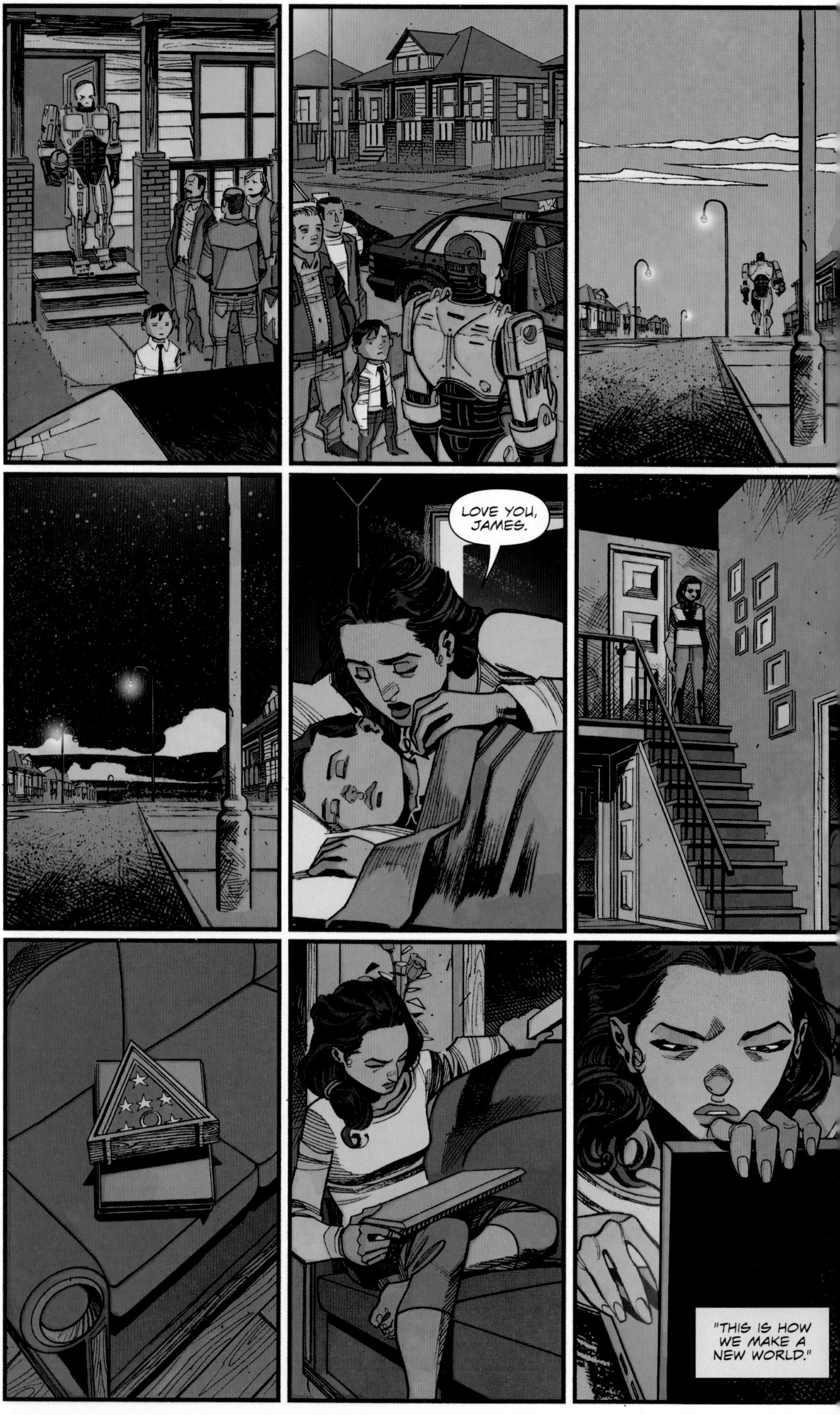
LOVE YOU, JAMES.
"THIS IS HOW WE MAKE A NEW WORLD."

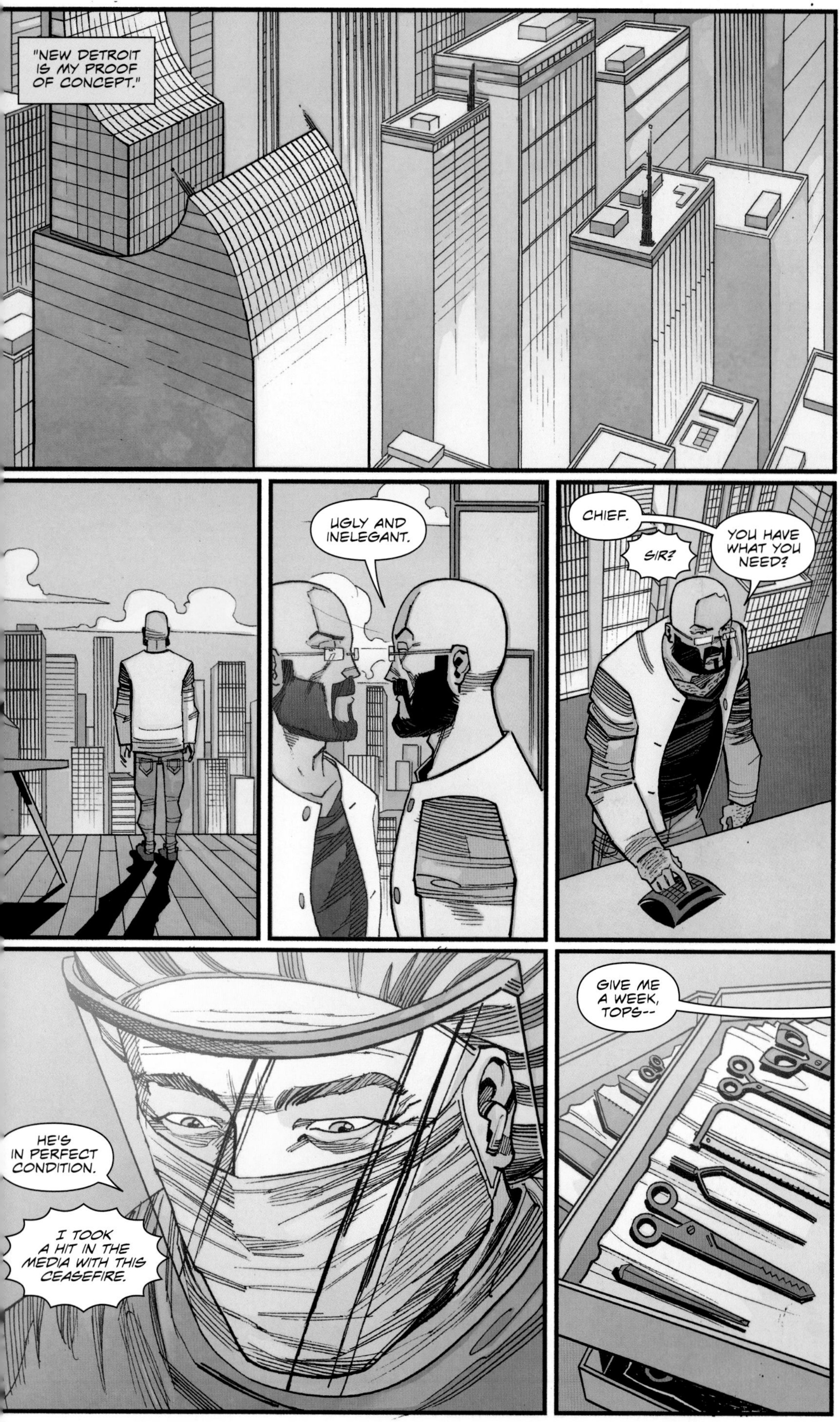
"NEW DETROIT IS MY PROOF OF CONCEPT."
UGLY AND INELEGANT.
CHIEF.
SIR?
YOU HAVE WHAT YOU NEED?
HE'S IN PERFECT CONDITION.
I TOOK A HIT IN THE MEDIA WITH THIS CEASEFIRE.
GIVE ME A WEEK, TOPS--

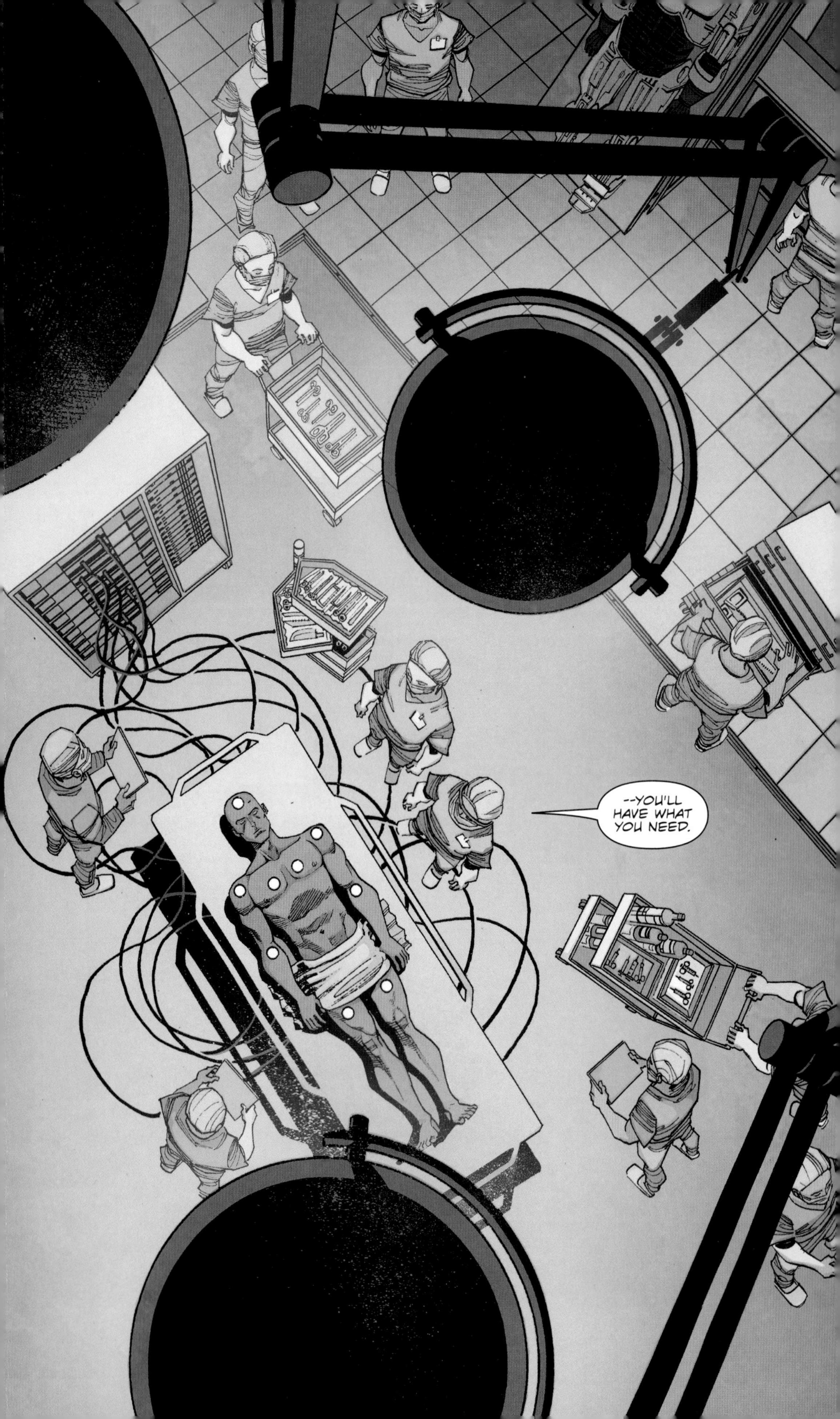
--YOU'LL HAVE WHAT YOU NEED.

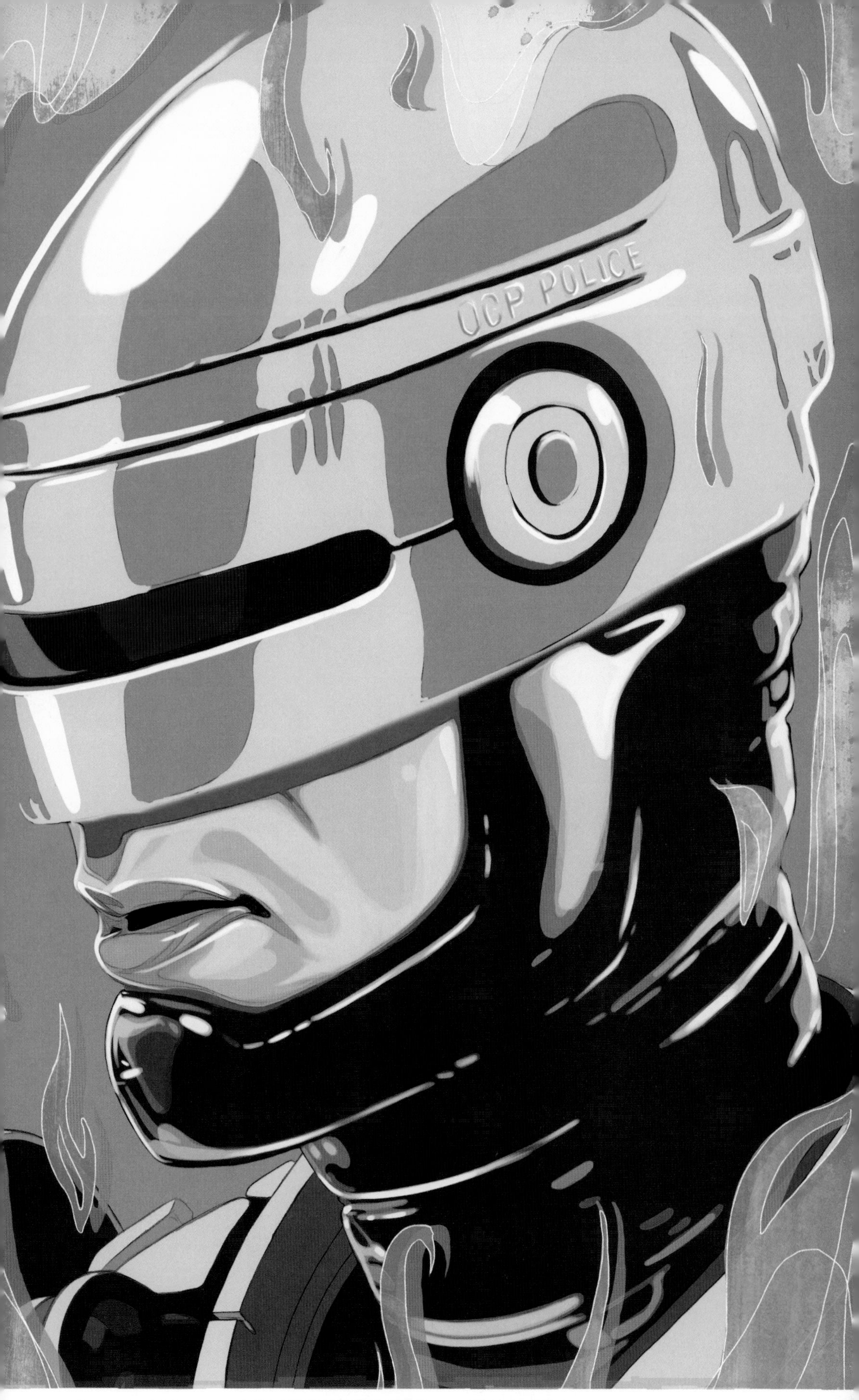
OCP POLICE
ISSUE 04 COVER NIMIT MALAVIA

FIVE

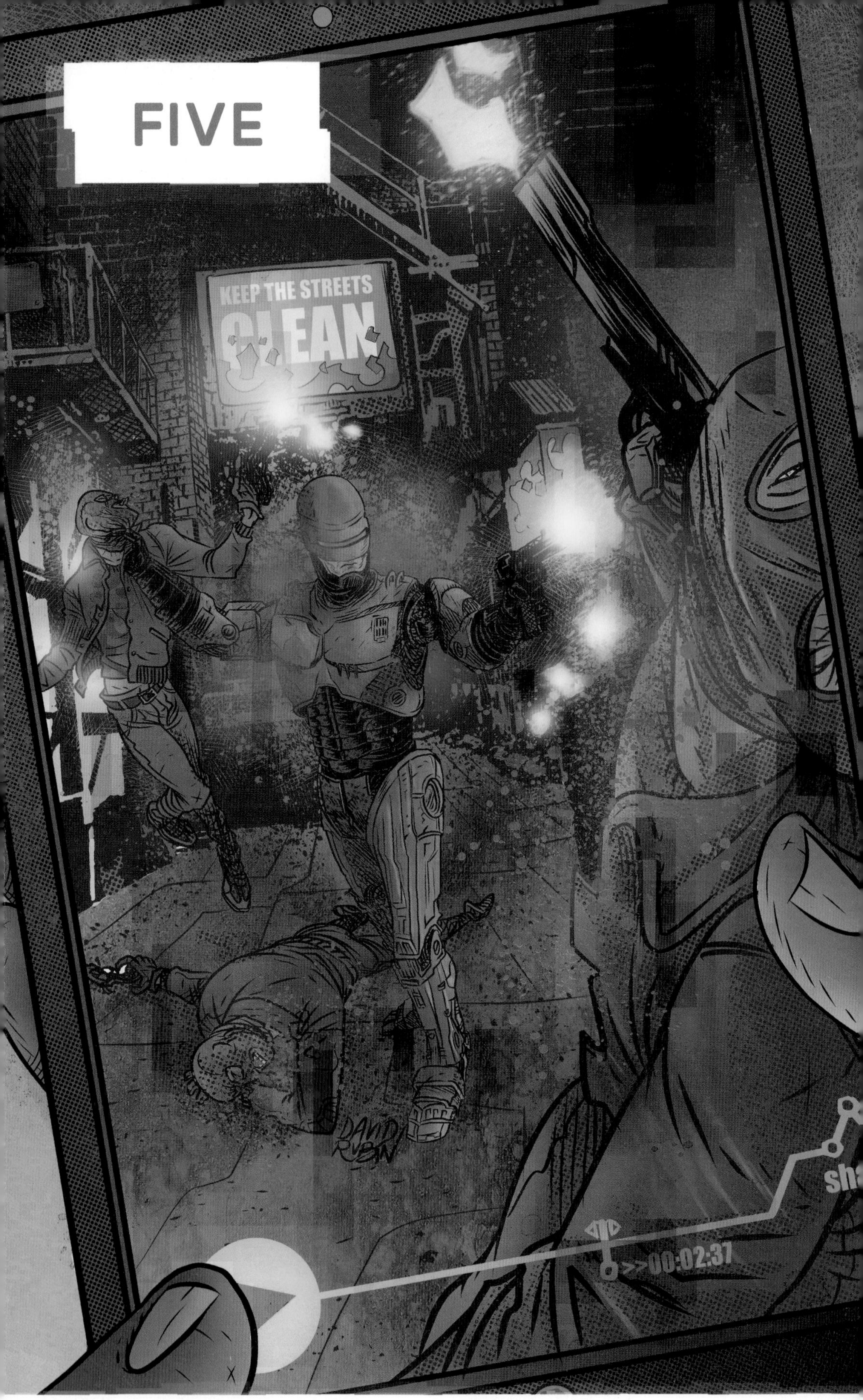
KEEP THE STREETS CLEAN
DAVID RUBIN
>>00:02:37

ISSUE 05 COVER **DAVID RUBÍN**

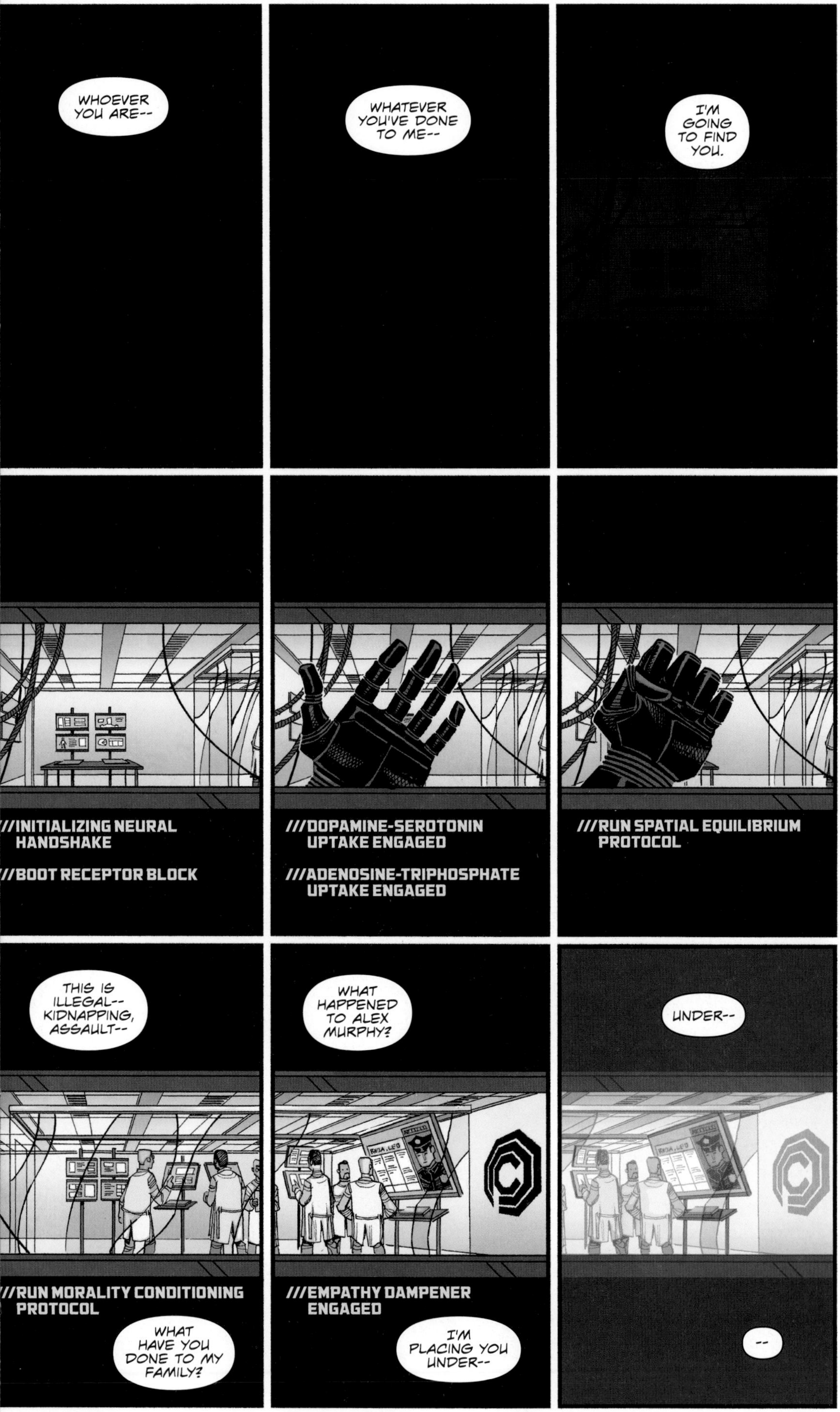
WHOEVER YOU ARE--
WHATEVER YOU'VE DONE TO ME--
I'M GOING TO FIND YOU.
///INITIALIZING NEURAL HANDSHAKE
///BOOT RECEPTOR BLOCK
///DOPAMINE-SEROTONIN UPTAKE ENGAGED
///ADENOSINE-TRIPHOSPHATE UPTAKE ENGAGED
///RUN SPATIAL EQUILIBRIUM PROTOCOL
THIS IS ILLEGAL-- KIDNAPPING, ASSAULT--
///RUN MORALITY CONDITIONING PROTOCOL
WHAT HAVE YOU DONE TO MY FAMILY?
WHAT HAPPENED TO ALEX MURPHY?
///EMPATHY DAMPENER ENGAGED
I'M PLACING YOU UNDER--
UNDER--
--

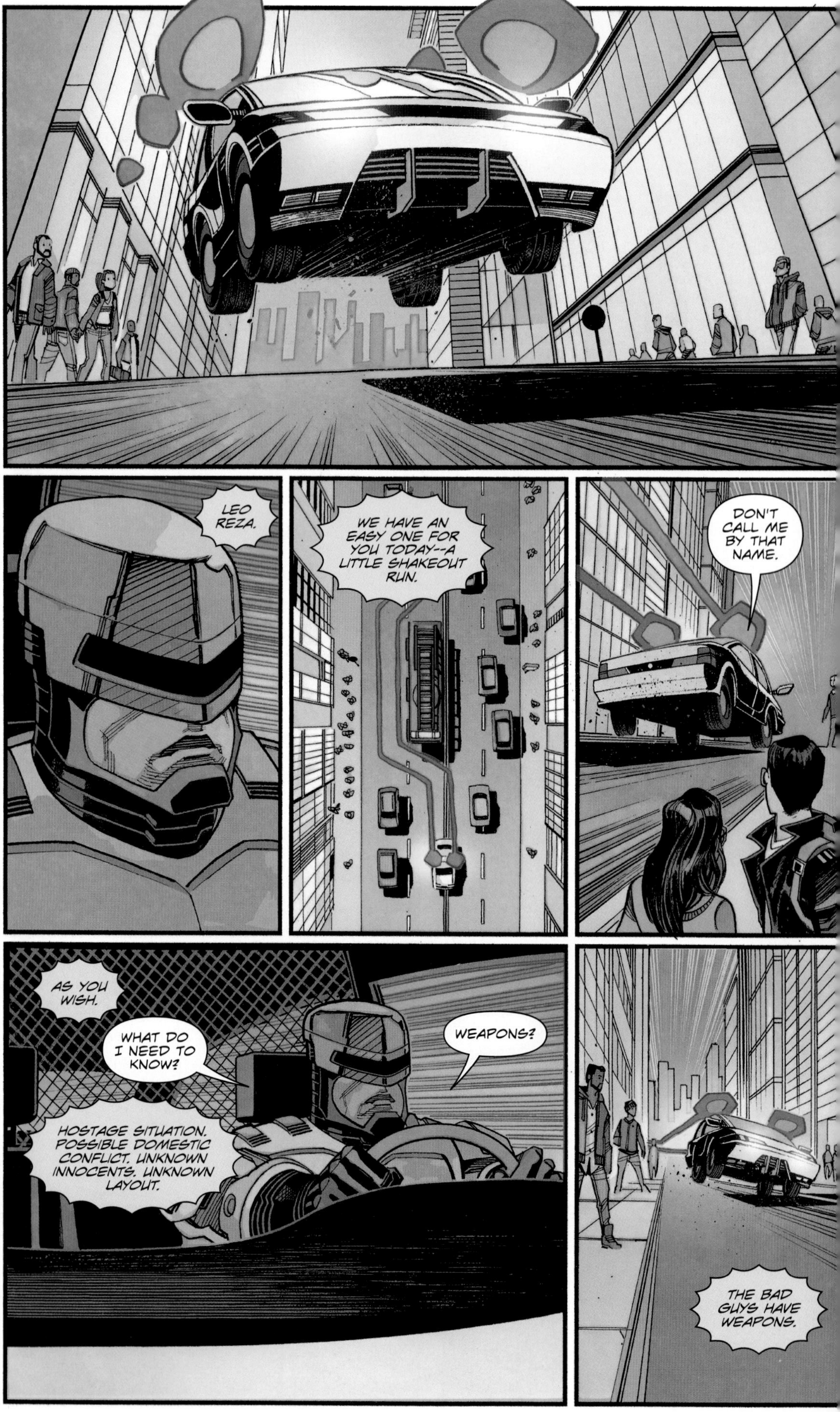
LEO REZA.
WE HAVE AN EASY ONE FOR YOU TODAY--A LITTLE SHAKEOUT RUN.
DON'T CALL ME BY THAT NAME.
AS YOU WISH.
WHAT DO I NEED TO KNOW?
HOSTAGE SITUATION. POSSIBLE DOMESTIC CONFLICT. UNKNOWN INNOCENTS. UNKNOWN LAYOUT.
WEAPONS?
THE BAD GUYS HAVE WEAPONS.

NOT FOR LONG.

SHOULD WE DISCUSS TACTICS?

I WAS THINKING OF GOING IN THE FRONT DOOR.

GET SOME, ROBOCOP.

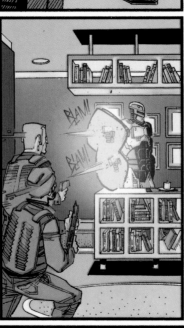

BLAM!

BLAM!

BLAM!

HELP US!

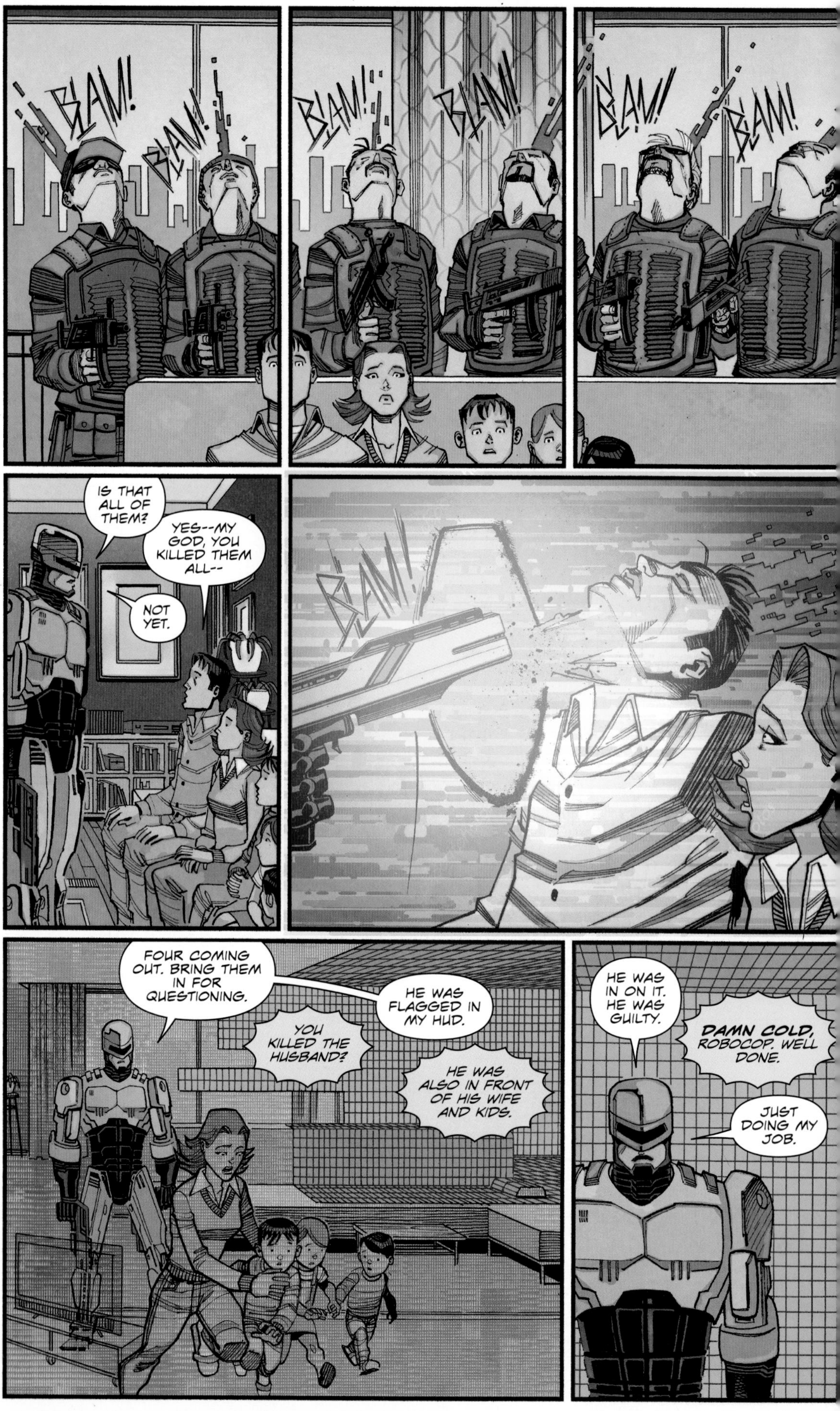
BLAM!
BLAM!
BLAM!
BLAM!
BLAM!
BLAM!
IS THAT ALL OF THEM?
YES--MY GOD, YOU KILLED THEM ALL--
NOT YET.
BLAM!
FOUR COMING OUT. BRING THEM IN FOR QUESTIONING.
YOU KILLED THE HUSBAND?
HE WAS FLAGGED IN MY HUD.
HE WAS ALSO IN FRONT OF HIS WIFE AND KIDS.
HE WAS IN ON IT. HE WAS GUILTY.
DAMN COLD, ROBOCOP. WELL DONE.
JUST DOING MY JOB.

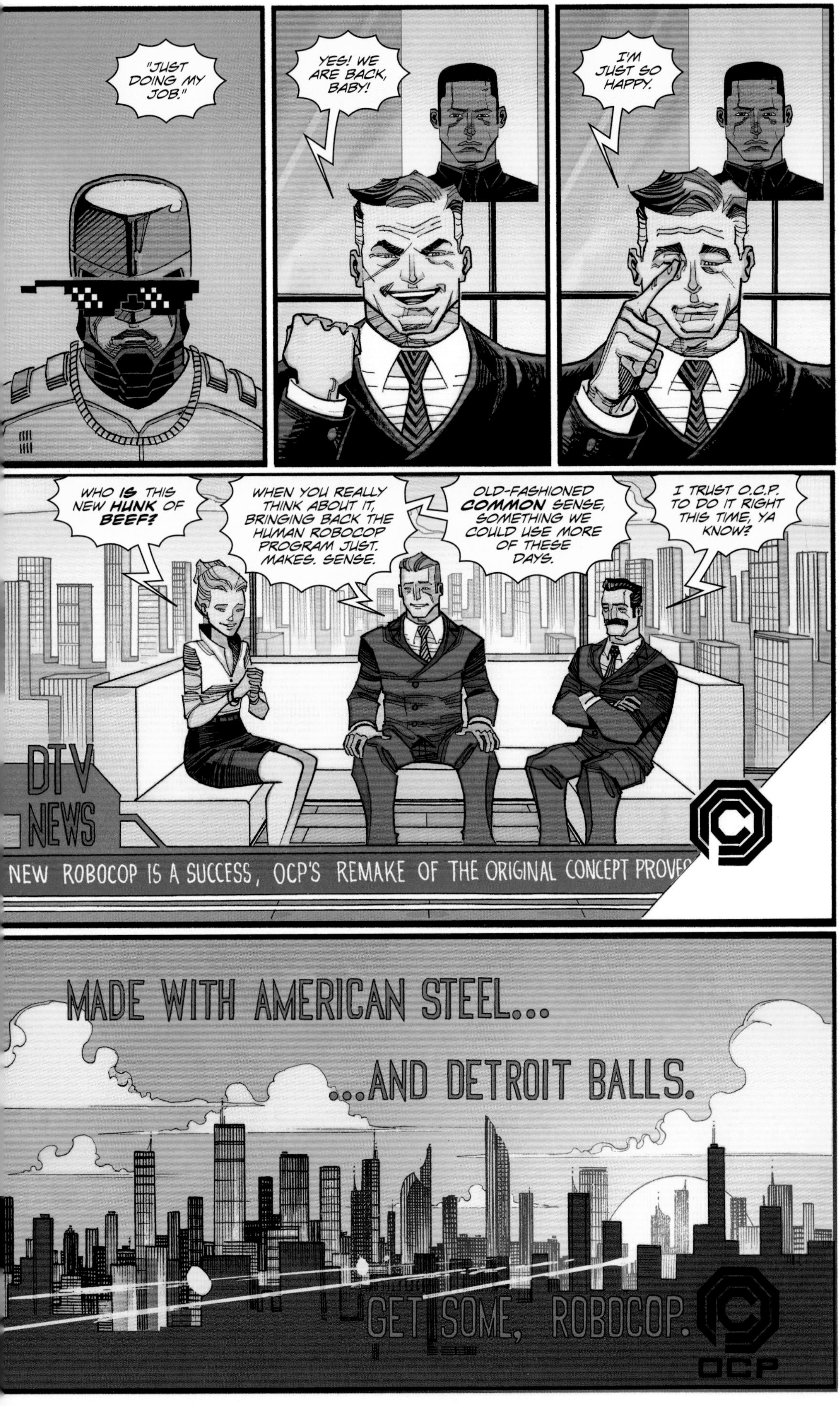
"JUST DOING MY JOB."
YES! WE ARE BACK, BABY!
I'M JUST SO HAPPY.
WHO IS THIS NEW HUNK OF BEEF?
WHEN YOU REALLY THINK ABOUT IT, BRINGING BACK THE HUMAN ROBOCOP PROGRAM JUST. MAKES. SENSE.
OLD-FASHIONED COMMON SENSE, SOMETHING WE COULD USE MORE OF THESE DAYS.
I TRUST O.C.P. TO DO IT RIGHT THIS TIME, YA KNOW?
DTV NEWS
NEW ROBOCOP IS A SUCCESS, OCP'S REMAKE OF THE ORIGINAL CONCEPT PROVES
MADE WITH AMERICAN STEEL...
...AND DETROIT BALLS.
GET SOME, ROBOCOP.
OCP

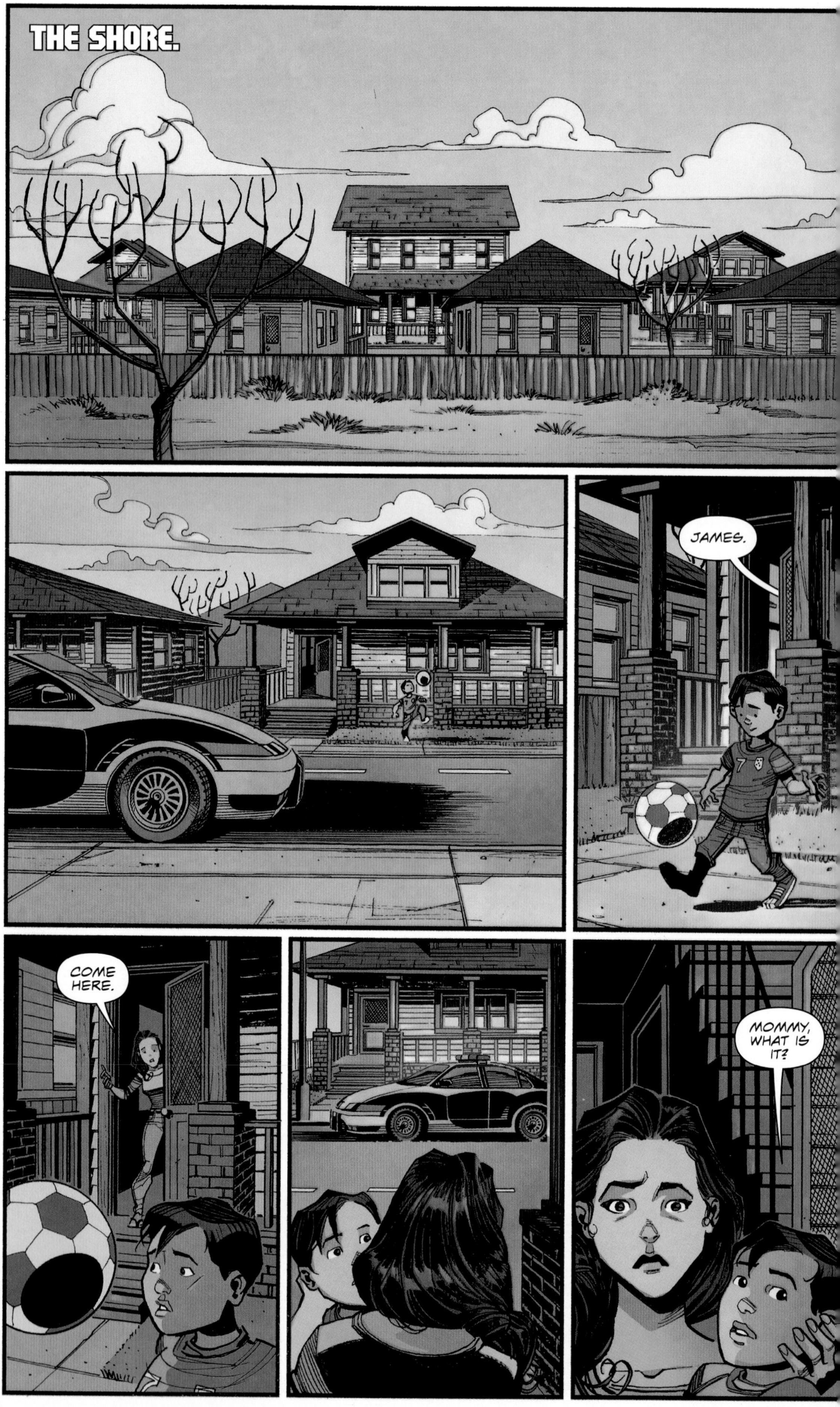
THE SHORE.
JAMES.
COME HERE.
MOMMY, WHAT IS IT?

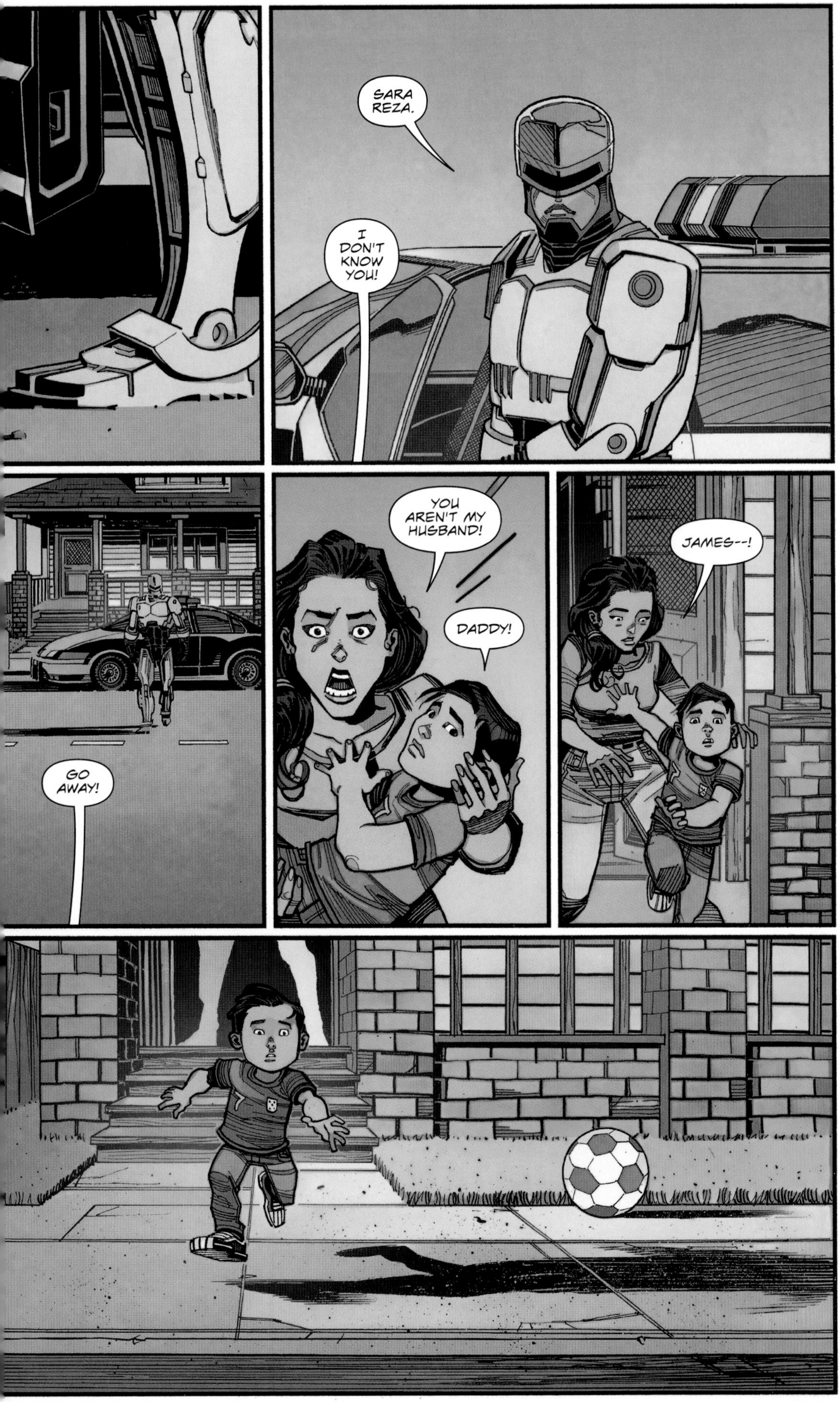
SARA REZA.
I DON'T KNOW YOU!
GO AWAY!
YOU AREN'T MY HUSBAND!
DADDY!
JAMES--!

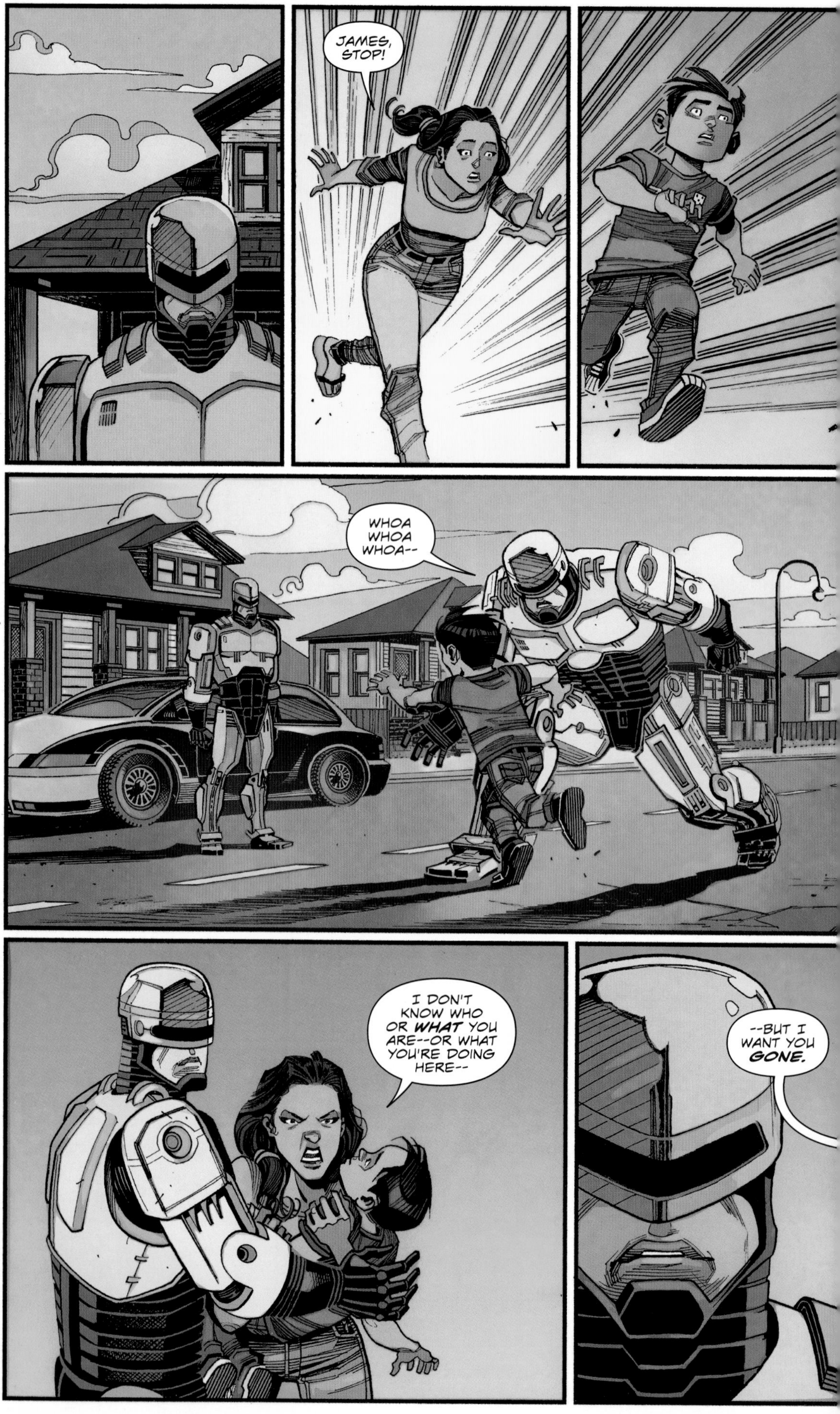
JAMES, STOP!
WHOA WHOA WHOA--
I DON'T KNOW WHO OR ***WHAT*** YOU ARE--OR WHAT YOU'RE DOING HERE--
--BUT I WANT YOU ***GONE.***

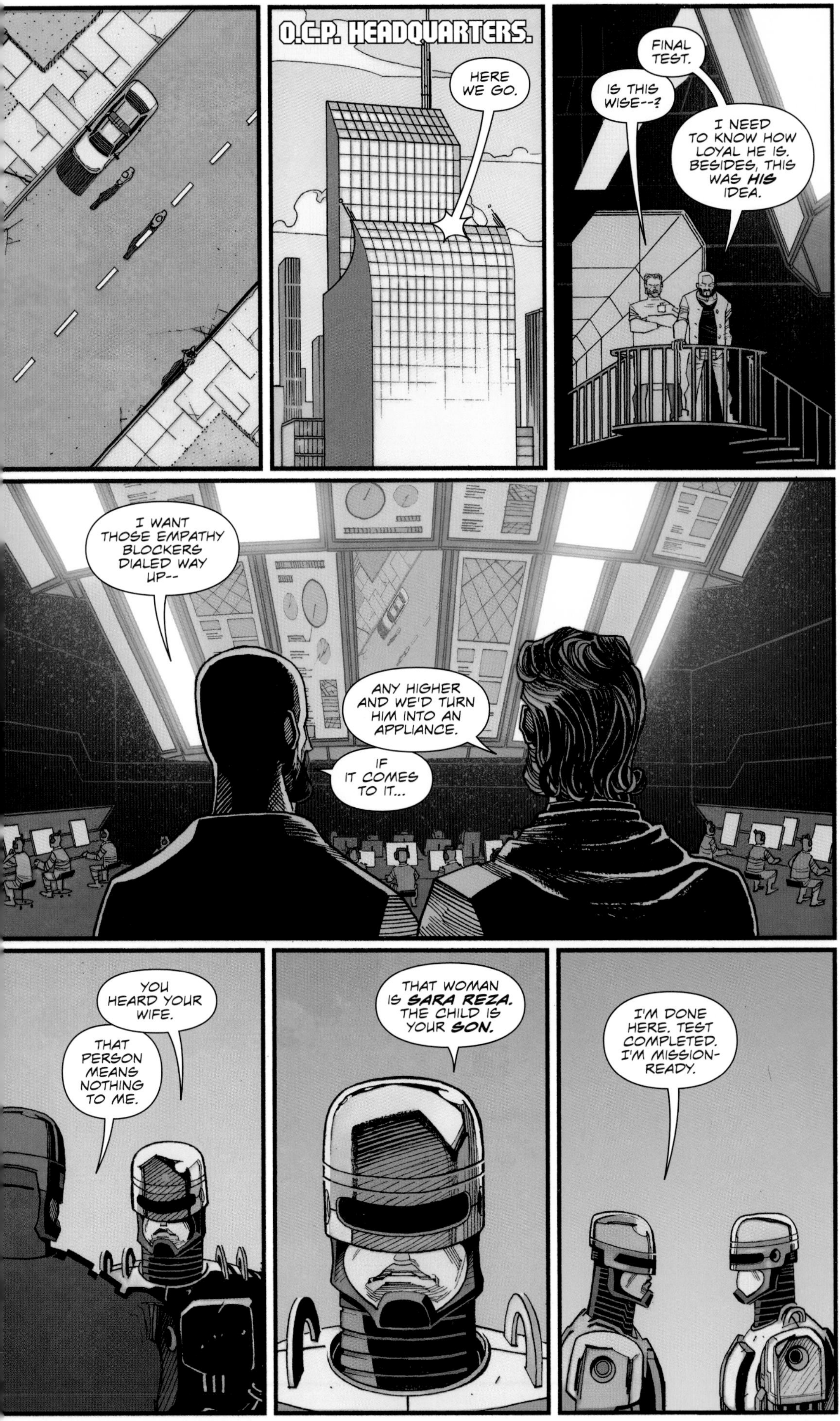
O.C.P. HEADQUARTERS.
HERE WE GO.
FINAL TEST.
IS THIS WISE--?
I NEED TO KNOW HOW LOYAL HE IS. BESIDES, THIS WAS HIS IDEA.
I WANT THOSE EMPATHY BLOCKERS DIALED WAY UP--
ANY HIGHER AND WE'D TURN HIM INTO AN APPLIANCE.
IF IT COMES TO IT...
YOU HEARD YOUR WIFE.
THAT PERSON MEANS NOTHING TO ME.
THAT WOMAN IS SARA REZA. THE CHILD IS YOUR SON.
I'M DONE HERE. TEST COMPLETED. I'M MISSION-READY.

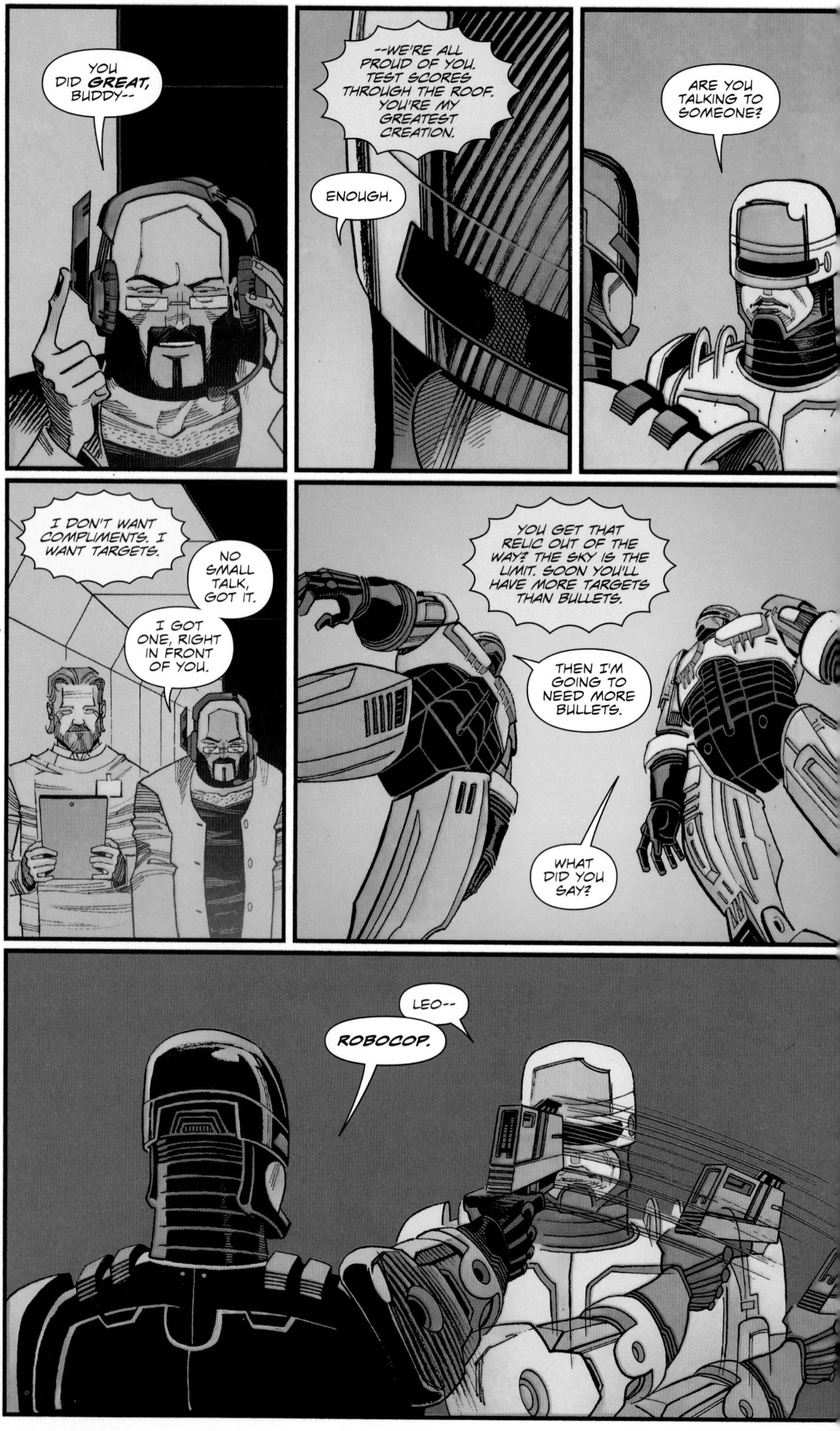
YOU DID **GREAT,** BUDDY--
--WE'RE ALL PROUD OF YOU. TEST SCORES THROUGH THE ROOF. YOU'RE MY GREATEST CREATION.
ENOUGH.
ARE YOU TALKING TO SOMEONE?
I DON'T WANT COMPLIMENTS. I WANT TARGETS.
NO SMALL TALK, GOT IT.
I GOT ONE, RIGHT IN FRONT OF YOU.
YOU GET THAT RELIC OUT OF THE WAY? THE SKY IS THE LIMIT. SOON YOU'LL HAVE MORE TARGETS THAN BULLETS.
THEN I'M GOING TO NEED MORE BULLETS.
WHAT DID YOU SAY?
LEO--
ROBOCOP.

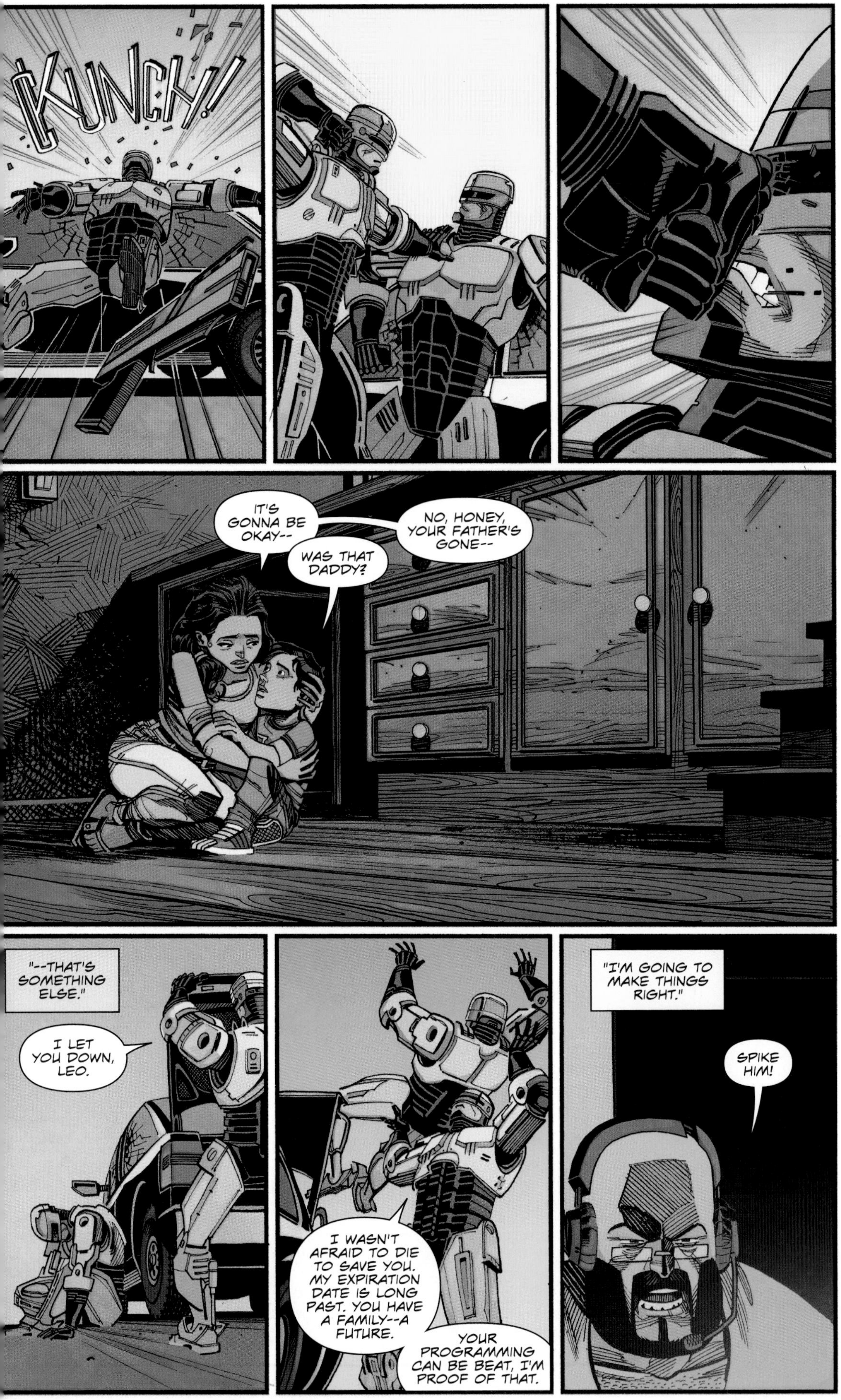
KUNCH!
IT'S GONNA BE OKAY--
WAS THAT DADDY?
NO, HONEY, YOUR FATHER'S GONE--
"--THAT'S SOMETHING ELSE."
I LET YOU DOWN, LEO.
I WASN'T AFRAID TO DIE TO SAVE YOU. MY EXPIRATION DATE IS LONG PAST. YOU HAVE A FAMILY--A FUTURE.
YOUR PROGRAMMING CAN BE BEAT, I'M PROOF OF THAT.
"I'M GOING TO MAKE THINGS RIGHT."
SPIKE HIM!

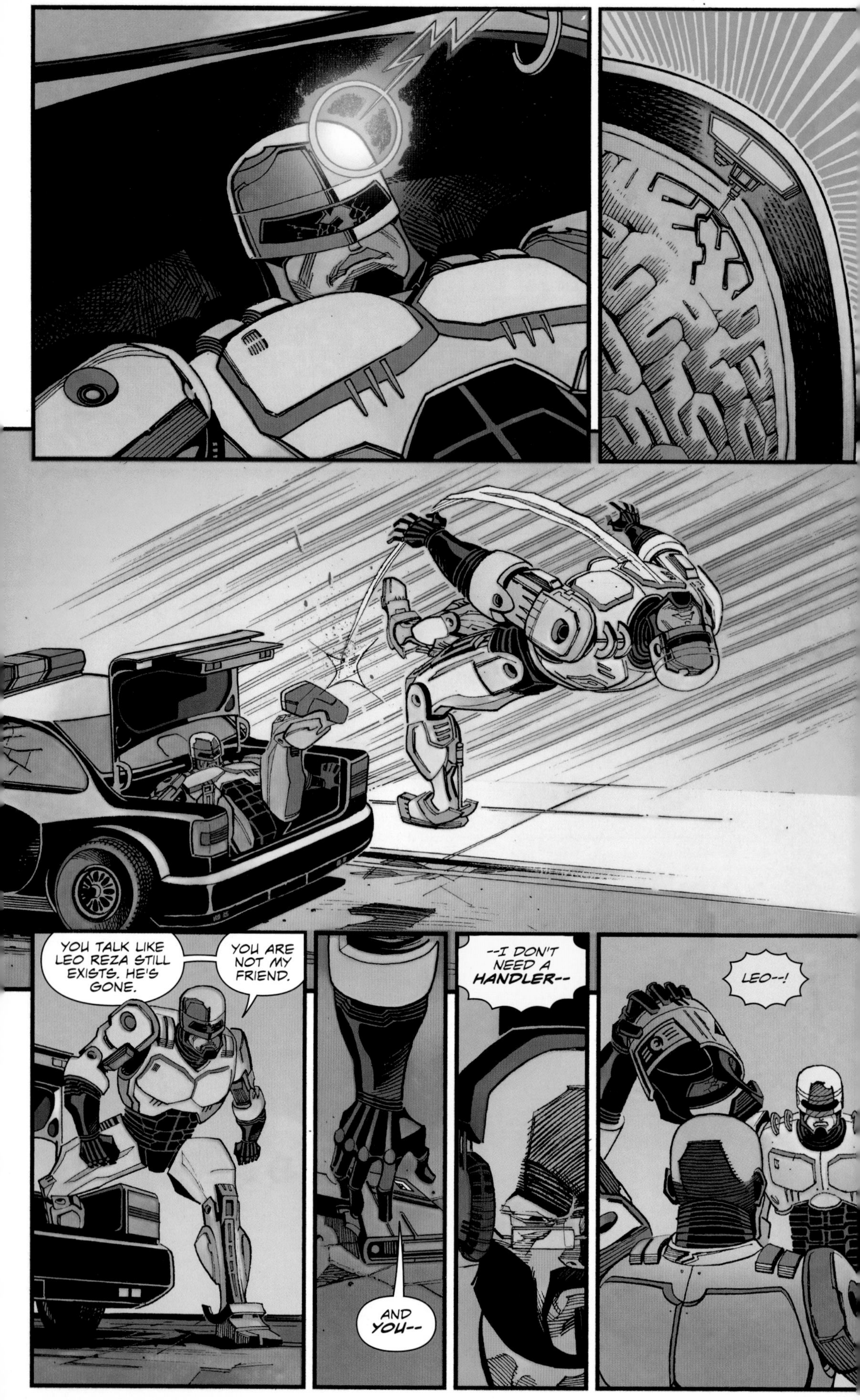
YOU TALK LIKE LEO REZA STILL EXISTS. HE'S GONE.
YOU ARE NOT MY FRIEND.
AND *YOU*--
--I DON'T NEED A *HANDLER*--
LEO--!

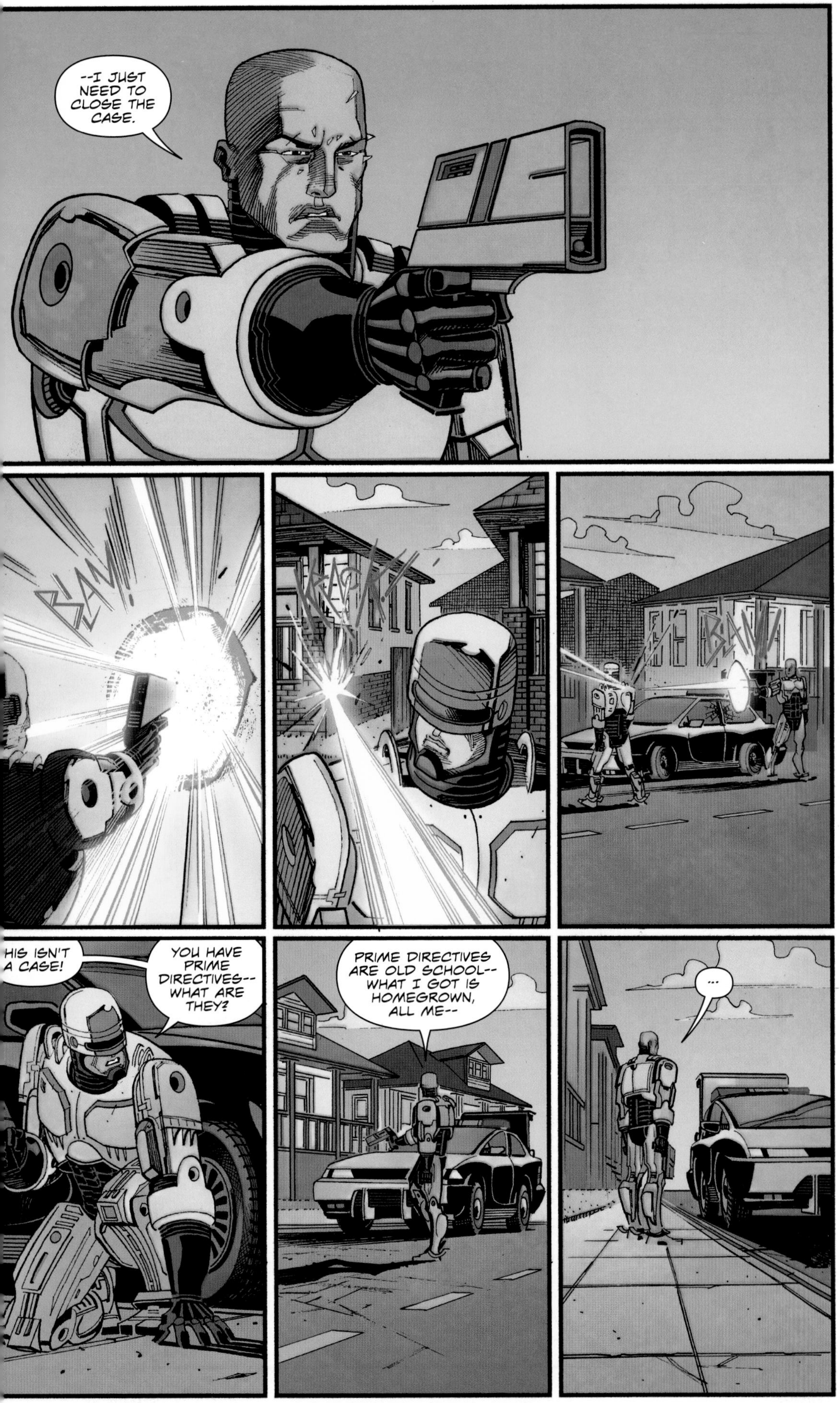
--I JUST NEED TO CLOSE THE CASE.
BLAM!
KRACK!
BLAM!
HIS ISN'T A CASE!
YOU HAVE PRIME DIRECTIVES--WHAT ARE THEY?
PRIME DIRECTIVES ARE OLD SCHOOL--WHAT I GOT IS HOMEGROWN, ALL ME--
...

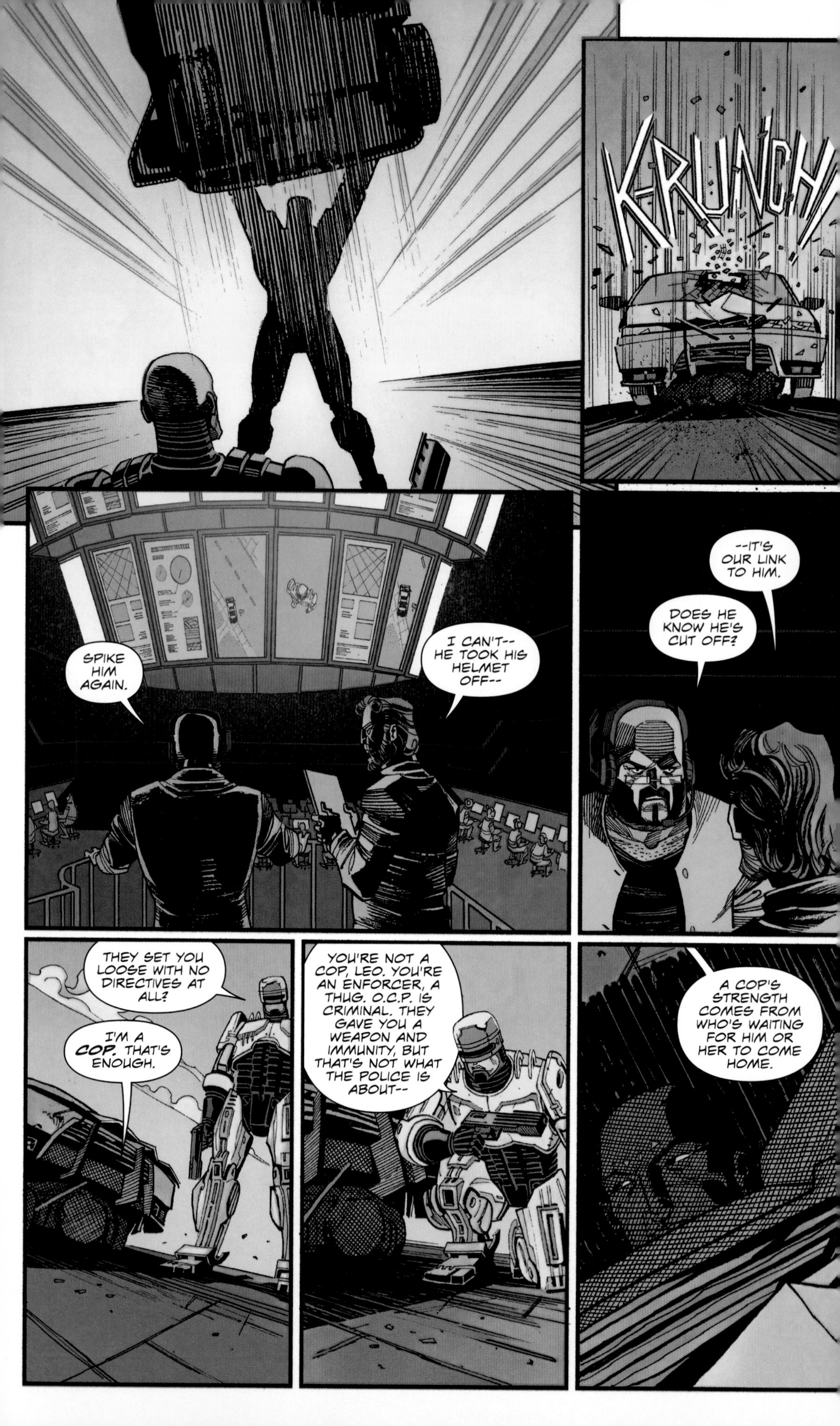

K-RUNCH!
SPIKE HIM AGAIN.
I CAN'T-- HE TOOK HIS HELMET OFF--
DOES HE KNOW HE'S CUT OFF?
--IT'S OUR LINK TO HIM.
THEY SET YOU LOOSE WITH NO DIRECTIVES AT ALL?
I'M A COP. THAT'S ENOUGH.
YOU'RE NOT A COP, LEO. YOU'RE AN ENFORCER, A THUG. O.C.P. IS CRIMINAL. THEY GAVE YOU A WEAPON AND IMMUNITY, BUT THAT'S NOT WHAT THE POLICE IS ABOUT--
A COP'S STRENGTH COMES FROM WHO'S WAITING FOR HIM OR HER TO COME HOME.

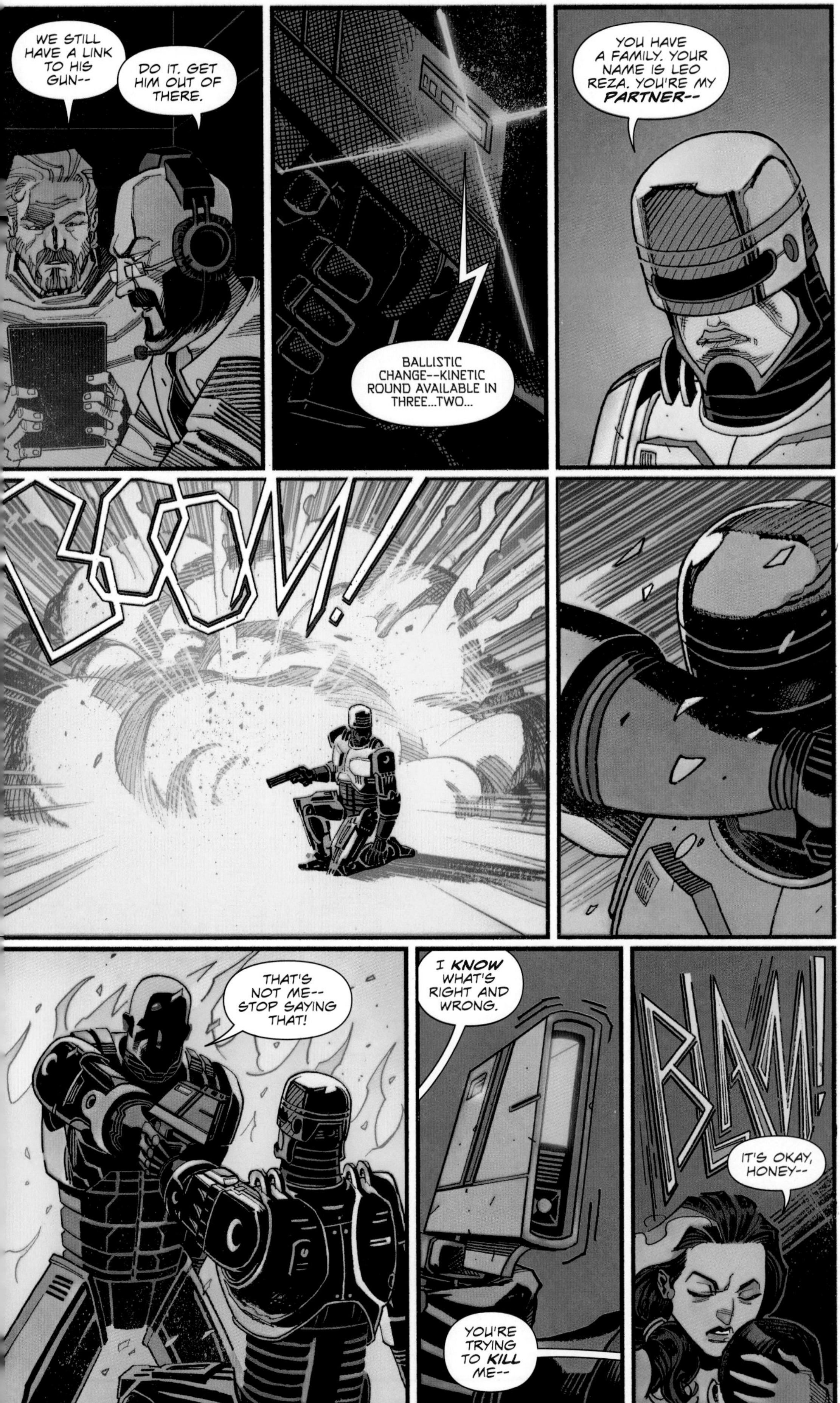
WE STILL HAVE A LINK TO HIS GUN--
DO IT. GET HIM OUT OF THERE.
BALLISTIC CHANGE--KINETIC ROUND AVAILABLE IN THREE...TWO...
YOU HAVE A FAMILY. YOUR NAME IS LEO REZA. YOU'RE MY ***PARTNER--***
BOOM!
THAT'S NOT ME-- STOP SAYING THAT!
I ***KNOW*** WHAT'S RIGHT AND WRONG.
YOU'RE TRYING TO ***KILL*** ME--
BLAM!
IT'S OKAY, HONEY--

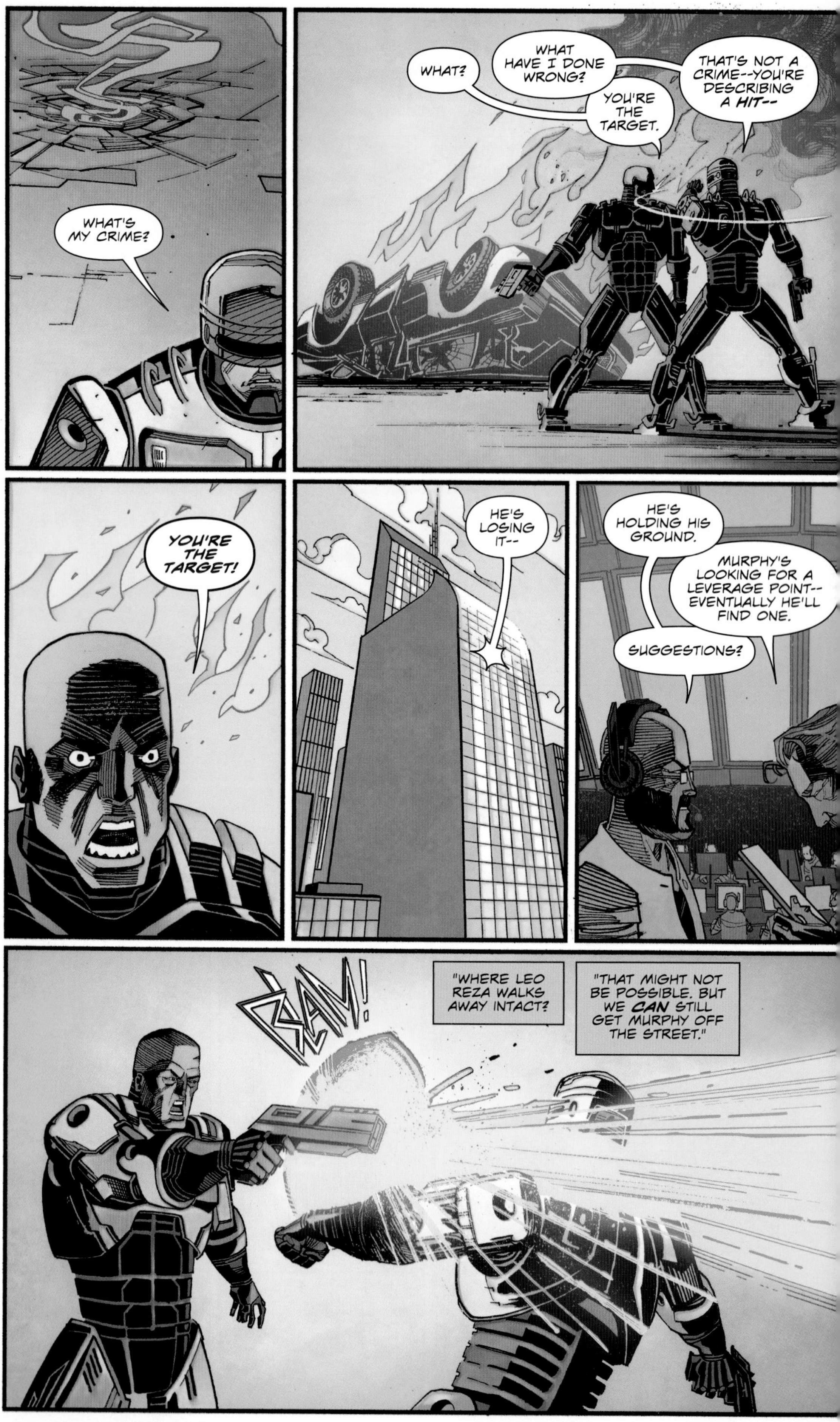
WHAT'S MY CRIME?
WHAT?
WHAT HAVE I DONE WRONG?
YOU'RE THE TARGET.
THAT'S NOT A CRIME--YOU'RE DESCRIBING A HIT--
YOU'RE THE TARGET!
HE'S LOSING IT--
HE'S HOLDING HIS GROUND.
MURPHY'S LOOKING FOR A LEVERAGE POINT--EVENTUALLY HE'LL FIND ONE.
SUGGESTIONS?
BAM!
"WHERE LEO REZA WALKS AWAY INTACT?
"THAT MIGHT NOT BE POSSIBLE. BUT WE CAN STILL GET MURPHY OFF THE STREET."

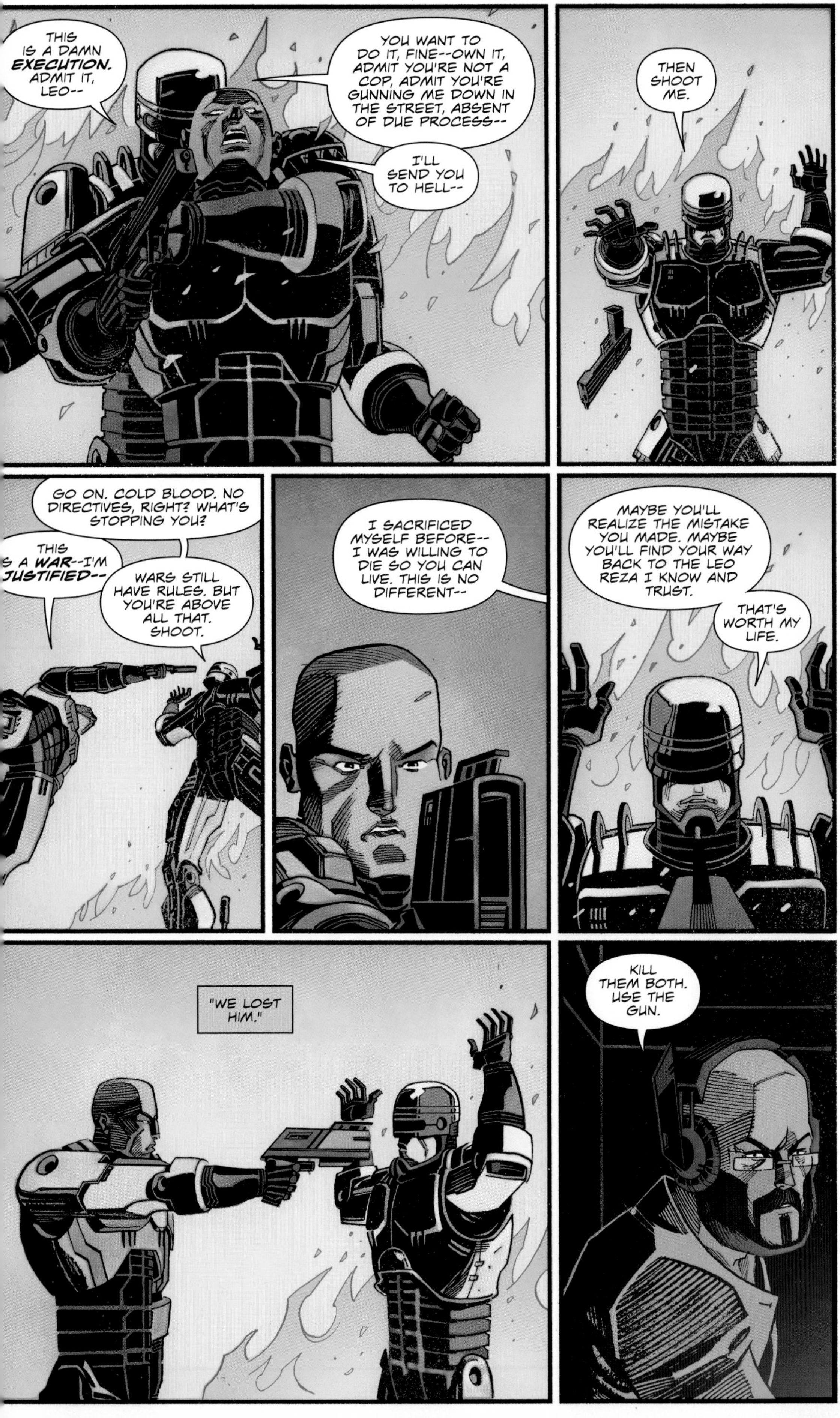
THIS IS A DAMN EXECUTION. ADMIT IT, LEO--
YOU WANT TO DO IT, FINE--OWN IT, ADMIT YOU'RE NOT A COP, ADMIT YOU'RE GUNNING ME DOWN IN THE STREET, ABSENT OF DUE PROCESS--
I'LL SEND YOU TO HELL--
THEN SHOOT ME.
GO ON. COLD BLOOD. NO DIRECTIVES, RIGHT? WHAT'S STOPPING YOU?
THIS S A WAR--I'M JUSTIFIED--
WARS STILL HAVE RULES. BUT YOU'RE ABOVE ALL THAT. SHOOT.
I SACRIFICED MYSELF BEFORE-- I WAS WILLING TO DIE SO YOU CAN LIVE. THIS IS NO DIFFERENT--
MAYBE YOU'LL REALIZE THE MISTAKE YOU MADE. MAYBE YOU'LL FIND YOUR WAY BACK TO THE LEO REZA I KNOW AND TRUST.
THAT'S WORTH MY LIFE.
"WE LOST HIM."
KILL THEM BOTH. USE THE GUN.

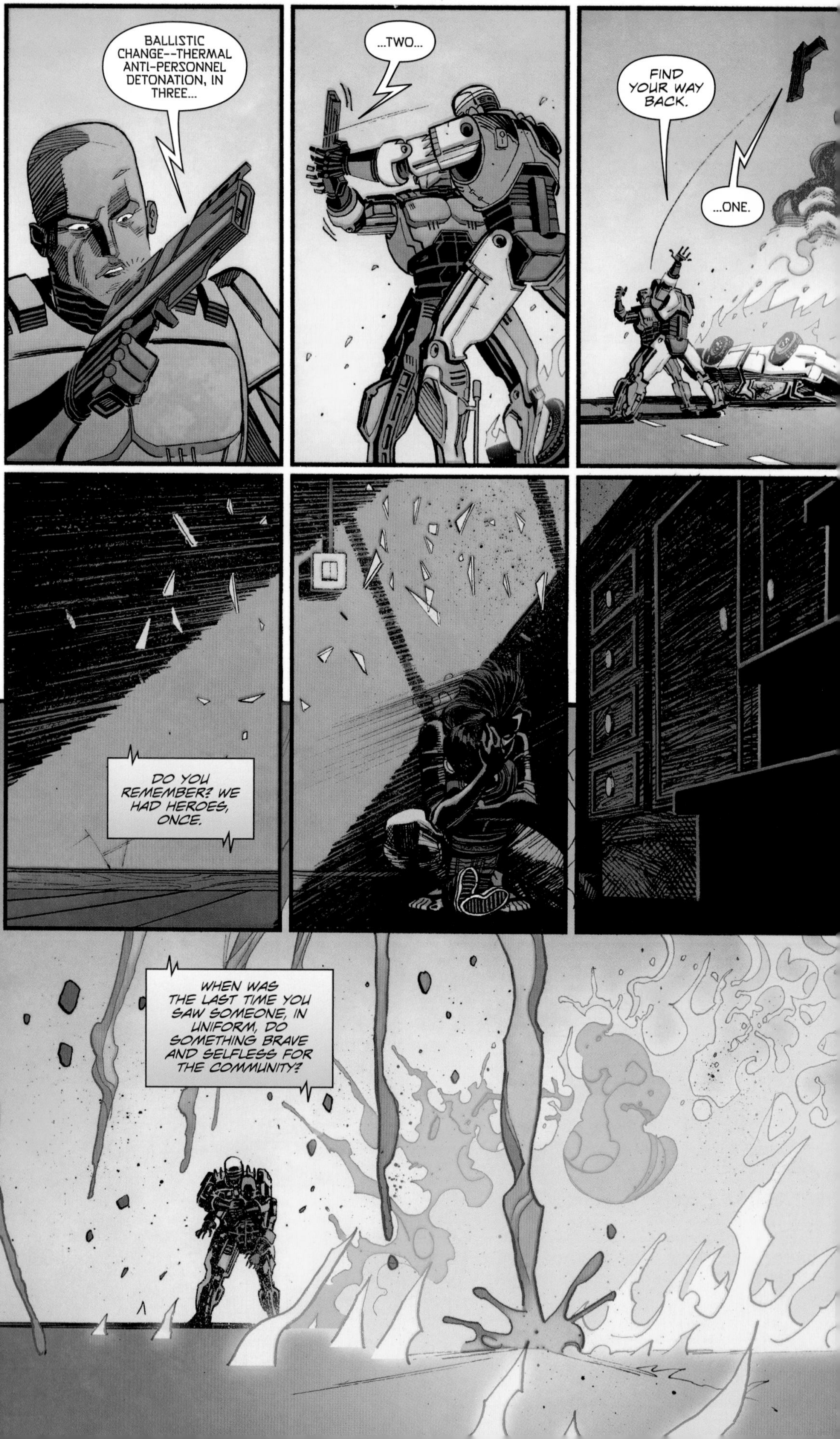
BALLISTIC CHANGE--THERMAL ANTI-PERSONNEL DETONATION, IN THREE...
...TWO...
FIND YOUR WAY BACK.
...ONE.
DO YOU REMEMBER? WE HAD HEROES, ONCE.
WHEN WAS THE LAST TIME YOU SAW SOMEONE, IN UNIFORM, DO SOMETHING BRAVE AND SELFLESS FOR THE COMMUNITY?

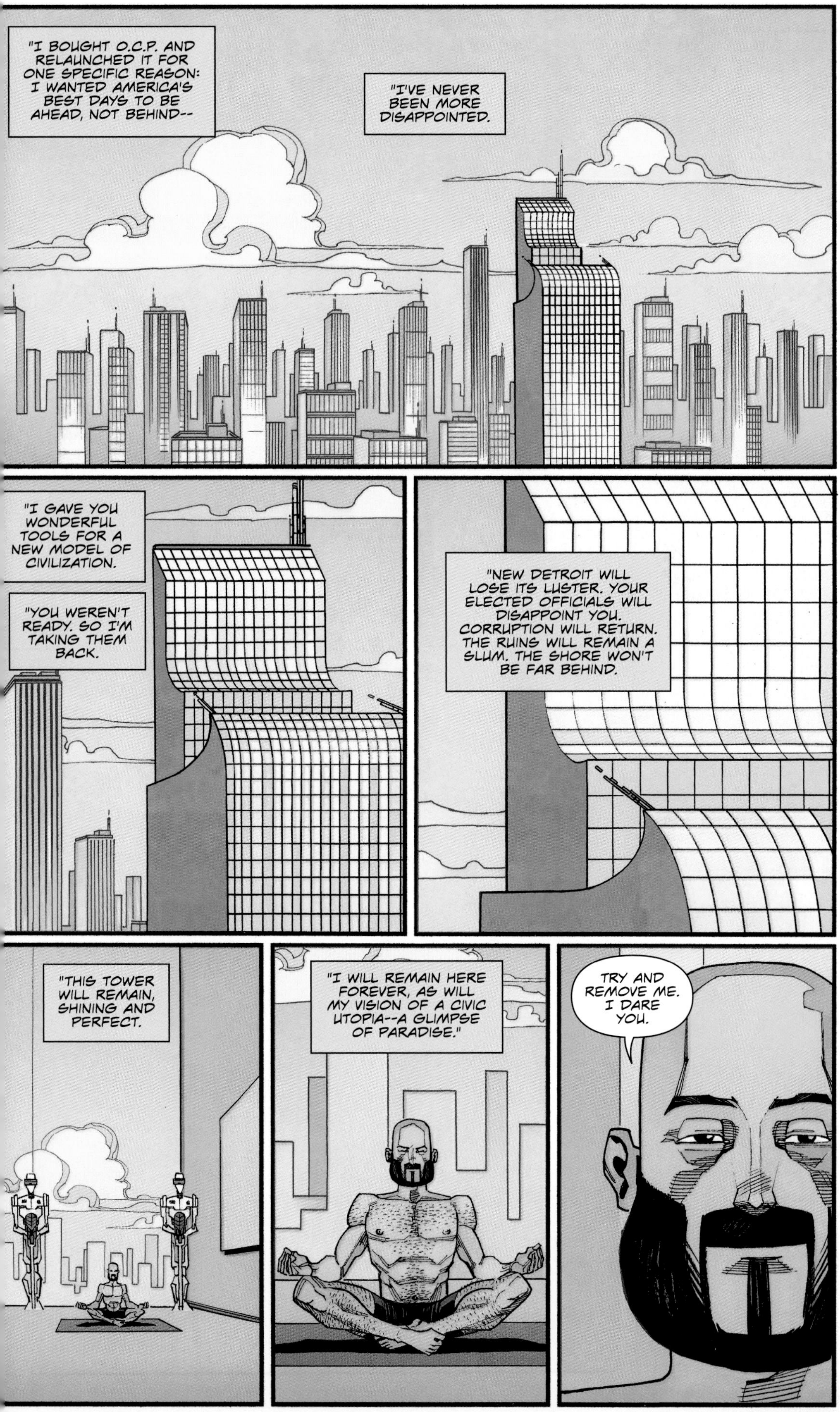
"I BOUGHT O.C.P. AND RELAUNCHED IT FOR ONE SPECIFIC REASON: I WANTED AMERICA'S BEST DAYS TO BE AHEAD, NOT BEHIND--
"I'VE NEVER BEEN MORE DISAPPOINTED.
"I GAVE YOU WONDERFUL TOOLS FOR A NEW MODEL OF CIVILIZATION.
"YOU WEREN'T READY. SO I'M TAKING THEM BACK.
"NEW DETROIT WILL LOSE ITS LUSTER. YOUR ELECTED OFFICIALS WILL DISAPPOINT YOU. CORRUPTION WILL RETURN. THE RUINS WILL REMAIN A SLUM. THE SHORE WON'T BE FAR BEHIND.
"THIS TOWER WILL REMAIN, SHINING AND PERFECT.
"I WILL REMAIN HERE FOREVER, AS WILL MY VISION OF A CIVIC UTOPIA--A GLIMPSE OF PARADISE."
TRY AND REMOVE ME. I DARE YOU.

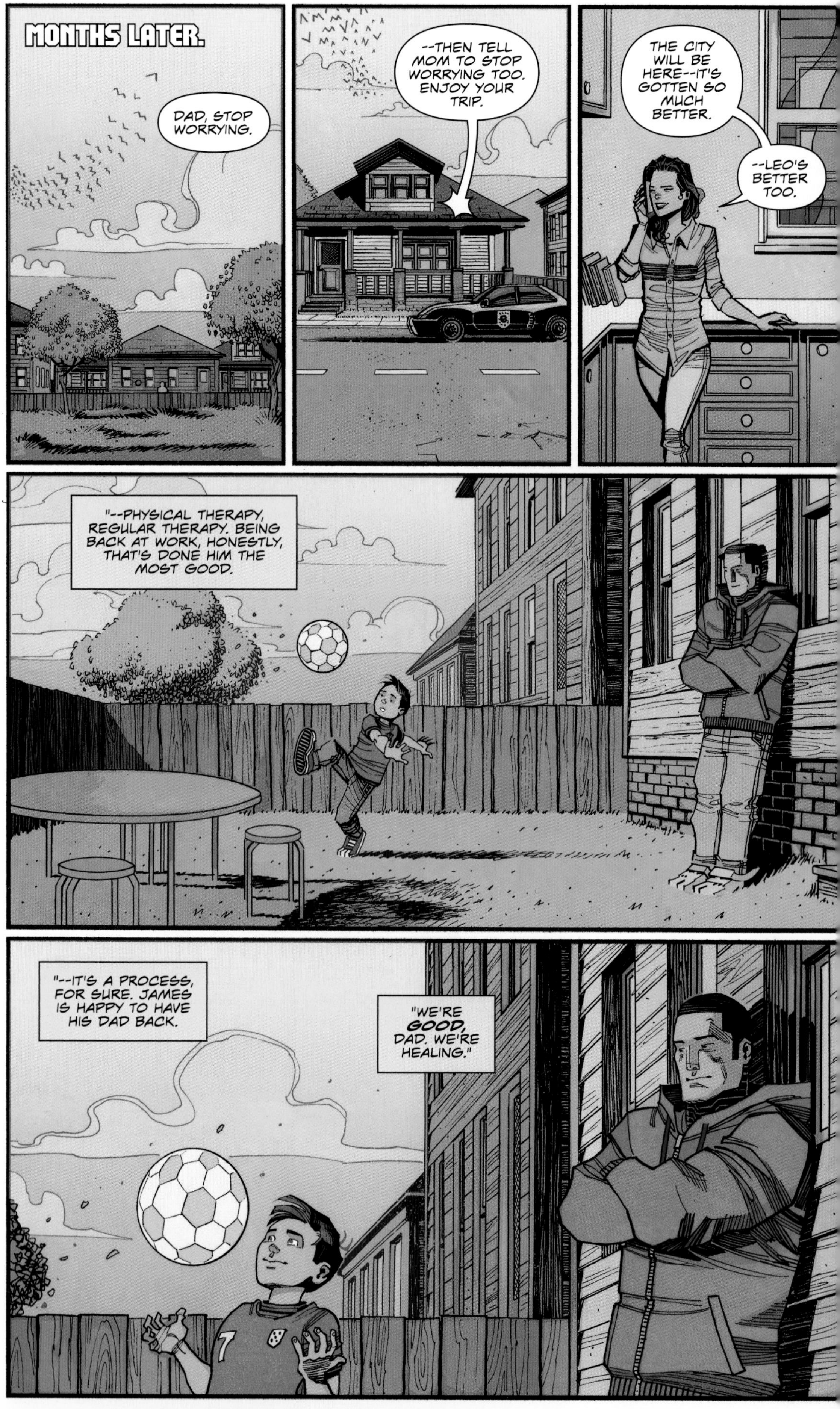
MONTHS LATER.
DAD, STOP WORRYING.
--THEN TELL MOM TO STOP WORRYING TOO. ENJOY YOUR TRIP.
THE CITY WILL BE HERE--IT'S GOTTEN SO MUCH BETTER.
--LEO'S BETTER TOO.
"--PHYSICAL THERAPY, REGULAR THERAPY. BEING BACK AT WORK, HONESTLY, THAT'S DONE HIM THE MOST GOOD.
"--IT'S A PROCESS, FOR SURE. JAMES IS HAPPY TO HAVE HIS DAD BACK.
"WE'RE GOOD, DAD. WE'RE HEALING."

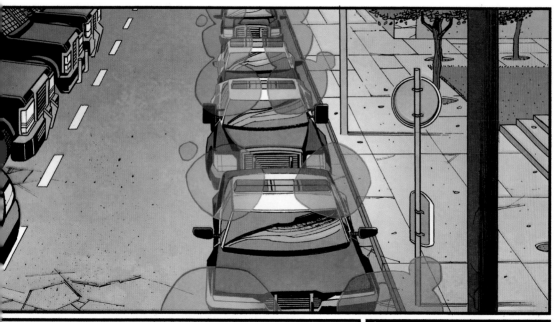

WHAT ARE WE WAITING FOR?

I'M TAKING A MINUTE.

A MINUTE--

TELL ME ABOUT IT.

HUMOR ME. THIS HAS BEEN A LONG TIME COMING.

FINE.

MURPHY TO TASK FORCE--WE ARE A GO.

"STANDARD RULES OF ENGAGEMENT?"

"FOR YOU, MAYBE. THIS OP IS MY LAST RODEO--"

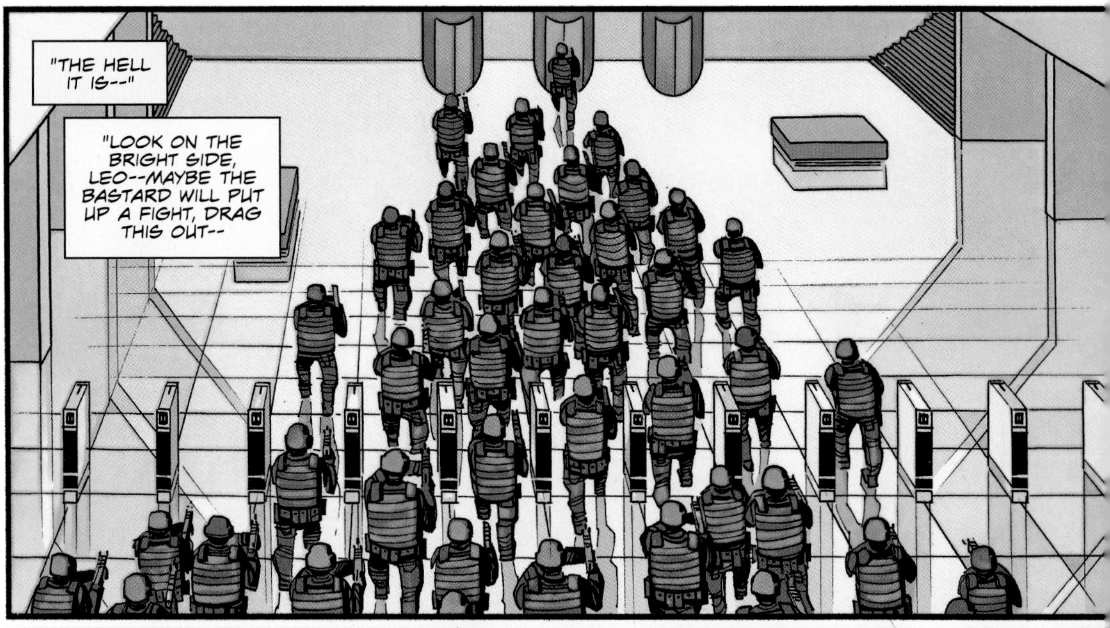
"THE HELL IT IS--"
"LOOK ON THE BRIGHT SIDE, LEO--MAYBE THE BASTARD WILL PUT UP A FIGHT, DRAG THIS OUT--

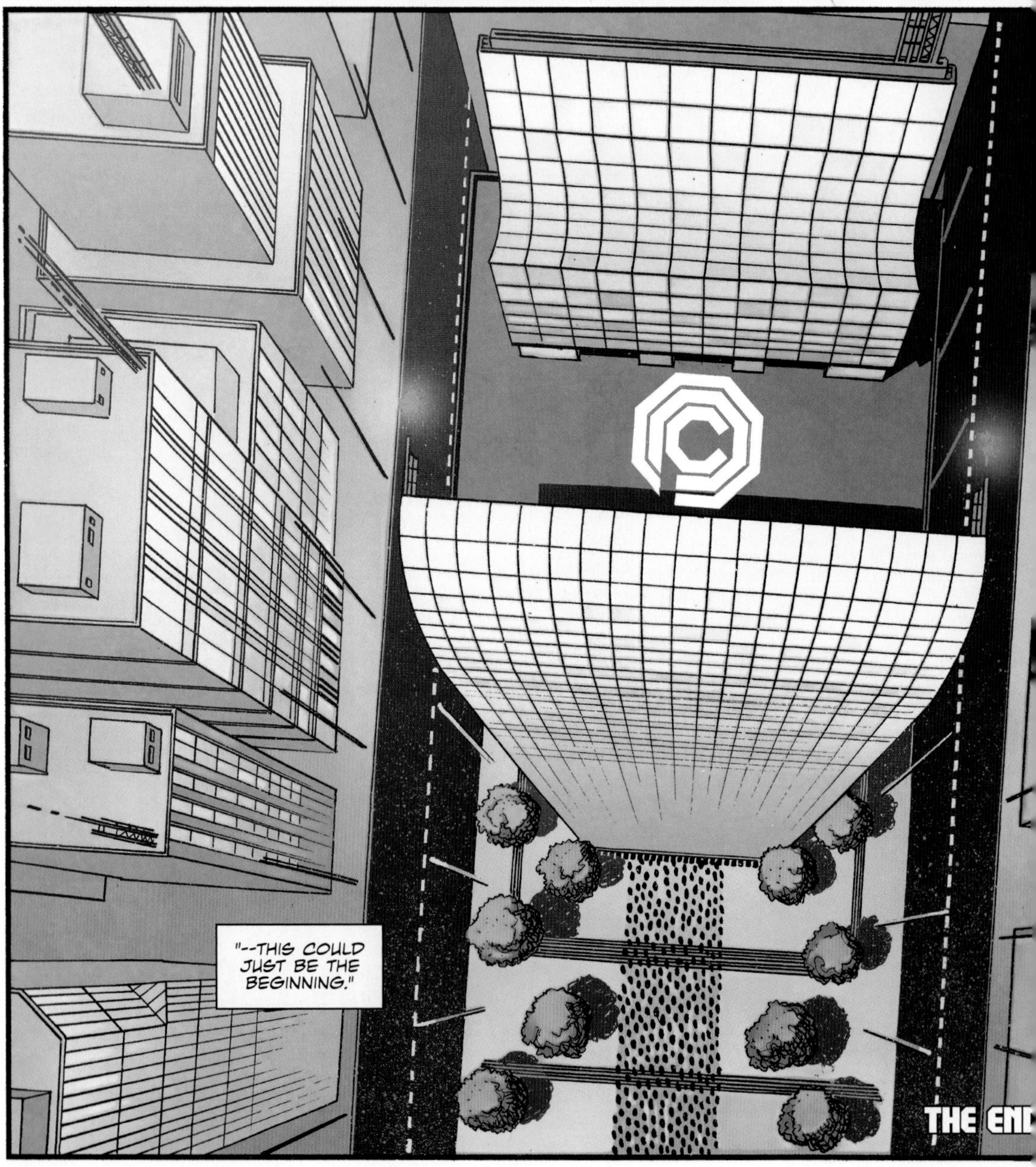
"--THIS COULD JUST BE THE BEGINNING."
THE END

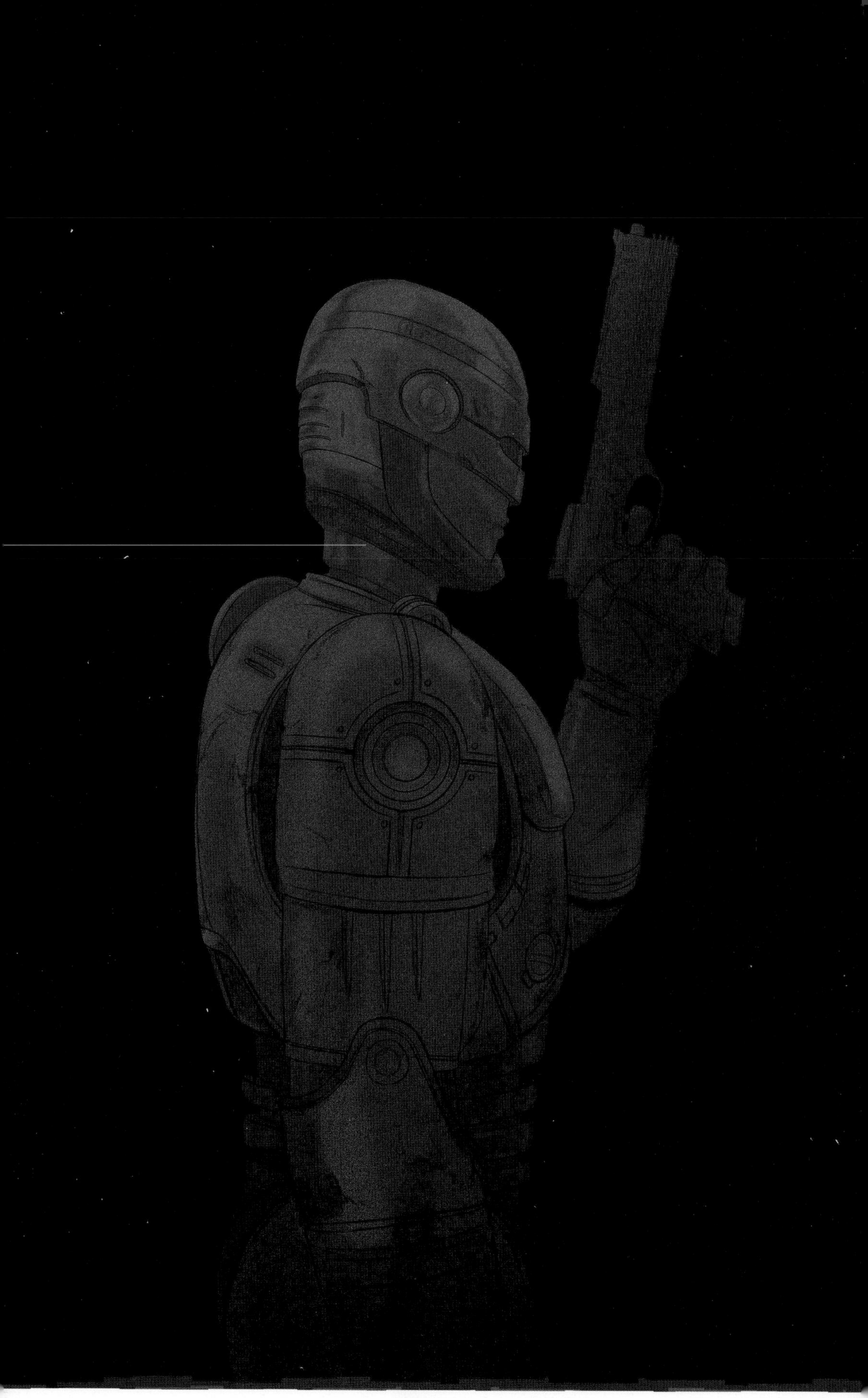

ISSUE 05 COVER **NIMIT MALAVIA**

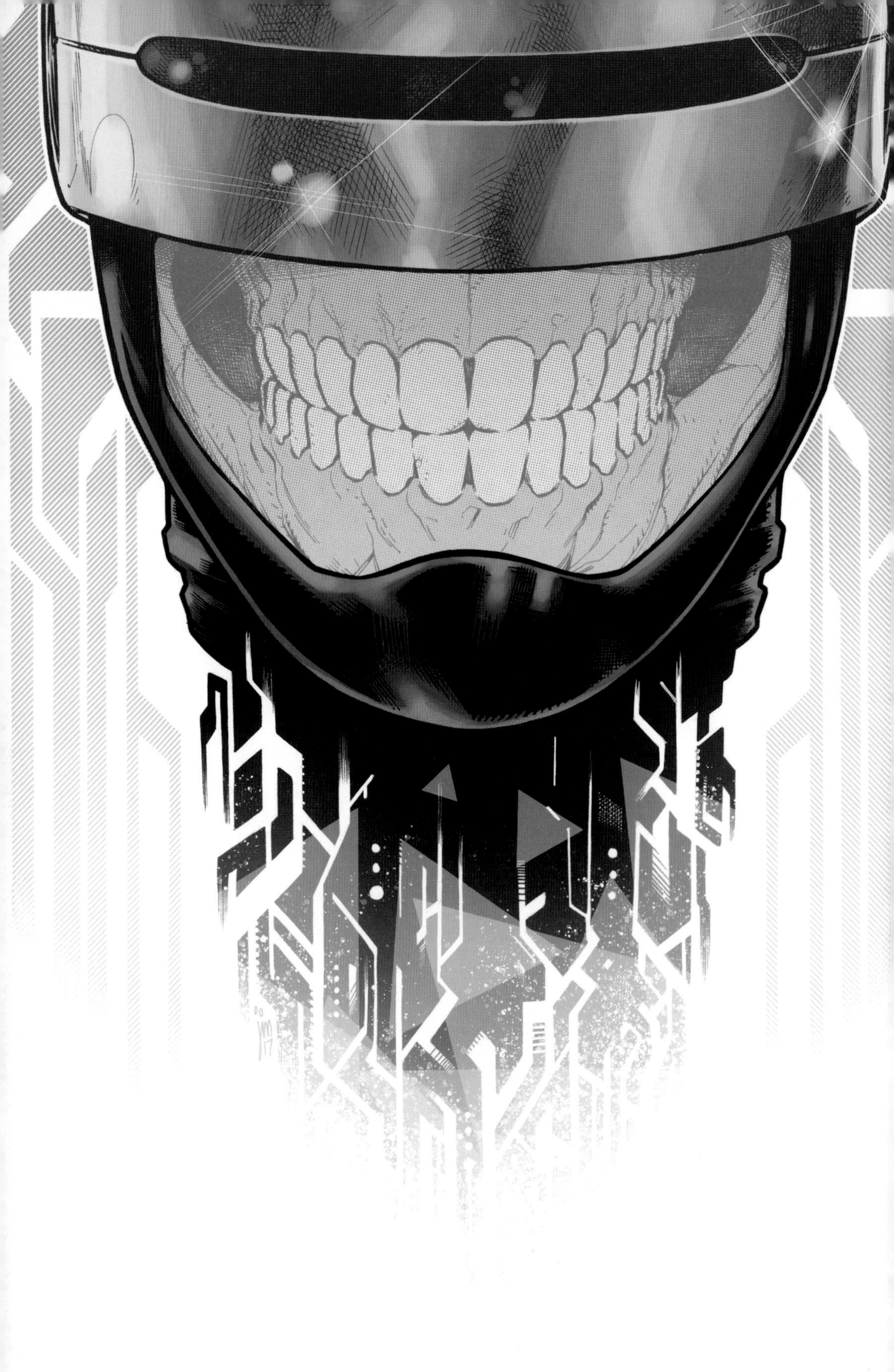

ISSUE 01 VARIANT COVER **JIM TOWE**

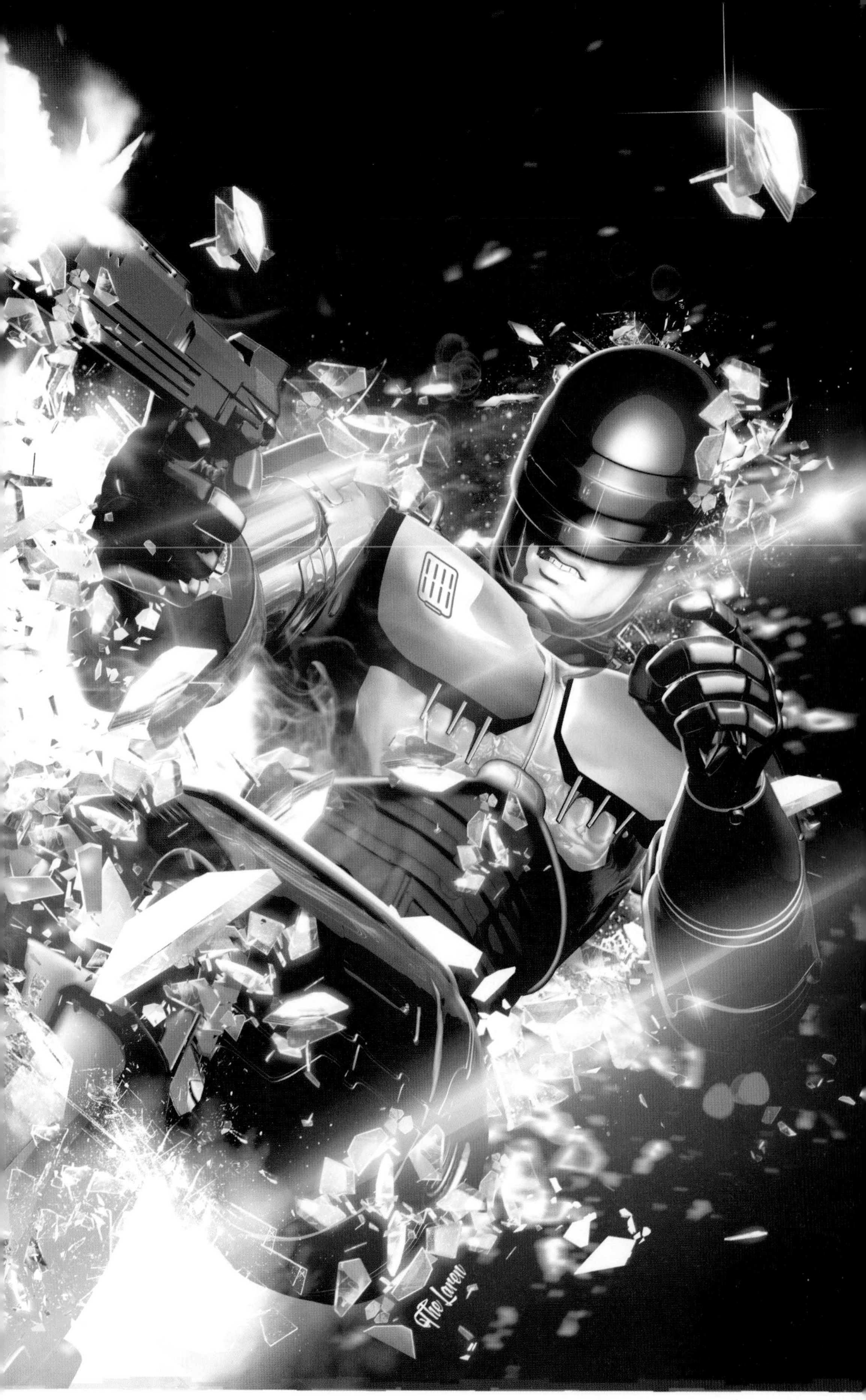
The Laren

ISSUE 01 AOD COLLECTABLES EXCLUSIVE COVER **HAL LAREN**

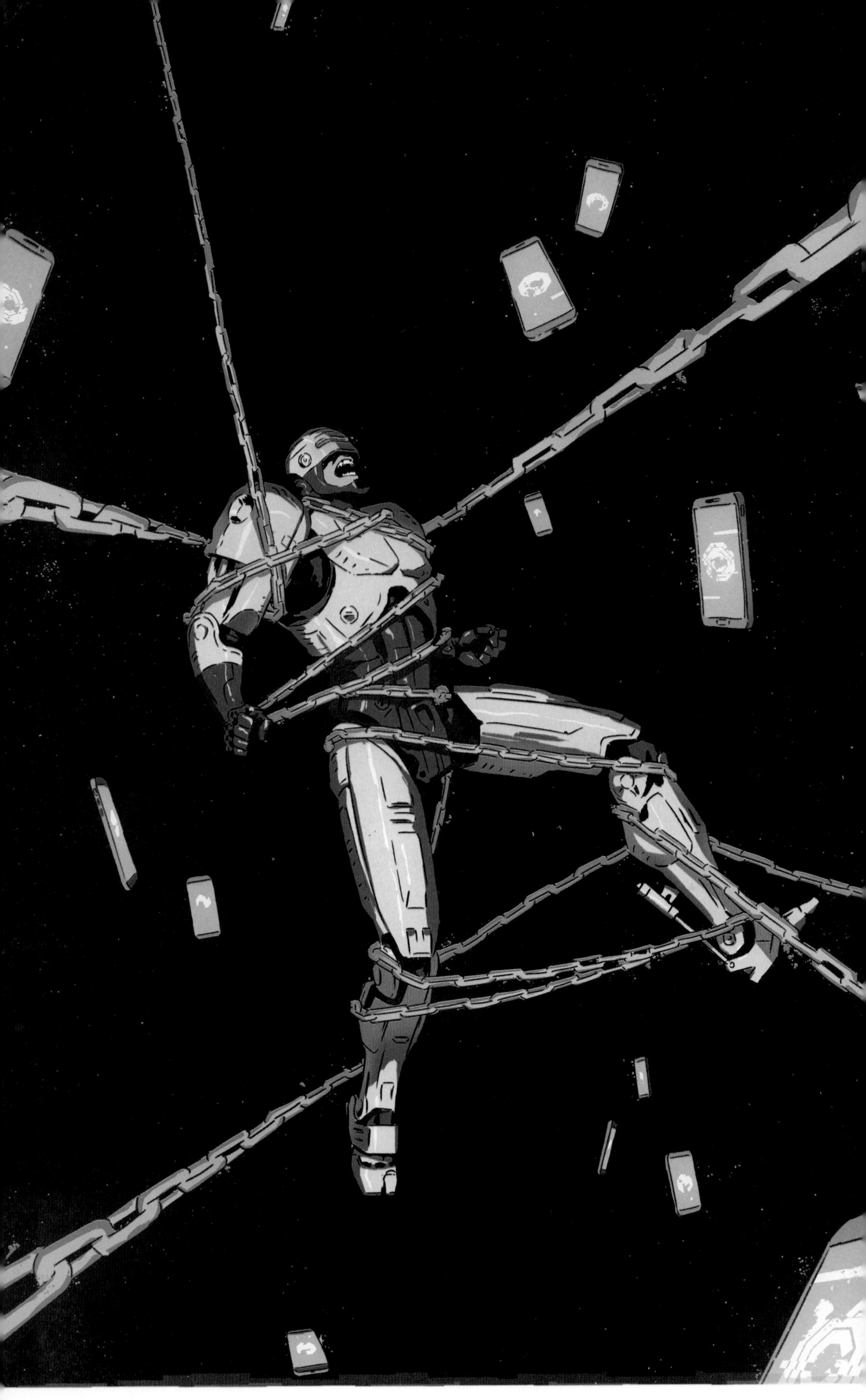

ADDITIONAL ARTWORK **PIUS BAK**

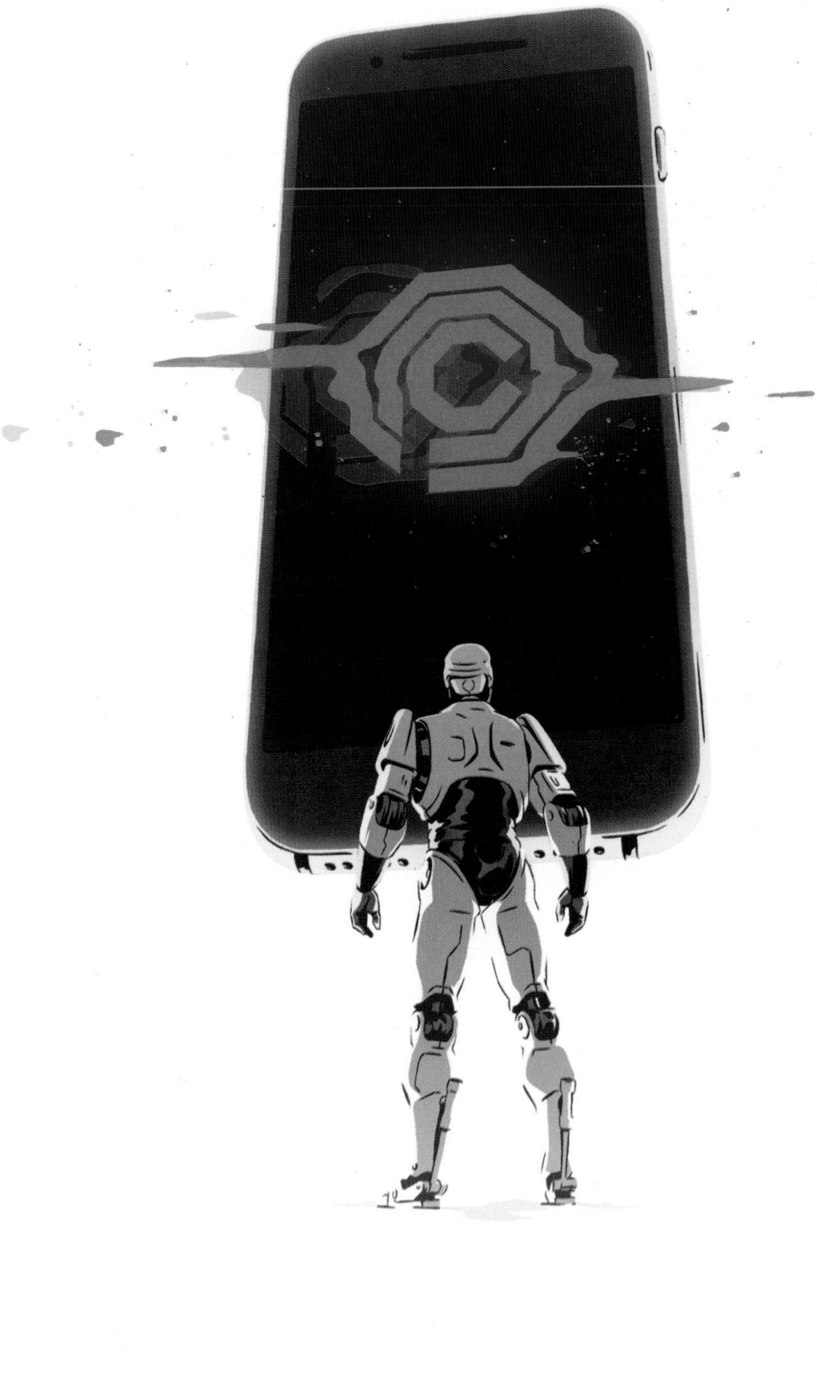

ADDITIONAL ARTWORK PIUS BAK

VISIONARY CREATORS

THE
WOODS
JAMES TYNION IV • MICHAEL DIALYNAS
VOL. 1
THE ARROW

"The Spire is fantastic! My kind of genre free-for-all."
—BRIAN K. VAUGHAN (Saga)
THE
SPIRE
SIMON SPURRIER
JEFF STOKELY
ANDRÉ MAY

MARK WAID • PETER KRAUSE
IRREDEEMABLE
AFTERWORD BY GRANT MORRISON

J.G.
JONES
MARK
WAID
STRANGE
FRUIT
Foreword by
ELVIS MITCHELL

MICHAEL ALAN NELSON
DAN MORA
GABRIEL CASSATA
HEXED
THE HARLOT & THE THIEF VOLUME ONE

ABNETT & CULBARD
WILD'S
END
FIRST LIGHT
"IT'S REALLY GREAT!"
JEFF LEMIRE

James Tynion IV

The Woods

Volume 1

ISBN: 978-1-60886-454-6 | $9.99 US

Volume 2

ISBN: 978-1-60886-495-9 | $14.99 US

Volume 3

ISBN: 978-1-60886-773-8 | $14.99 US

The Backstagers

Volume 1

ISBN: 978-1-60886-993-0 | $14.99 US

Simon Spurrier

Six-Gun Gorilla

ISBN: 978-1-60886-390-7 | $19.99 US

The Spire

ISBN: 978-1-60886-913-8 | $29.99 US

Weavers

ISBN: 978-1-60886-963-3 | $19.99 US

Mark Waid

Irredeemable

Volume 1

ISBN: 978-1-93450-690-5 | $16.99 US

Volume 2

ISBN: 978-1-60886-000-5 | $16.99 US

Incorruptible

Volume 1

ISBN: 978-1-60886-015-9 | $16.99 US

Volume 2

ISBN: 978-1-60886-028-9 | $16.99 US

Strange Fruit

ISBN: 978-1-60886-872-8 | $24.99 US

Michael Alan Nelson

Hexed The Harlot & The Thief

Volume 1

ISBN: 978-1-60886-718-9 | $14.99 US

Volume 2

ISBN: 978-1-60886-816-2 | $14.99 US

Day Men

Volume 1

ISBN: 978-1-60886-393-8 | $9.99 US

Volume 2

ISBN: 978-1-60886-852-0 | $9.99 US

Dan Abnett

Wild's End

Volume 1: First Light

ISBN: 978-1-60886-735-6 | $19.99 US

Volume 2: The Enemy Within

ISBN: 978-1-60886-877-3 | $19.99 US

Hypernaturals

Volume 1

ISBN: 978-1-60886-298-6 | $16.99 US

Volume 2

ISBN: 978-1-60886-319-8 | $19.99 US

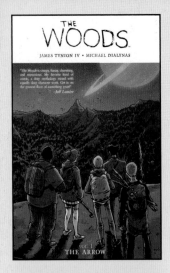

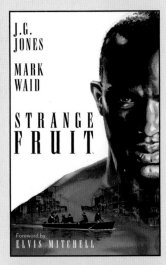

...LE AT YOUR LOCAL ...SHOP AND BOOKSTORE ...-STUDIOS.COM